PUFFIN BOOKS

Books by Rick Riordan

The Percy Jackson series:
PERCY JACKSON AND THE LIGHTNING THIEF
PERCY JACKSON AND THE SEA OF MONSTERS
PERCY JACKSON AND THE TITAN'S CURSE
PERCY JACKSON AND THE BATTLE OF THE LABYRINTH
PERCY JACKSON AND THE LAST OLYMPIAN
THE DEMIGOD FILES

PERCY JACKSON AND THE GREEK GODS
PERCY JACKSON AND THE GREEK HEROES

For more about Percy Jackson, try:
PERCY JACKSON: THE ULTIMATE GUIDE

The Heroes of Olympus series:
THE LOST HERO
THE SON OF NEPTUNE
THE MARK OF ATHENA
THE HOUSE OF HADES
THE BLOOD OF OLYMPUS
THE DEMIGOD DIARIES

The Kane Chronicles series:
THE RED PYRAMID
THE THRONE OF FIRE
THE SERPENT'S SHADOW

For more about the Kane Chronicles, try:
THE KANE CHRONICLES: SURVIVAL GUIDE

Percy Jackson/Kane Chronicles Adventures (ebooks):
THE SON OF SOBEK
THE STAFF OF SERAPIS
THE CROWN OF PTOLEMY

www.rickriordan.co.uk

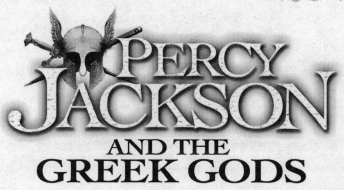

PERCY JACKSON
AND THE
GREEK GODS

RICK RIORDAN

PUFFIN

PUFFIN BOOKS

UK | USA | Canada | Ireland | Australia
India | New Zealand | South Africa

Puffin Books is part of the Penguin Random House group of companies
whose addresses can be found at global.penguinrandomhouse.com.

puffinbooks.com

First published in the USA by Disney•Hyperion, an imprint of Disney Book Group, 2014
Published simultaneously in Great Britain by Puffin Books 2014
This edition published 2015
009

Text copyright © Rick Riordan, 2014

The moral right of the author has been asserted

Set in Centaur
Printed in Great Britain by Clays Ltd, St Ives plc

A CIP catalogue record for this book is available from the British Library

ISBN: 978–0–141–35868–0

www.greenpenguin.co.uk

To my father, Rick Riordan, Sr, who read me my first book of mythology
− R. R.

TABLE OF CONTENTS

INTRODUCTION

I HOPE I'M GETTING EXTRA CREDIT FOR THIS.

A publisher in New York asked me to write down what I know about the Greek gods, and I was like, 'Can we do this anonymously? Because I don't need the Olympians mad at me again.'

But if it helps you to know your Greek gods, and survive an encounter with them if they ever show up in your face, then I guess writing all this down will be my good deed for the week.

If you don't know me, my name is Percy Jackson. I'm a modern-day demigod – a half-god, half-mortal son of Poseidon – but I'm not going to say much about myself. My story has already been written down in some books that are total fiction (wink, wink) and I am just a character from the story (*cough* – yeah, right – *cough*).

Just go easy on me while I'm telling you about the gods, all right? There's like forty bajillion different versions of the myths, so don't be all *Well, I heard it a different way, so you're WRONG!*

I'm going to tell you the versions that make the most sense to me. I promise I didn't make any of this up. I got all these stories straight from the Ancient Greek and Roman dudes who wrote them down in the first place. Believe me, I couldn't make up stuff this weird.

So here we go. First I'll tell you how the world got made. Then I'll run down a list of gods and give you my two cents about each of them. I just hope I don't make them so mad they incinerate me before I –

AGGHHHHHHHHH!

Just kidding. Still here.

Anyway, I'll start with the Greek story of creation, which by the way is seriously *messed up*. Wear your safety glasses and your raincoat. There will be blood.

THE BEGINNING
AND STUFF

IN THE BEGINNING, I wasn't there. I don't think the Ancient Greeks were, either. Nobody had a pen and paper to take notes, so I can't vouch for what follows, but I can tell you it's what the Greeks *thought* happened.

At first, there was pretty much nothing. A lot of nothing.

The first god, if you can call it that, was Chaos – a gloomy, soupy mist with all the matter in the cosmos just drifting around. Here's a fact for you: *Chaos* literally means the *Gap*, and we're not talking about the clothing store.

Eventually Chaos got less chaotic. Maybe it got bored with being all gloomy and misty. Some of its matter collected and solidified into the earth, which unfortunately developed a living personality. She called herself Gaia, the Earth Mother.

Now Gaia *was* the actual earth – the rocks, the hills, the valleys, the whole enchilada. But she could also take on humanlike form. She liked to walk across the earth – which was basically walking across herself – in the shape of a matronly woman with a flowing green dress, curly black hair and a serene smile on her face. The smile hid a nasty disposition. You'll see that soon enough.

After a long time alone, Gaia looked up into the misty nothing above the earth and said to herself: 'You know what would be good? A sky. I could really go for a sky. And it would be nice if he was also a handsome man I could fall in love with, because I'm kind of lonely down here with just these rocks.'

Either Chaos heard her and cooperated, or Gaia simply willed it to happen. Above the earth, the sky formed – a protective dome that was blue in the daytime and black at night. The sky named himself Ouranos – and, yeah, that's another spelling for Uranus. There's pretty much no way you can pronounce that name without people snickering. It just sounds *wrong*. Why he didn't choose a better name for himself – like Deathbringer or José – I don't know, but it might explain why Ouranos was so cranky all the time.

Like Gaia, Ouranos could take human shape and visit the earth – which was good, because the sky is way up there and long-distance relationships never work out.

In physical form, he looked like a tall, buff guy with long-ish dark hair. He wore only a loincloth, and his skin changed colour – sometimes blue with cloudy patterns across his muscles, sometimes dark with glimmering stars. Hey, Gaia dreamed him up to look like that. Don't blame me. Sometimes you'll see pictures of him holding a zodiac wheel, representing all the constellations that pass through the sky over and over for eternity.

Anyway, Ouranos and Gaia got married.

Happily ever after?

Not exactly.

Part of the problem was that Chaos got a little creation-happy. It thought to its misty, gloomy self, Hey, Earth and Sky. That was fun! I wonder what else I can make.

Soon it created all sorts of other problems – and by that I mean gods. Water collected out of the mist of Chaos, pooled in the deepest parts of the earth and formed the first seas, which naturally developed a consciousness – the god Pontus.

Then Chaos really went nuts and thought, I know! How about a dome like the sky, but at the *bottom* of the earth! That would be awesome!

So another dome came into being beneath the earth, but it was dark and murky and generally not very nice, since it was always hidden from the light of the sky. This was Tartarus, the Pit of Evil; and as you can guess from the name, when he developed a godly personality, he didn't win any popularity contests.

The problem was both Pontus and Tartarus liked Gaia, which put some pressure on her relationship with Ouranos.

A bunch of other primordial gods popped up, but if I tried to name them all we'd be here for weeks. Chaos and Tartarus had a kid together (don't ask how; I don't know) called Nyx, who was the embodiment of Night. Then Nyx, somehow all by herself, had a daughter named Hemera, who was Day. Those two never got along because they were as different as . . . well, you know.

According to some stories, Chaos also created Eros, the god of procreation . . . in other words, mommy gods and daddy gods having lots of little baby gods. Other stories claim Eros was the son of Aphrodite. We'll get to her later. I don't know which version is true, but I *do* know Gaia and Ouranos started having kids — with *very* mixed results.

First, they had a batch of twelve — six girls and six boys called the Titans. These kids looked human, but they were much taller and more powerful. You'd figure twelve kids would be enough for anybody, right? I mean, with a family that big, you've basically got your own reality TV show.

Plus, once the Titans were born, things started to go sour with Ouranos and Gaia's marriage. Ouranos spent a lot more time hanging out in the sky. He didn't visit. He didn't help with the kids. Gaia got resentful. The two of them started fighting. As the kids grew older, Ouranos would yell at them and basically act like a horrible dad.

A few times, Gaia and Ouranos tried to patch things up. Gaia decided maybe if they had another set of kids it would bring them closer . . .

I know, right? Bad idea.

She gave birth to triplets. The problem: these new kids defined the word UGLY. They were as big and strong as Titans, except hulking and brutish and in desperate need of a body wax. Worst of all, each kid had a single eye in the middle of his forehead.

Talk about a face only a mother could love. Well, Gaia loved these guys. She named them the Elder Cyclopes, and eventually they would spawn a whole race of other, lesser Cyclopes. But that was much later.

When Ouranos saw the Cyclops triplets, he freaked. 'These cannot be my kids! They don't even look like me!'

'They *are* your children, you deadbeat!' Gaia screamed back. 'Don't you dare leave me to raise them on my own!'

'Don't worry, I won't,' Ouranos growled.

He stormed off and came back with thick chains made from the night sky's pure darkness. He bound up the Cyclopes and tossed them into Tartarus, which was the only part of creation where Ouranos wouldn't have to look at them.

Harsh, right?

Gaia screamed and wailed, but Ouranos refused to release the Cyclopes. No one else dared to oppose his orders, because by this time he was getting a reputation as a pretty scary dude.

'I am king of the universe!' he bellowed. 'How could I *not* be? I am literally above everything else.'

'I hate you!' Gaia wailed.

'Bah! You will do as I say. I am the first and best of the primordial gods.'

'I was born *before* you!' Gaia protested. 'You wouldn't even be here if I didn't –'

'Don't test me,' he snarled. 'I've got plenty more chains of darkness.'

As you can guess, Gaia threw a total earthquake fit, but she didn't see what else she could do. Her first kids, the Titans, were almost adults now. They felt bad for Mom. They didn't like their dad much either – Gaia was always bad-mouthing him, with good reason – but the Titans were scared of Ouranos and felt helpless to stop him.

I have to keep it together for the kids, Gaia thought. Maybe I should give it one more try with Ouranos.

She arranged a nice romantic evening – candles, roses, soft music. They must have rekindled some of the old magic. A few months later, Gaia gave birth to one more set of triplets.

As if she needed more proof that her marriage to Ouranos was dead . . .

The new kids were even more monstrous than the Cyclopes. Each one had a hundred arms all around his chest like sea urchin spines, and fifty teeny, tiny heads clustered on his shoulders. It didn't matter to Gaia. She loved their little faces – all hundred and fifty of them. She called the triplets the Hundred-Handed Ones. She'd barely had time to give them names, though, when Ouranos marched over, took one look at them and snatched them from Gaia's arms. Without a word, he wrapped them in chains and tossed them into Tartarus like bags of recycling.

Clearly, the sky dude had issues.

Well, that was pretty much it for Gaia. She wailed and moaned and caused so many earthquakes that her Titan kids came running to see what was wrong.

'Your father is a complete _____!'

I don't know what she called him, but I have a feeling that's when the first swear words were invented.

She explained what had happened. Then she raised her arms and caused the ground to rumble beneath her. She summoned the hardest substance she could find from her earthy domain, shaped it with her anger and created the first weapon ever made – a curved iron blade about three feet long. She fixed it to a wooden handle made from a nearby tree branch, then showed her invention to the Titans.

'Behold, my children!' she said. 'The instrument of my revenge. I will call it a scythe!'

The Titans muttered among themselves: *What is that for? Why is it curved? How do you spell* scythe?

'One of you needs to step up!' Gaia cried. 'Ouranos isn't worthy to be the king of the cosmos. One of you will kill him and take his place.'

The Titans looked pretty uncomfortable.

'So . . . explain this whole *killing* thing,' said Oceanus. He was the oldest Titan boy, but he mostly hung out in the far reaches of the sea with the primordial water god, whom he called Uncle Pontus. 'What does it mean, to kill?'

'She wants us to exterminate our dad,' Themis guessed. She was one of the smartest girls, and she immediately got the concept of punishing someone for a crime. 'Like, make him not exist any more.'

'Is that even possible?' asked her sister Rhea. 'I thought we were all immortal.'

Gaia snarled in frustration. 'Don't be cowards! It's very simple. You take this sharp pointy blade and you cut your dad into small pieces so he can't bother us again. Whichever of you does this will be the ruler of the universe! Also, I will make you those cookies you used to like, with the sprinkles.'

Now, in modern times, we have a word for this sort of behaviour. We call it *psycho*.

Back then, the rules of behaviour were a lot looser. Maybe you'll feel better about your own relatives, knowing that the first family in creation was also the first *dysfunctional* family.

The Titans started mumbling and pointing to each other, like, 'Hey, you'd be good at killing Dad.'

'Uh, no, I think *you* should do it.'

'I'd love to kill Dad, honestly, but I've got this thing I have to do, so –'

'*I'll* do it!' said a voice from the back.

The youngest of the twelve shouldered his way forward. Kronos was smaller than his brothers and sisters. He wasn't the smartest or the strongest or the fastest. But he *was* the most power-hungry. I suppose when you're the youngest of twelve kids, you're always looking for ways to stand out and get noticed. The youngest Titan loved the idea of taking over the world, especially if it meant being the boss of all his siblings. The offer of cookies with sprinkles didn't hurt, either.

Kronos stood about nine feet tall, which was runty for a Titan. He didn't look as dangerous as some of his brothers, but the kid was crafty. He'd already got the nickname 'the Crooked One' among his siblings, because he would fight dirty in their wrestling matches and was never where you expected him to be.

He had his mother's smile and dark curly hair. He had his father's cruelty. When he looked at you, you could never tell if he was about to punch you or tell you a joke. His beard was kind of unnerving, too. He was young for a beard, but he'd already started growing his whiskers into a single spike that jutted from his chin like the beak of a raven.

When Kronos saw the scythe, his eyes gleamed. He wanted that iron blade. Alone among his siblings, he understood how much damage it could cause.

And as for killing his dad – why not? Ouranos barely noticed him. Neither did Gaia, for that matter. His parents probably didn't even know his name.

Kronos hated being ignored. He was tired of being the smallest and wearing all those stupid Titan hand-me-downs.

'I'll do it,' he repeated. 'I'll chop up Dad.'

'My favourite son!' Gaia cried. 'You are *awesome*! I knew I could count on you, uh . . . which one are you again?'

'Kronos.' He managed to keep his smile. Hey, for a scythe, cookies and a chance to commit murder, Kronos could hide his true feelings. 'I will be honoured to kill for you, Mother. But we'll have to do it my way. First, I want you to trick Ouranos into visiting you. Tell him you're sorry. Tell him it's all your fault and you're going to cook him a fancy dinner to apologize. Just get him here tonight and act like you still love him.'

'Ugh!' Gaia gagged. 'Are you crazy?'

'Just pretend,' Kronos insisted. 'Once he's in human form and sitting next to you, I'll jump out and attack him. But I'll need some help.'

He turned to his siblings, who were all suddenly very interested in their own feet.

'Look, guys,' said Kronos, 'if this goes bad, Ouranos is going to take revenge on *all* of us. We can't have any mistakes. I'll need four of you to hold him down and make sure he doesn't escape back into the sky before I finish killing him.'

The others were silent. They were probably trying to picture their shrimpy little brother Kronos taking on their huge violent dad, and they weren't liking the odds.

'Oh, come on!' Kronos chided. 'I'll do the actual slicing and dicing. Four of you just need to hold him. When I'm king, I'll reward those four! I'll give them each a corner of the earth to rule – north, south, east and west. One-time offer. Who's with me?'

The girls were too wise to get involved in murder. They made their excuses and quickly left. The eldest son, Oceanus, chewed his thumb nervously. 'I have to get back to the sea, for some, uh, aquatic stuff. Sorry . . .'

That left only four of Kronos's brothers – Koios, Iapetus, Krios and Hyperion.

Kronos smiled at them. He took the scythe from Gaia's hands and tested its point, drawing a drop of golden blood from his own finger. 'So, four volunteers! Nice!'

Iapetus cleared his throat. 'Uh, actually –'

Hyperion jabbed Iapetus with his elbow. 'We're in, Kronos!' he promised. 'You can count on us!'

'Excellent,' Kronos said, which was the first time an evil genius ever said *excellent*. He told them the plan.

That night, amazingly, Ouranos showed up.

He wandered into the valley where he usually met Gaia and frowned when he saw the sumptuous dinner laid out on the table. 'I got your note. Are you serious about making up?'

'Absolutely!' Gaia was dressed in her best green sleeveless dress. Her curly hair was braided with jewels (which were easy for her to get, being the earth) and she smelled of roses and jasmine. She reclined on a sofa in the soft light of the candles and beckoned her husband to come closer.

Ouranos felt underdressed in his loincloth. He hadn't brushed his hair or anything. His night-time skin was dark and covered with stars, but that probably didn't count as 'black tie' for a fancy dinner. He was starting to think he should've at least brushed his teeth.

Was he suspicious? I don't know. Remember, nobody in the history of the cosmos had been lured into an ambush and chopped to pieces before. He was going to be the first. Lucky guy. Also, he got lonely hanging out in the sky so much. His only company was the stars, the air god Aither (who was, in fact, a total airhead), and Nyx and Hemera, mother and daughter, who argued with each other every dawn and dusk.

'So . . .' Ouranos's palms felt sweaty. He'd forgotten how beautiful Gaia could be when she wasn't all yelling up in his face. 'You're not angry any more?'

'Not at all!' Gaia assured him.

'And . . . you're okay with me wrapping our kids in chains and throwing them into the abyss?'

Gaia gritted her teeth and forced a smile. 'I am *okay* with it.'

'Good,' he grunted. 'Because those little guys were UGLY.'

Gaia patted the couch. 'Come sit with me, my husband.'

Ouranos grinned and lumbered over.

As soon as he settled in, Kronos whispered from behind the nearest boulder: 'Now.'

His four brothers jumped out from their hiding places. Krios had disguised himself as a bush. Koios had dug a hole for himself and covered it with branches. Hyperion had tucked himself under the couch (it was a large couch), and Iapetus was attempting to look like a tree with his arms out for branches. For some reason, it had worked.

The four brothers grabbed Ouranos. Each one took an arm or a leg and they wrestled their dad to the ground, stretching him out spread-eagled.

Kronos emerged from the shadows. His iron scythe gleamed in the starlight. 'Hello, Father.'

'What is the meaning of this?' Ouranos bellowed. 'Gaia, tell them to release me!'

'HA!' Gaia rose from her couch. 'You gave our children no mercy, my husband, so you deserve no mercy. Besides, who wears a loincloth to a fancy dinner? I am disgusted!'

Ouranos struggled in vain. 'How dare you! I am the lord of the cosmos!'

'Not any more.' Kronos raised the scythe.

'Beware! If you do this, uh . . . what was your name again?'

'KRONOS!'

'If you do this, Kronos,' said Ouranos, 'I will curse you! Someday, your *own* children will destroy you and take your throne, just as you are doing to me!'

Kronos laughed. 'Let them try.'

He brought down the scythe.

It hit Ouranos right in the . . . well, you know what? I can't even say it. If you're a guy, imagine the most painful place you could possibly be hit.

Yep. That's the place.

Kronos chopped, and Ouranos howled in pain. It was like the most disgusting cheap-budget horror movie you can imagine. Blood was everywhere – except the blood of the gods is golden, and it's called *ichor*.

Droplets of it splattered over the rocks, and the stuff was so powerful that later on, when no one was looking, creatures arose from the ichor – three hissing winged demons called the Furies, the spirits of punishment. They immediately fled into the darkness of Tartarus. Other drops of sky blood fell on fertile soil, where they eventually turned into wild but gentler creatures called *nymphs* and *satyrs*.

Most of the blood just splattered everything. Seriously, those stains were *never* going to come out of Kronos's shirt.

'Well done, brothers!' Kronos grinned ear to ear, his scythe dripping gold.

Iapetus got sick on the spot. The others laughed and patted each other on the back.

'Oh, my children!' Gaia said. 'I am so proud! Cookies and punch for everyone!'

Before the celebration, Kronos gathered up the remains of his father in the tablecloth. Maybe because he resented his eldest brother, Oceanus, for not helping with the murder, Kronos toted the stuff to the sea and tossed it in. The blood mixed with the salty water, and . . . well, you'll see what came from that later.

Now you're going to ask, *Okay, so, if the sky was killed, why do I look up and still see the sky?*

Answer: *I dunno.*

My guess is that Kronos killed Ouranos's physical form, so the sky god could no longer appear on the earth and claim kingship. They basically exiled him into the air. So he's not dead, exactly, but now he can't do anything but be the harmless dome over the world.

Anyway, Kronos returned to the valley, and all the Titans had a party.

Gaia named Kronos lord of the universe. She made him a cool one-of-a-kind collector's edition golden crown and everything. Kronos kept his promise and gave his four helpful brothers control over the four corners of the earth. Iapetus became the Titan of the west. Hyperion got the east. Koios took the north, and Krios got the south.

That night, Kronos lifted his glass of nectar, which was the immortals' favourite drink. He tried for a confident smile, since kings should always look confident, though truthfully he was already starting to worry about Ouranos's curse – that some day Kronos's own children would depose him.

In spite of that, he yelled, 'My siblings, a toast! We have begun a Golden Age!'

And if you like lots of lying, stealing, backstabbing and cannibalism, then read on, because it definitely was a Golden Age for all that.

THE GOLDEN AGE OF CANNIBALISM

A T FIRST, KRONOS WASN'T SO BAD. He had to work his way up to being a *complete* slime bucket.

He released the Elder Cyclopes and the Hundred-Handed Ones from Tartarus, which made Gaia happy. The monstrous guys turned out to be useful, too. They had spent all their time in the abyss learning how to forge metal and build with stone (I guess that's pretty much all there was to do), so in gratitude for their freedom they constructed a massive palace for Kronos on top of Mount Othrys, which back then was the tallest mountain in Greece.

The palace was made from void-black marble. Towering columns and vast halls gleamed in the light of magical torches. Kronos's throne was carved from a solid block of obsidian, inlaid with gold and diamonds — which sounds impressive, but probably wasn't very comfortable. That didn't matter to

Kronos. He could sit there all day, surveying the entire world below him, cackling evilly, 'Mine! All mine!'

His five Titan brothers and six Titan sisters didn't argue with him. They had pretty much staked out their favourite territories already – and besides, after seeing Kronos wield that scythe, they didn't want to get on his bad side.

In addition to being king of the cosmos, Kronos became the Titan of time. He couldn't pop around the time stream like Doctor Who or anything, but he *could* occasionally make time slow down or speed up. Whenever you're in an incredibly boring lecture that seems to take forever, blame Kronos. Or when your weekend is *way* too short, that's Kronos's fault, too.

He was especially interested in the destructive power of time. Being immortal, he couldn't believe what a few short years could do to a mortal life. Just for kicks, he used to travel around the world, fast-forwarding the lives of trees, plants and animals so he could watch them wither and die. He never got tired of that.

As for his brothers, the four who helped with the murder of Ouranos were given the four corners of the earth – which is weird, since the Greeks thought the world was a big flat circle like a shield, so it didn't really *have* corners, but whatever.

Krios was the Titan of the south. He took the ram for his symbol, since the ram constellation rose in the southern sky. His navy blue armour was dotted with stars. Ram's horns jutted from his helmet. Krios was the dark, silent type. He would stand down there at the southern edge of world, watching the constellations and thinking deep thoughts – or maybe he was just thinking he should have requested a more exciting job.

Koios, the Titan of the north, lived at the opposite end of the world (obviously). He was sometimes called Polus, because he controlled the northern pole. This was way before Santa Claus moved in. Koios was also the first Titan to have the gift of prophecy. In fact, *Koios* literally means *question*. He could ask questions of the sky, and sometimes the sky would whisper answers. Creepy? Yes. I don't know if he was communing with the spirit of Ouranos or what, but his glimpses of the future were so useful that other Titans started asking him burning questions like: *What's the weather going to be on Saturday? Is Kronos going to kill me today? What should I wear to Rhea's dance?* That kind of thing. Eventually Koios would pass down the gift of prophecy to his children.

Hyperion, Titan of the east, was the flashiest of the four. Since the light of day came from the east every morning, he called himself the Lord of Light. Behind his back, everybody else called him Kronos Lite, because he did whatever Kronos told him, and was basically like Kronos with half the calories and none of the taste. Anyway, he wore blazing golden armour and was known to burst into flames at random moments, which made him fun at parties.

His counterpart, Iapetus, was more laid-back, being the Titan of the west. A good sunset always makes you want to kick back and chill. Despite that, you didn't want to get this guy mad at you. He was an excellent fighter who knew how to use a spear. *Iapetus* literally means *the Piercer*, and I'm pretty sure he didn't get that name by doing ear-piercings at the mall.

As for the last brother, Oceanus, he took charge of the outer waters that circled the world. That's how the big expanses of water bordering the earth came to be called *oceans*. It could have been worse. If Iapetus had taken over the waters, today we'd be talking about the *Atlantic Iapet* and *sailing the iapet blue*, and that just doesn't have the same ring to it.

Now, before I turn to the six lady Titans, let me get some nasty business out of the way.

See, eventually the guy Titans started thinking, Hey, Dad had Gaia for a wife. Who are *we* going to have for wives? Then they looked at the lady Titans and thought, Hmm . . .

I know. You're screaming, *GROSS! The brothers wanted to marry their own* sisters?!

Yeah. I find that pretty disgusting myself, but here's the thing: Titans didn't see family relationships the same way we do.

First off, like I said before, the rules of behaviour were a lot looser back then. Also, there weren't many choices when it came to marriage partners. You couldn't simply log into TitansMatch .com and find your perfect soul mate.

Most important, immortals are just *different* from humans. They live forever, more or less. They have cool powers. They have ichor instead of blood and DNA, so they aren't concerned about bloodlines not mixing well. Because of that, they don't see the whole brother–sister thing in the same way. You and the girl you like might have been born of the same mom, but once you grew up and you were both adults, you wouldn't necessarily think of her as your sister any more.

That's my theory. Or maybe the Titans were all just freaks. I'll let you decide.

Anyway, not *all* the brothers married all the sisters, but here's the rundown.

The oldest girl was Theia. If you wanted her attention, all you had to do was wave something shiny in her face. She *loved* sparkly things and bright scenic views. Every morning she would dance with happiness when daylight returned. She would climb mountains just so she could see for miles around. She would even delve underground and bring out precious gems, using her magic powers to make them gleam and sparkle. Theia is the one who gave gold its lustre and made diamonds glitter.

She became the Titan of clear sight. Because she was all about bright and glittery, she ended up marrying Hyperion, the lord of light. As you can imagine, they got along great, though how they got any sleep with Hyperion glowing all night and Theia giggling, 'Shiny! Shiny!' I don't know.

Her sister Themis? Totally different. She was quiet and thoughtful and never tried to draw attention to herself, always wearing a simple white shawl over her hair. She realized from an early age that she had a natural sense of right and wrong. She understood what was fair and what wasn't. Whenever she was in doubt, she claimed that she could draw wisdom straight from the earth. I don't think she meant from *Gaia*, though, because Gaia wasn't really hung up on right and wrong.

Anyway, Themis had a good reputation among her brothers and sisters. She could mediate even the worst arguments. She became the Titan of natural law and fairness. She didn't marry any of her six brothers, which just proves how wise she was.

Third sister: Tethys, and I promise this is the last 'T' name for the girls, because even *I'm* getting confused. She loved rivers, springs and fresh running water of any kind. She was very kind, always offering her siblings something to drink, though the others got tired of hearing that the average Titan needs twenty-four large glasses of water a day to stay hydrated. At any rate, Tethys thought of herself as the nursemaid for the whole world, since all living things need to drink. She ended up marrying Oceanus, which was kind of a no-brainer. 'Hey, you like water? I like water too! We should totally go out!'

Phoebe, the fourth sister, lived right in the geographic centre of the world, which for the Greeks meant the Oracle of Delphi – a sacred spring where you could sometimes hear whispers of the future if you knew how to listen. The Greeks called this place the *omphalos*, literally the belly button of the earth, though they never specified whether it was an innie or an outie.

Phoebe was one of the first people to figure out how to hear the voices of Delphi, but she wasn't a gloomy, mysterious sort of fortune-teller. Her name meant *bright*, and she always looked on the positive side of things. Her prophecies tended to be like fortune cookies – only good stuff. Which was fine, I guess, if you only wanted to hear good news, but not so great if you had a serious problem. Like if you were going to die tomorrow, Phoebe might just tell you, 'Oh, um, I foresee that you won't have to worry about your maths test next week!'

Phoebe ended up marrying Koios, the northern dude, because he also had the gift of prophecy. Unfortunately, they only saw each other once in a while since they lived very far apart. Bonus fact: much later, Phoebe's grandson, a guy named Apollo, took over the Oracle. Because he inherited her powers, Apollo was sometimes called Phoebus Apollo.

Titan sister five was Mnemosyne – and, man, with my dyslexia I had to spell-check that name about twenty times, and it's probably still wrong. Pretty sure it's pronounced 'NEMO-sign'. Anyway, Mnemosyne was born with a photographic memory long before anyone knew what a photograph was. Seriously, she remembered *everything* – her sisters' birthdays, her homework, putting out the garbage, feeding the cats. In some ways, that was good. She kept the family records and never *ever* forgot anything. But in some ways, having her around was a drag, because she would never *let* you forget anything.

That embarrassing thing you did when you were eight years old? Yep, she remembered. That promise you made three years ago that you would pay her back that loan? She remembered.

What was worse, Mnemosyne expected everybody else to have a good memory, too. Just to be helpful, she invented letters and writing so the rest of us poor schmucks who didn't have perfect recall could keep permanent records of everything. She became the Titan of memory, especially rote memorization. Next time you have to study for a spelling test or memorize the capitals of all fifty states for no apparent reason, thank Mnemosyne. That kind of assignment was *totally* her idea. None of her fellow Titans wanted to marry her. Go figure.

Finally, there was sister number six: Rhea. Poor Rhea. She was the sweetest and most beautiful of the lady Titans, which of course meant she had the worst luck and the hardest life. Her name either means *flow* or *ease*. Both definitions fit. She always went with the flow, and she totally put people at ease. She would wander the valleys of the earth, visiting her brothers and sisters, talking to the nymphs and satyrs who had sprung from the blood of Ouranos. She loved animals, too. Her favourite was the lion. If you see pictures of Rhea, she almost always has a couple of lions with her, which made it *very* safe for her to walk around, even in the worst neighbourhoods.

Rhea became the Titan of motherhood. She adored babies and always helped her sisters during their deliveries. Eventually she would earn the title *the Great Mother* when she had kids of her own. Unfortunately, she had to get married before any of that happened, which is how all the trouble started . . .

Oh, but everything was so great! What could possibly go wrong?

That's what the Earth Mother Gaia thought. She was so pleased to see her kids in charge of the world, she decided to sink back down into the earth for a while and just be, well . . . the earth. She'd been through a lot. She'd had eighteen kids. She deserved a rest.

She was sure Kronos would take care of things and be a good king forever and ever. (Yeah, right.) So she lay down for a quick nap, which in geological terms meant a few millennia.

Meanwhile, the Titans started having kids of their own, who were second-generation Titans. Oceanus and Tethys, Mr and Mrs Water, had a daughter named Klymene, who became the Titan goddess of fame. I'm guessing she was into fame because she grew up at the bottom of the ocean where nothing ever happened. She was *all* about gossip and reading the tabloids and catching up on the latest Hollywood news . . . or she would've been, if Hollywood existed. Like a lot of folks who are obsessed with fame, she headed west. She ended up falling for the Titan of the west, Iapetus.

I know, he was technically her uncle. Disgusting. But like I said before, the Titans were different. My advice is not to think about it too much.

Anyway, Iapetus and Klymene had a son named Atlas, who turned out to be an excellent fighter, and also kind of a jerk. When he grew up, he became Kronos's right-hand man and main enforcer.

Next, Iapetus and Klymene had a son named Prometheus, who was almost as clever as Kronos. According to some legends, Prometheus invented a minor life form you may have heard of – humans. One day he was just messing around at the riverbank, building stuff out of wet clay, when he sculpted a couple of funny-looking figures similar to Titans, only much smaller and easier to smash. Maybe some blood of Ouranos got into the clay, or maybe Prometheus breathed life into the figures on purpose – I don't know. But the clay creatures came to life and became the first two humans.

Did Prometheus get a medal for that? Nah. The Titans looked on humans the way we might look on gerbils. Some Titans thought humans were kind of cute, though they died awfully quick and didn't really serve any purpose. Other Titans thought they were repulsive rodents. Some Titans didn't pay them any attention at all. As for the humans, they mostly just cowered in their caves and scurried around trying not to get stepped on.

The Titans kept having more baby Titans. I won't mention all of them or we'll be here for as long as Gaia napped, but Koios and Phoebe, the prophecy couple, had a girl named Leto, who decided she wanted to be the Titan protector of the young. She was the world's first babysitter. All the dad and mom Titans were really happy to see her.

Hyperion and Theia, Mr and Mrs Shiny, had twins named Helios and Selene, who were in charge of the sun and the moon. Makes sense, right? You can't get much shinier than the sun and the moon.

Helios would drive the chariot of the sun across the sky every day, even though it got terrible mileage. Helios thought he looked pretty hot, and he had an annoying habit of calling the sun his 'chick magnet'.

Selene wasn't quite so flashy. She drove her silver moon chariot across the sky at night and mostly kept to herself, though the one time she *did* fall in love it was the saddest story ever. But that's for later.

At any rate, one particular Titan wasn't getting married or having kids . . . namely Kronos, the lord of the universe. He just sat on his throne in the palace of Mount Othrys and got very, very grumpy watching everyone else have a good time.

Remember that curse Ouranos warned him about — that some day Kronos's own kids would overthrow him? Kronos couldn't get that out of his head.

At first he told himself, *Well, no biggie. I just won't get married or have kids!*

But it's a pain to be on your own when everyone around you is settling down and starting families. Kronos had earned the throne fair and square, but that curse took all the fun out of chopping up his dad. Now he had to worry about getting overthrown while everyone else got to enjoy the good life. Uncool.

His relatives didn't visit him much any more. Once Gaia went back into the earth, they stopped coming by the palace for Sunday dinner. They said they were busy, but Kronos suspected that his brothers, sisters, nieces and nephews were simply scared of him. He *did* have his father's temper and sense of cruelty. His scythe was intimidating. Plus, he had the slightly off-putting tendency to scream, 'I'll kill you all!' whenever someone made him mad. But was that *his* fault?

One morning he really snapped. He woke up to a Cyclops hammering on a piece of bronze right outside his bedroom window. Seven in the morning, on a *weekend*!

Kronos had promised his mom he would free the Elder Cyclopes and the Hundred-Handed Ones from Tartarus, but he was getting really tired of his ugly relatives. They'd become more and more disgusting as they grew up. They smelled like Porta Potties. They had, like, *zero* personal hygiene, and they were constantly making noise – building things, hammering metal, cutting stone. They'd been useful for building the palace, but now they were just annoying.

Kronos called Atlas and Hyperion and a couple of his other goons. They rounded up the Cyclopes and Hundred-Handed Ones and told them they were going for a nice drive in the country to look at wildflowers. Then they jumped the poor guys, wrapped them in chains again and tossed them back into Tartarus.

If Gaia woke up, she wouldn't be happy – but so what? Kronos was the king now. Mom would just have to deal with it.

Things were much quieter at the palace after that, but Kronos still had a major case of the grumpies. It wasn't fair that he couldn't have a girlfriend.

In fact, he had a particular girl in mind.

Secretly, he had a crush on Rhea.

She was *gorgeous*. Every time the Titan family got together, Kronos stole glances at her. If he noticed any of the other guys flirting with her, he would pull them aside for a private conversation with his scythe in hand, and warn them never to do it again.

He loved how Rhea laughed. Her smile was brighter than Helios's chick magnet . . . uh, I mean the sun. He loved the way her dark curly hair swept her shoulders. Her eyes were as green as meadows, and her lips . . . well, Kronos dreamed about kissing those lips.

Also, Rhea was sweet and kind and everyone loved her. Kronos thought, If I just had a wife like that, my family wouldn't fear me as much. They'd come to the palace more often. Rhea would teach me to be a better Titan. Life would be awesome!

But another part of him thought, No! I can't get married, because of that stupid curse!

Kronos grumbled in frustration. He was the king of the freaking universe! He could do whatever he wanted! Maybe Ouranos had just been messing with him and there *was* no curse. Or maybe he would get lucky and he wouldn't have kids.

Note to self: if you're trying not to have kids, don't marry a lady who is the Titan of motherhood.

Kronos tried to restrain himself, but finally he couldn't stand it any longer. He invited Rhea to a romantic dinner and poured out his feelings. He proposed to her on the spot.

Now, I don't know if Rhea loved the guy or not. If she didn't, I imagine she was too afraid to say so. This was Kronos the Crooked One, after all – the dude who had killed their dad. The king of the freaking universe.

It didn't help that the whole time they ate dinner, his scythe was resting on a hook on the wall right behind him, its blade gleaming in the candlelight like it was still covered in golden ichor.

Rhea agreed to marry him.

Maybe she thought she could make him into a better guy. Maybe *Kronos* believed that, too. They had a nice honeymoon. A few weeks later, when Kronos heard that (surprise, surprise) Rhea was expecting their first child, he tried to convince himself everything was fine. He was happy! He would never be a bad father like Ouranos. It didn't matter if the baby was a boy Titan or a girl Titan. Kronos would love him or her and forget all about that old curse.

Then the kid was born – a beautiful baby girl.

Rhea had been secretly worried her child might turn out to be a Cyclops or a Hundred-Handed One. Maybe Kronos had been stressing about that, too. But nope. The child was perfect.

In fact, she was a little *too* perfect.

Rhea named her Hestia. She swaddled the baby in soft blankets and showed her to her proud papa. At first, Kronos smiled. The kid was not a monster – sweet! But, as he tickled her chin and looked into her eyes and made the usual cute *goo-goo* noises, Kronos realized Hestia wasn't exactly a Titan.

She was smaller than a Titan baby, but heavier and perfectly proportioned. Her eyes were much too intelligent for a newborn. She radiated power. With Kronos's understanding of time, he could easily envision what this girl would look like when she grew up. She would be smaller than a Titan, but capable of great things. She would surpass any Titan at whatever she chose to do.

Hestia was like an improved version of the Titans – Titan 2.0, the Next Big Thing. In fact, she wasn't a Titan at all. She was a *goddess* — the first member of an entirely new branch of immortal evolution.

Looking at her, Kronos felt like an old cell phone staring at the latest model smartphone. He knew his days were numbered.

His proud papa smile faded. This kid could *not* be allowed to grow up, or the prophecy of Ouranos would come true. Kronos had to act fast. He knew Rhea would never agree to have her child killed, and she'd brought those stupid lions with her as usual. He couldn't have a fight in the throne room. Besides, he couldn't reach for his scythe while holding the baby. He had to get rid of Hestia immediately and irreversibly.

He opened his mouth — super, super wide, wider than even he realized he could. His lower jaw was hinged like on one of those massive snakes that can eat a cow. He stuffed Hestia in his mouth and swallowed her whole.

Just like: *GULP.* She was gone.

As you can imagine, Rhea completely freaked.

'My baby!' she screamed. 'You — you just —'

'Oh, wow.' Kronos belched. 'My bad. Sorry.'

Rhea's eyes bugged out. She screamed some more. She would have launched herself at Kronos and pummelled him with her fists, or ordered her lions to attack, but she was afraid of hurting the baby that was now stuck inside him.

'Cough her up!' Rhea demanded.

'Can't,' Kronos said. 'I have this super-strong stomach. Once something goes down, it doesn't come back up.'

'How could you swallow her?' she shouted. 'That was our child!'

'Yeah, about that . . .' Kronos tried to look apologetic. 'Listen, babe, it wasn't going to work out with that kid.'

'*Work out?*'

'There was this curse.' Kronos told her what Ouranos had prophesied. 'I mean, come on, sweetcakes! That baby wasn't even a proper Titan. She was trouble, I could tell! The next kid will be better, I'm sure.'

This sounded perfectly reasonable to Kronos, but for some reason Rhea wasn't satisfied. She stormed off in a rage.

You'd think Rhea would never forgive him. I mean, your husband eats your firstborn child like a slider hamburger . . . Your typical mother isn't going to forget that.

But Rhea's situation was complicated.

First, Kronos had swallowed the baby Hestia *whole*. Hestia, like her parents, was technically immortal. She couldn't die, even inside her father's stomach. Gross in there? Yes. A little claustrophobic? You bet. But fatal? No.

She's still alive, Rhea consoled herself. *I can find a way to get her back.*

That calmed her down a little, though she didn't have a plan. She couldn't use force to get her way. Rhea was a gentle goddess. Even if she tried to fight, most of the strongest Titans, like Hyperion and that big goon Atlas, would back Kronos up.

She couldn't risk a sneak attack with a knife or the scythe or even her lions, because that might hurt the baby.

Maybe you're thinking, *Wait a minute. If the kid is immortal, why is Rhea worried about hurting her?* But, see, immortals can be hurt badly, crippled or mutilated. An injury might not kill them, but they also don't always *heal* from damage. They just stay crippled forever. You'll see some examples of that later on.

Rhea wasn't about to cut open Kronos and risk chopping up her baby, because being in pieces is no way to live, especially when you live forever.

She couldn't divorce Kronos, because nobody had invented divorce yet. And, even if they had, Rhea would have been too scared to try. Can you blame her? As you may have noticed, Kronos was one crazy piece of work. Rhea had known that fact ever since he chopped up their dad with the scythe and then walked around the after-party in his ichor-stained shirt shouting, 'Awesome murder, guys! High five!'

She couldn't run, because Kronos was lord of the whole world. Unless she wanted to jump into Tartarus (which she didn't), there was no place to go.

Her best bet was to stick it out, bide her time and wait until she found a way to get Hestia back.

Kronos tried to be nice to her. He bought her presents and took her out to dinner, as if that could make her forget about the baby in his stomach.

When Kronos thought enough time had passed – like three or four days – he insisted that they try to have more kids.

Why? Maybe he had a secret death wish. Maybe he became obsessed with Ouranos's prophecy and wanted to see if the next kid would be a proper Titan or one of those horrible, too-powerful, too-perfect little *gods*.

So Rhea had another baby – a little girl even cuter than the first. Rhea named her Demeter.

Rhea dared to hope. Demeter was *so* adorable that maybe she would melt Kronos's heart. He couldn't possibly feel threatened by this little bundle of joy.

Kronos took the child in his arms and saw right away that Demeter was another goddess. She glowed with an aura even more powerful than Hestia's. She was trouble with a capital *tau*.

This time he didn't hesitate. He opened his jaws and swallowed her down.

Cue the screaming fit from Mom. Cue the apologies.

Rhea was *seriously* tempted to call out her lions, but now the stakes were even higher. Kronos had two kids in there.

I know, you're thinking it must've been getting crowded in the Titan lord's gut. But gods are kind of flexible about their size. Sometimes they are huge. Sometimes they're no bigger than humans.

I was not there in Kronos's stomach, thankfully, but I'm guessing the little immortal babies just made themselves small. They continued to mature, but they didn't get any bigger. They were like springs getting wound up tighter and tighter, hoping that some day they would get to burst out fully grown. And every day praying that Kronos wouldn't have hot sauce with his dinner.

Poor Rhea. Kronos insisted they try again.

'The next child will be better,' he promised. 'No more swallowing babies!'

The third kid? Also a girl. Rhea named her Hera, and she was the least Titan-ish, most godly yet. Rhea was indeed the Great Mother. In fact, she was a little *too* good at it. Every child she had was better and more powerful than the one before.

Rhea didn't want to take little Hera to Kronos, but it was a tradition back then. Dad got to hold the baby. It was one of those natural laws that Themis always insisted on. (There was also a natural law against eating your kids, but Themis was too afraid to mention that to Kronos.)

And so Rhea mustered her courage. 'My lord, may I present your daughter Hera.'

GULP.

This time, Rhea left the throne room without throwing a fit. She was too numb with pain and misery and disbelief. She had married a pathological liar who was also a murderer and a cannibal baby-eater.

Could things be any worse?

Oh, wait! He was also the king of the universe with lots of powerful henchmen, so she couldn't fight back or run away.

Yeah. Things were worse.

Two more times she gave birth to perfect, lovely god babies. The fourth child was a boy named Hades. Rhea hoped Kronos would let him live, because every dad wants a son to play catch with, right? Nope. Down the hatch, matey!

The fifth child was another boy, Poseidon. Same story. *SNARF.*

At this point, Rhea fled the palace. She wept and wailed and didn't know *what* to do. She went to her brothers and sisters, her nieces and nephews, anyone who would listen. She pleaded for help. The other Titans were either too scared of Kronos (like Themis), or they *worked* for Kronos (like Hyperion) and told her to stop whining.

Finally Rhea visited her sister Phoebe at the Oracle of Delphi, but sadly even the Oracle had no advice for her. Rhea ran to the nearest meadow, threw herself on the ground and began to cry. Suddenly she heard whispering from the earth. It was the voice of Gaia, who was still asleep, but even in her dreams the Earth Mother couldn't stand to hear the wailing of her lovely daughter.

When you are ready to deliver your next child, Gaia's voice whispered, *go to Crete to give birth! You will find help there! This child will be different! He will save the others!*

Rhea sniffled and tried to pull herself together. 'Where is Crete?'

It's an island in the south, Gaia's voice said. *You take the Ionian Sea down to, like, Kalamata. Then you turn left and – You know what? You'll find it.*

When the time came and Rhea started to get very big in the belly, she took a few deep breaths, composed herself and waddled into the throne room.

'My lord Kronos,' she said, 'I am off to Crete. I will be back with the baby.'

'Crete?' Kronos scowled. 'Why Crete?'

'Um, well,' Rhea said, 'you know how Koios and Phoebe sometimes have glimpses of the future?'

'Yeah?'

'I didn't want to spoil the surprise, but they prophesied that if I had this child in Crete it would please you best of all! And of course, my lord, I am all about pleasing you!'

Kronos frowned. He was suspicious, but he also thought, Hey, I've eaten five kids, and Rhea is still here. If she were going to try something fishy, she would've done it already.

Plus, by now his thoughts were getting a little sluggish. He had five young gods shifting around in his gut, fighting for space, so he always felt like he'd just eaten a massive dinner and needed a nap.

I mean, five gods in one stomach – *dang.* That's enough for doubles tennis, including an umpire. They'd been down there so long they were probably hoping Kronos would swallow a deck of cards or a Monopoly game.

Anyway, Kronos looked at Rhea and said, 'You'll bring the baby to me immediately?'

'Of course.'

'Okay. Off you go. Where is Crete?'

'Not sure,' Rhea said. 'I'll find it.'

And she did. Once she got there, she was immediately met by some helpful nymphs who had also heard the voice of Gaia. They brought Rhea to a cosy, well-hidden cave at the base of Mount Ida. The nymphs' stream ran nearby, so Rhea would have lots of fresh water. The bountiful forest offered plenty to eat.

Yes, I know: immortals live mostly on nectar and ambrosia, but in a pinch they could eat other stuff. Being a god wouldn't be much fun if you couldn't enjoy the occasional pizza.

Rhea gave birth to a healthy baby boy god. He was the most beautiful and perfect one yet. Rhea named him Zeus, which, depending on who you ask, either means *Sky* or *Shining* or simply *Living*. I personally vote for the last one, because I think at this point Rhea had simple hopes for this kid – keep him alive and away from hostile stomachs.

Zeus began to cry, maybe because he sensed his mother's anxiety. The sound echoed through the cave and out into the world – so loud that everyone and their Titan mother knew a baby had been born.

'Oh, great,' Rhea muttered. 'I promised to bring the child to Kronos immediately. Now word will get back to Kronos that it's baby-swallowing time.'

The cave floor rumbled. A large stone emerged from the dirt — a smooth, oval rock exactly the same size and weight as a baby god.

Rhea wasn't stupid. She knew this was a gift from Gaia. Normally, you would not be excited if your mom gave you a rock for a present, but Rhea understood what to do with it. She wrapped the stone in swaddling clothes and gave the real baby Zeus to the nymphs to take care of. She just hoped she could pull off the switcheroo once she got back to the palace.

'I'll visit as often as I can,' Rhea promised the nymphs. 'But how will you care for the baby?'

'Don't sweat it,' said Neda, one of the nymphs. 'We can feed him honey from the bees nearby. And for milk we have an *awesome* immortal goat.'

'A what, now?' Rhea asked.

The nymphs brought in their goat Amaltheia, who produced excellent magical goat milk in many different flavours, including low fat, chocolate and baby formula.

'Nice goat,' Rhea admitted. 'But what if the baby cries? Kronos has incredible hearing up there on Mount Othrys. You may have noticed this kid has a set of lungs on him. Kronos will suspect something.'

Neda considered this. She led Rhea to the cave entrance and called out to the Earth Mother: 'Oh, Gaia! I know you're asleep and all. Sorry to disturb you. But we could use some help guarding this kid! Preferably some very loud help!'

The ground rumbled again. Three new helpers emerged, born of soil and the spilled blood of Ouranos (like I said, that stuff got *everywhere*). The new guys were large, hairy humanoids, dressed in fur and feathers and leather like they were on their way to some primeval festival deep in the rainforest. They were armed with spears and shields, so they looked more like headhunters than nursemaids.

'WE ARE THE KOURETES!' one shouted at the top of his lungs. 'WE WILL HELP!'

'Thank you,' Rhea said. 'Do you have to speak so loudly?'

'THIS IS MY INSIDE VOICE!' the warrior yelled.

Baby Zeus began crying again. The three warriors immediately busted out some sweet tribal dance moves, beating their spears on their shields and shouting and chanting. They covered up the crying just fine.

For some reason, Baby Zeus seemed to like the noise. He went to sleep in the nymph Neda's arms, and the Kouretes stopped.

'Okay, well,' Rhea said, her ears popping, 'looks like you have things under control here.' She hefted her fake baby. 'Wish me luck.'

Once she got back to Mount Othrys, Rhea stormed into the throne room with her swaddled boulder. She was terrified her plan wouldn't work, but after so many years married to Kronos she was learning to be a good actress. She marched right up to King Cannibal and shouted, 'This is the best baby yet! A fine little boy named, uh, Rocky! And I suppose you're going to eat him!'

Kronos grimaced. Honestly, he wasn't excited about swallowing another baby god. He was full! But when you're king you do what you have to do.

'Yeah – sorry, hon,' he said. 'I have to. Prophecy and all.'

'I hate you!' she screamed. 'Ouranos was a horrible father, but at least he didn't swallow us!'

Kronos snarled. 'Give me that child!'

'No!'

Kronos roared. He unhinged his jaw and showed his extreme mouth-opening skills. 'NOW!'

He snatched up the swaddled boulder and stuffed it down his throat without even looking at it, just as Rhea had hoped.

In Kronos's belly, the five undigested young gods heard the rock rolling down the oesophagus.

'Incoming!' yelled Poseidon.

They shifted – as much as they could in the cramped space – and Rocky landed in their midst.

'This is not a baby,' Hades noticed. 'I think it's a rock.'

He was observant that way.

Meanwhile, in the throne room, Rhea threw an Oscar-worthy tantrum. She screamed and stomped her feet and called Kronos all kinds of unflattering names.

'RO-O-CCCKY!' she wailed. 'NO-O-O-O-O-O-O!'

Kronos started to get a bad stomach ache.

'That kid was *filling*,' he complained. 'What have you been feeding him?'

'Why should you care?' Rhea wailed. 'I will never have another child again!'

That was okay with Kronos. He was stuffed.

Rhea ran screaming out of the throne room, and he didn't try to stop her.

Eventually, things quieted down in the palace. Kronos was now convinced he had thwarted the curse of Ouranos. No way could his children displace him, since he knew exactly where they all were. He was the king of the cosmos and would never be overthrown!

Meanwhile, Rhea visited Mount Ida whenever she could. Her baby boy began to grow up, and Rhea made sure he heard lots of bedtime stories about his horrible father and his five undigested siblings who were just waiting to be rescued from Kronos's gut.

So you *know* that when Zeus comes of age, there's going to be a father–son smackdown of epic proportions. If you want a 'happily ever after' ending for Kronos and his Titans, I would stop reading now. Because in the next chapter Zeus goes nuclear.

THE OLYMPIANS BASH SOME HEADS

ZEUS HAD A GOOD CHILDHOOD ON MOUNT IDA. He spent his days romping around the countryside with nymphs and satyrs, learning to fight with his loud friends the Kouretes, eating his fill of honey and magical goat milk (yum!), and of course never going to school, because school hadn't been invented yet.

By the time he was a young adult god, he had grown into a good-looking dude – all tan and ripped from his time in the forest and at the beach. He had short black hair, a neatly trimmed beard and eyes as blue as the sky, though they could cloud over *very* fast when he got angry.

One day his mom, Rhea, came to visit on her chariot pulled by lions.

'Zeus,' she said, 'you need a summer job.'

Zeus scratched his beard. He liked the word *summer.* He

wasn't so sure about the word *job*. 'What did you have in mind?'

Rhea's eyes gleamed. She had been planning her revenge on Kronos for a long time. Now, looking at her son – so confident, strong and handsome – she knew the time had come.

'There's an opening at the palace for a cupbearer,' she said.

'But I have no experience bearing cups,' Zeus said.

'It's easy,' Rhea promised. 'Whenever King Kronos asks for a drink, you bring it to him. The pay isn't great, but the job has good side benefits, such as overthrowing your father and becoming lord of the cosmos.'

'I'm down with that,' Zeus said. 'But won't Kronos recognize me as a god?'

'I've been thinking about that,' Rhea said. 'Your siblings have survived in Kronos's gut all these years and, like you, they're fully grown by now. That means they must have the power to change their size and shape. *You* should have that power, too. See if you can make yourself appear less godly, more . . . Titan-ish.'

Zeus considered that. He had already discovered his ability to change shape. Once, he'd scared his caretaker nymphs by transforming into a bear. Another time he'd won a footrace with some satyrs by transforming into a wolf. The satyrs claimed he'd cheated, but he *totally* hadn't. It was a footrace. Wolves ran on their feet. It's not like he'd turned into an eagle (which he could also do).

The only Titan that Zeus had ever seen up close was his mother, but he knew Titans were generally bigger than he was. They didn't radiate power the way he did. They gave off a slightly different vibe – more violent and rougher around the edges. He imagined himself as a Titan. When he opened his eyes, he was taller than his mom for the first time. He felt as if he'd slept badly after a hard day strangling his enemies.

'Well done!' Rhea said. 'Now, let's go to your job interview.'

When Zeus saw Mount Othrys for the first time, his jaw dropped. The palace was *huge*. Its gleaming black towers rose into the clouds like greedy fingers grasping for the stars.

The fortress was meant to inspire fear. Zeus understood that immediately. But it also seemed lonely and dismal – not a fun place to be king. Zeus decided that if he ever got his own crib it would be much cooler than Othrys. He wouldn't go so heavy on the whole 'Lord of Darkness' look. His palace would be brilliant, blinding white.

One thing at a time, he told himself. *I have to bear cups first.*

Rhea escorted her son into the royal hall, where Old King Cannibal was snoozing on his throne. The years had not been kind to Kronos, which was ironic, since he was the lord of time. He hadn't *aged*, exactly, but he seemed tired and listless. Making mortal life forms wither and die no longer amused him. Stepping on humans didn't make him laugh like it used to, despite their cute little shrieks.

He'd put on weight from eating and drinking so much. The five gods in his stomach didn't help. They'd got bigger and heavier over the years. They were constantly trying to break out by climbing up Kronos's throat. Their attempts were unsuccessful, but they gave Kronos terrible acid reflux.

Rhea approached the throne. 'My lord, I have someone for you to meet!'

Kronos snorted and opened his eyes. 'I wasn't asleep!' He

blinked at the handsome young Titan who stood before him. 'Who . . . ?'

The young immortal bowed low. 'I am Zeus, my lord.' Zeus had decided to use his real name, because – why not? Kronos had never heard it. 'I would like to be your cupbearer.'

Kronos studied the newcomer's face. Something about him seemed vaguely familiar – the sparkle in his eyes, the crooked way he smiled. Of course *all* the Titans were related. Maybe that was it. Kronos had so many nieces and nephews these days, he couldn't keep track of them all. Still, he found this young one unsettling . . .

He looked around, trying to remember exactly who had introduced the boy, but Rhea had already faded into the shadows. Kronos's stomach was too full and his thoughts were too sluggish for him to stay suspicious for very long.

'Well,' he said to the boy, 'do you have any experience bearing cups?'

Zeus grinned. 'No, my lord. But I'm a quick learner. I can also sing, dance and tell satyr jokes.'

Zeus burst into a song the nymphs had taught him. Then he demonstrated some Kouretes dance moves. It was the most interesting thing that had happened on Mount Othrys in a long time. Other Titans gathered in the throne room to watch. Soon they were cheering and laughing. Even Kronos had a smile on his face.

'You're hired,' Kronos said. 'In fact, I'm thirsty.'

'One cup, coming up!' Zeus hustled off to find the kitchen, where he filled a golden chalice with ice-cold nectar.

In no time, Zeus became the most popular servant in the palace. He bore cups like nobody's business. His singing was as clear as the streams on Mount Ida. His satyr jokes were so edgy I can't tell them in a family-friendly book.

He always knew exactly what Kronos would like to drink — hot spiced nectar, cold nectar with a twist of lemon, nectar spritzer with a little cranberry juice. He also introduced the Titans to drinking contests, which were very popular with the satyrs back on Mount Ida. Everybody at the table started chugging at the same time. The fastest drinker won. What did he win? Well, nothing — but it was a great way to show off, because nothing looks more manly (or Titanly) than having nectar dribbling down your chin and all over your shirt.

These contests rekindled some of Kronos's competitive spirit. Sure, he was king of the universe, but he was still the youngest of twelve kids. He couldn't allow his brothers or nephews to be better than him at anything. Despite his constantly full stomach, he got to the point where he could chug a full goblet of nectar in three seconds, and Titan goblets are the size of water-cooler bottles.

He trusted Zeus to fill his glass with whatever would go down the smoothest.

Which was exactly Zeus's plan.

One night when Kronos was dining with his favourite lieutenants, Zeus mixed some special brews for the drinking contest. The nymphs back on Mount Ida had taught him a lot about herbs and stuff. He knew which plants could make you drowsy, which ones could make you dizzy, and which could make you feel so *terrible* that your stomach would want to exit your body.

For the king's guests, Zeus mixed some sleepy-time extra-dizzy nighty-night nectar. For Kronos, he mixed a special blend of nectar and mustard. Some versions of the story will say Zeus used wine, but that can't be right, because wine hadn't been invented yet. We'll get to that later.

Anyway, the stuff in Kronos's goblet was über-nasty. Zeus set it aside and waited for the right moment.

Dinner started out as usual, with lots of drinking, eating and catching up on the Titan news of the day. Zeus kept the nectar flowing. He entertained the guests with his jokes and his singing. Towards the end of the evening, when everybody was content and relaxed and sleepy, Zeus began boasting about the king's drinking skill.

'Kronos is the boss at drinking!' he proclaimed. 'You should *see* him. The guy is *insane*. I mean his record is, what – three seconds?'

'Urg,' Kronos said. He was full already and had been hoping to avoid a drinking contest.

'If he wanted to,' Zeus said, 'he could drink faster than all of you! I bet he would set a new world record tonight. Wouldn't you love to see that?'

Atlas, Hyperion, Koios and the others cheered and called for a contest.

Kronos *really* wasn't in the mood, but he couldn't decline. His honour as a super-chugger was at stake. He gestured for Zeus to bring in another round.

Zeus ran to the kitchen and fetched his special concoctions. He offered the guests their sleepy-time nectar, then served Kronos last, giving the king no time to smell his brew before yelling, 'Ready, set, go!'

The Titans gulped down their tasty beverages. Kronos

immediately noticed that his nectar tasted weird, but it was a contest. He couldn't stop chugging. The whole point was to drain the cup! Maybe his taste buds were just a little off. After all, Zeus had never steered him wrong.

Kronos drained his nectar in two and a half seconds. He slammed the goblet upside down on the table and shouted, 'I win! I –'

The next sound out of his mouth was like a walrus getting the Heimlich manoeuvre.

There's no pleasant way to say it. Kronos puked. He puked a puke worthy of the king of the universe. It was a *kingly* puke.

His stomach tried to propel itself out his throat. His mouth hinged open all by itself – the better to upchuck you with, my dear – and shot out five gods, a very slimy rock, quite a lot of nectar, some biscuits and a chariot licence plate. (No, I don't know how *that* got in there.)

The five disgorged gods immediately grew to full-size adults right there on the dining table. The Titan guests stared in amazement, their minds working slowly due to the spiked nectar.

As for Kronos, he was still trying to catapult his guts across the throne room.

'Get –' he retched – 'them!'

Atlas was the first to react. He yelled, 'Guards!' and tried to stand, but he was so dizzy he fell right into Hyperion's lap.

Zeus wanted to lunge for his father's scythe. He wanted to slice up the old cannibal on the spot, but the other Titans were starting to recover from their shock. They might be slow and sleepy, but they had weapons. Meanwhile, Zeus's only weapon was a serving tray. His army consisted of five slimy, unarmed gods who had spent very little time outside a stomach, much less in combat.

Guards started pouring into the throne room.

Zeus turned to his confused siblings. 'I'm your brother Zeus. Follow me, and I will give you freedom and revenge. Also honey and goat milk.'

That was good enough for the gods. While Kronos retched and his fighters fumbled with their weapons, Zeus and his siblings turned into eagles and soared out of the palace.

'Now what?' Hades asked.

The six gods had gathered at Zeus's secret lair on Mount Ida, which his siblings refused to call the Zeus Cave. Zeus had briefed them on what was happening in the world, but they all knew they couldn't stay on Mount Ida very long. The nymphs had heard rumours whispered through the earth: Kronos was sending his Titans to scour the world for the escapees. He wanted them brought back, either in chains or in small pieces. He wasn't particular.

'Now we fight,' Zeus said.

Poseidon grunted. He'd only been out of Kronos's gut for a day, but he was already starting to dislike his youngest brother – this upstart *Zeus*, who thought he should be in charge just because he had rescued them.

'I'm all for fighting Dad,' Poseidon said, 'but that requires weapons. Do you have any?'

Zeus scratched his ear. He hadn't really thought that far ahead. 'Well, no . . .'

'Perhaps we can make peace,' Hestia suggested.

The others stared at her as if she were crazy. Hestia was the eldest and gentlest of the gods, but her siblings didn't take her seriously. You have to wonder how the world might've been different if Hestia had been put in charge, but, alas, she wasn't.

'Uh, no,' said Demeter. 'I will never forgive our father. Perhaps we could steal his scythe. We could chop him up like he did Ouranos! Then I could use the scythe for something better – like cutting wheat! Did you see those beautiful fields we flew over?'

Hera scowled at her sister. 'What is it with you and crops? All those years in Kronos's gut, all you ever talked about was plants, which you never even saw before today!'

Demeter blushed. 'I don't know. I always dream about green fields. They're so peaceful and beautiful and –'

'My children!' said a voice from the woods.

Mother Rhea stepped into the clearing. She hugged each of her precious sons and daughters, weeping tears of joy over their freedom. Then she drew them together and said, 'I know where you can get weapons.'

She told them the story of the Hundred-Handed Ones and the Elder Cyclopes, whom Kronos had exiled to Tartarus for a second time.

'The Hundred-Handed Ones are incredible stonemasons,' Rhea said. 'They built Kronos's palace.'

'Which is pretty awesome,' Zeus admitted.

'They are strong, and they hate Kronos,' Rhea continued. 'They would be good in battle. As for the Cyclopes, they are talented blacksmiths. If anyone can forge weapons more powerful than your father's scythe, they can.'

Hades's dark eyes gleamed. The idea of descending into

the most dangerous, vilest part of creation somehow appealed to him. 'So we go to Tartarus, and we bring back the Cyclopes and Hundred-Handed Ones.'

'Piece of cake,' said Hera. She knew about cake, because Kronos had eaten lots of it. The crumbs and icing were always getting in her hair. 'Let's go.'

A Tartarus jailbreak may not sound like an easy thing for you or me, but six gods can accomplish a lot when they put their minds to it. Hades found a cave system that led deep into the Underworld. He seemed to have a knack for navigating the tunnels. He led his siblings along the course of a subterranean river called the Styx until it spilled over a cliff into the void of Tartarus. The gods became bats (you could argue that they were already bats, but you know what I mean) and flew into the abyss.

At the bottom, they found a gloomy landscape of rock spires, grey wastes, fiery pits and poisonous fog, with all sorts of nasty monsters and evil spirits roaming about. Apparently Tartarus, the spirit of the pit, had been breeding more primordial gods down there in the darkness, and they'd been having kids of their own.

The six young gods crept around until they found the maximum-security zone, surrounded by a high brass wall and patrolled by demons. In bat form the gods could fly over the wall easily, but once inside they spotted the jailer and almost lost their nerve.

Kronos had personally hired the most horrible monster in Tartarus to make sure his high-value prisoners never escaped.

Her name was Kampê.

I don't know if Kronos found her on Craigslist or what, but if the worst creatures from your nightmares had nightmares of their own they would probably dream about Kampê. From the waist up, she was a humanoid female with snakes for hair. (If that sounds familiar, it's because the hairdo really caught on with other monsters later.) From the waist down, she was a four-legged dragon. Thousands of vipers sprouted from her legs like grass skirts. Her waist was ringed with the heads of fifty hideous beasts – bears, boars, wombats, you name it – always snapping and snarling and trying to eat Kampê's shirt.

Large, dark reptilian wings grew from her shoulder blades. Her scorpionlike tail swished back and forth, dripping venom. Basically, Kampê didn't get invited on many dates.

The gods watched from behind a pile of boulders as the monstrous jailer trudged back and forth, lashing the Elder Cyclopes with a fiery whip and stinging the Hundred-Handed Ones with her scorpion tail whenever they got out of line.

The poor prisoners were forced to work without any break – no water, no sleep, no food, nothing. The Hundred-Handed Ones spent their time at the far end of the yard, quarrying stone blocks from the hard volcanic floor. The Cyclopes worked at the closer end. They each had a forge where they smelted metals and hammered out sheets of bronze and iron. If the Cyclopes tried to sit down, or even pause long enough to catch their breaths, Kampê would leave fresh burning lash marks across their backs.

Even worse, the prisoners weren't allowed to finish anything they started. As soon as the Hundred-Handed Ones had a goodly stack of building blocks, Kampê forced them to break their quarried stone into rubble. Whenever the Cyclopes were on the verge of finishing a weapon or a shield or even a tool that might be dangerous, Kampê confiscated it and threw it into the bubbling pits of magma.

You're probably thinking, *Hey, there were six big dudes and only one Kampê. Why didn't they overpower her?*

But Kampê had the whip. The venom in her tail could incapacitate even an Elder Cyclops for hours, leaving him writhing in pain. The dragon lady was straight-up *terrifying*, and the prisoners were chained around their feet so they couldn't run far.

Besides, the Hundred-Handed Ones and the Cyclopes were gentle souls. Despite their looks, they were builders, not fighters. Give these dudes a bucket of Lego and they'd be happy for days.

Zeus waited until Kampê marched to the far end of the prison yard. Then he sneaked up to the nearest Cyclops.

'Psst!' he called.

The Cyclops lowered his hammer. He turned towards Zeus, but his one big eye had been staring into the flames so long that he couldn't see who was talking.

'I am not Psst,' the Cyclops said. 'I am Brontes.'

Oh, boy, Zeus thought. This may take a while.

'Hey, Brontes.' Zeus spoke slowly and cheerfully, like he was trying to coax a puppy out of its box. 'I'm Zeus. I've come to rescue you.'

Brontes scowled. 'I have heard that before. Kronos tricked us.'

'Yeah, I know,' Zeus said. 'Kronos is my enemy too. Together, we can get revenge and throw *him* down here. How does that sound?'

'Sounds good,' Brontes said. 'But how?'

'First we need weapons,' Zeus said. 'Can you make us some?'

Brontes shook his head. 'Kampê is always watching. She will not let us finish any project.'

'How about you each make a different part of each weapon?' Zeus suggested. 'Then you can assemble them at the last second and toss them over to us. Kampê will never know.'

'You are smart.'

'I know, right? Spread the word to your friends.' Zeus crept back behind the boulders.

Brontes whispered the plan to his brothers Arges and Steropes. Then they tapped their hammers on their anvils in a secret code they'd developed, sending the message across the yard to the Hundred-Handed Ones – Briares, Kottos and Gyes.

I know that's a bunch of horrible names, but remember Gaia didn't have much time to hold her monstrous triplets before Ouranos pitched them into Tartarus. At least they didn't end up named Huey, Dewey and Louie.

The gods waited in the darkness while the Cyclopes forged pieces of the new weapons, making each one look like a harmless, incomplete doohickey. I don't know if the stuff would've got through airport security, but it was good enough to fool Kampê.

The next time the she-dragon turned her back and marched towards the far side of the yard, Brontes quickly assembled the first magic weapon and tossed it to Zeus. It looked like a bronze rocket, about four feet long, with nose cones on both ends. Zeus's hand fit perfectly around the centre. As soon as he lifted it, his whole body tingled with power.

Poseidon frowned. 'What *is* that? It's not a scythe.'

Sparks flew from the points. Electricity arced from one end to the other. Zeus aimed the thing at a nearby boulder, and a thousand tendrils of lightning zapped it into dust.

'Oh, yeah,' Zeus said. 'I can work with this.'

Fortunately, Kampê didn't seem to notice the blast. Maybe things exploded a lot in Tartarus.

A few minutes later, Brontes tossed them a second weapon – a spear with three prongs. Poseidon caught it.

He immediately fell in love with the trident. He liked pointy things! Also, he could feel the power of storms humming through the spear. When he concentrated, a miniature tornado swirled around its three points, getting faster and larger the more he focused. When he planted the spear on the ground, the floor of the pit began to shake and crack.

'Best weapon,' he announced. 'Right here.'

Brontes tossed them a third item. Hades caught this one – a gleaming bronze war helmet decorated with scenes of death and destruction.

'You get weapons,' Hades grumbled. 'I get a hat.'

He put it on and disappeared.

'Dude, you're invisible,' Zeus said.

'Yeah.' Hades sighed miserably. 'I'm used to it.'

'No, I mean you're *actually* invisible.'

'Huh.' Hades willed himself to turn visible again.

'That is one scary hat,' Demeter said.

'Yeah,' Hades agreed. 'Yeah, it is.'

He decided to try something else. He glared at his brothers, and waves of terror radiated from the helmet. Zeus and Poseidon turned pale. They started to sweat. Zeus almost dropped his new lightning maker.

'Stop that!' Zeus hissed. 'You're freaking me out!'

Hades grinned. 'Okay, maybe the hat isn't so bad.'

Hera crossed her arms and sniffed disdainfully. 'Boys and their toys. I don't suppose *we* get weapons? Are we just supposed to stand back and be cheerleaders while you three do the fighting?'

Zeus winked at her. 'Don't worry, baby. I'll protect you.'

'I think I'm going to be sick,' Hera said.

It's possible the Cyclopes would have made weapons for the women. But at that moment Kampê turned and marched back towards the Cyclopes. Maybe she had noticed the smoke from Zeus's lightning blast, or the swirling clouds from Poseidon's trident. Maybe she could taste the residual fear in the air from Hades's helmet. Whatever tipped her off, she detected the presence of the gods.

She raised her whip and howled, 'RAWRGGGGWRRR!'

She charged towards their hiding place, her tail lashing, the thousands of vipers around her legs dripping poison.

'Great,' muttered Hera.

'I got this,' Zeus promised.

He stood and raised his bronze lightning bolt. He focused all his energy into the weapon.

KA-BLAM!

A column of white-hot power shot towards Kampê – the most blinding light that had ever been seen in Tartarus.

Kampê just had time to think, *Uh-oh*, before the bolt blasted her into a million sizzling pieces of reptile confetti.

'THAT'S what I'm talking about!' Zeus yelled happily.

Poseidon lowered his trident. 'Man, give the rest of us a chance.'

'You go free the Cyclopes and the Hundred-Handed Ones,' Zeus suggested.

Poseidon grumbled, but he used his trident to strike the dark chains from the prisoners' feet.

'Thank you,' Brontes said. 'We will help you fight Kronos.'

'Excellent!' Zeus said.

Hera cleared her throat. 'Yes, but about those weapons for the ladies –'

Outside the bronze walls, monstrous roars reverberated through the pit. Every spirit and beast in Tartarus had probably seen the flash of lightning, and now they were closing in to investigate.

'We should leave,' Demeter said. 'Like, right now.'

That was the best non-grain-related idea Demeter had ever had, so Hades led his siblings back to the upper world, along with their six large new friends.

Kronos wasn't an easy guy to defeat.

By most accounts, the Titan War took ten years – or maybe Kronos just used his time tricks to make it *seem* that long, hoping the gods would give up. If so, it didn't work.

Rhea the Great Mother visited every Titan she could, trying to persuade them to side with Zeus. Many listened. After all, Kronos wasn't the most popular leader. Almost all the female Titans either helped Zeus or stayed out of his way. Prometheus, the creator of humans, was smart enough to remain neutral. Oceanus kept to himself in the depths of the ocean. Helios and Selene, the sun and moon, agreed not to take sides as long as they got to keep their jobs.

That left Kronos and most of the other male Titans, with Atlas as his general and champion fighter.

The gods and Titans skirmished back and forth — blowing up an island here, vaporizing a sea there. The Titans were strong and well armed. At the beginning, they held the advantage. Even with magic Cyclops weapons, the gods weren't used to combat. It's a hard thing not to drop your trident and run when Atlas is barrelling down on you, screaming and waving his sword.

But the gods *did* learn to fight. The Cyclopes eventually armed all Zeus's allies with top-of-the-line weapons. The Hundred-Handed Ones learned to throw barrages of stones like living catapults.

You're thinking, *How hard can it be to throw rocks?*

Okay, *you* try throwing rocks with both hands at the same time and hitting your target. It's not as easy as it sounds. Now, imagine coordinating one hundred hands — all throwing rocks the size of refrigerators. If you're not careful, you'll spew rocks everywhere and crush yourself and your allies.

Once the gods learned to fight, the war *still* took a long time, because none of the combatants on either side could die. You couldn't just stab a guy, zap him or throw a house on him and call it a day. You had to actually capture each enemy and make sure he was hurt so badly that he would never heal. Then you had to figure out what to do with his crippled body. As Zeus knew, even throwing somebody into Tartarus wasn't a guarantee he would stay gone forever.

Little skirmishes weren't going to decide anything.

Finally Zeus came up with his big plan.

'We have to storm Mount Othrys,' he told his siblings at their weekly war meeting. 'A full frontal assault on their headquarters. If we do that, the hostile Titans will rally to protect Kronos. Then we can take them all down at once.'

'In other words,' Hades said, 'you want us to commit *suicide.*'

Poseidon leaned on his trident. 'For once, I agree with Hades. If we march up the slopes of Mount Othrys, Atlas will be ready for us. His troops will have the high ground. They'll smash us flat. If we try flying in, we'll get shot out of the air. They've got plenty of anti-god missile weapons.'

Zeus's eyes gleamed. 'But I've got a different plan. We'll soften them up by attacking from the next mountain over.'

'Do what, now?' asked Demeter. She looked uncomfortable in her armour, even though she'd designed it herself. She'd painted a sheaf of barley and a daisy on her shield, and for her main weapon she'd chosen a fearsome garden trowel.

Zeus drew a map of the Greek mainland in the ground. Near Mount Othrys was another Greek mountain – not quite as tall, not as well known. It was called Mount Olympus.

'We scale Olympus,' Zeus said. 'They won't be expecting that, but Othrys will be within range of our missile weapons. The Hundred-Handed Ones will launch volleys of boulders. I'll bust out the lightning. Poseidon will summon storms and earthquakes.'

'And I'll turn invisible,' Hades muttered.

Zeus clapped his brother on the shoulder. 'You have an important job, too. You send waves of terror through the enemy ranks. Once we've destroyed their defences, we all fly over there –'

'Including us three goddesses?' Demeter prompted. 'We can fight, too, you know.'

'Sure!' Zeus smiled nervously. 'Did you think I'd forgotten you?'

'Yes,' said Demeter.

'Uh, anyway,' Zeus continued, 'we fly over to Mount Othrys, smash anybody who's left standing and take them all prisoner.'

Hestia wrapped herself in her plain brown shawl. 'I still think we should make peace.'

'NO!' the others yelled.

Hera tapped the map. 'It's a crazy plan. I like it.'

So that night, under cover of darkness, the gods and their allies climbed Mount Olympus for the first time.

The next morning, as Helios rode his chick magnet into the sky, King Kronos awoke to a sound like thunder. Probably because it *was* thunder.

Storm clouds rolled in from every direction. Zeus hurled a lightning bolt that blasted the tallest tower into black marble shrapnel. The Hundred-Handed Ones chucked so many boulders towards Mount Othrys that when Kronos looked out of his window it seemed to be raining major appliances.

The beautiful palace domes imploded in mushroom clouds of dust. Walls crumbled. Columns fell like dominoes. The Hundred-Handed Ones had built Mount Othrys, and they knew exactly how to destroy it.

As the palace shook, Kronos grabbed his scythe and called

his brethren to attack. But the thing was a) scythes really don't do much against boulders and lightning, b) nobody could hear him over the noise, and c) the palace was disintegrating around him. Just as he was saying, 'Titans, let's go!' a three-ton section of the ceiling collapsed on his head.

The battle was a massacre, if you can have a massacre where nobody dies.

A few Titans tried to counterattack, only to be buried in an avalanche of rubble and boulders.

After the initial assault, the gods flew over and mopped up the resistance. Poseidon summoned earthquakes to swallow their enemies. Hades popped up in random places and yelled, 'Boo!' His helmet of terror (or his Boo Cap, as the others called it) sent Titans fleeing straight off the sides of cliffs, or into the waiting arms of the Elder Cyclopes.

When the dust settled and the storm clouds lifted, even the gods were in awe of what they'd done.

Not only was Kronos's palace gone, but the entire top of Mount Othrys had been sheared away with it.

Did I tell you Othrys was the highest mountain in Greece? Not any more. Today Mount Olympus, which *used* to be the smaller mountain, is over nine thousand feet tall. Mount Othrys is only five thousand and small change. Zeus and the Hundred-Handed Ones had basically cut the mountain in half.

The Cyclopes dug the Titans out of the rubble and began chaining them up. None of them got away. General Atlas and the four brothers who controlled the corners of the earth were dragged before Zeus and made to kneel.

'Ah, my dear uncles!' Zeus chuckled. 'Koios, Krios,

Hyperion, Iapetus – you four are going straight to Tartarus, where you will remain for all time!'

The four brothers hung their heads in shame, but General Atlas laughed at his captors.

'Puny gods!' he bellowed. Even wrapped in chains, he was intimidating. 'You know nothing of how the universe works. If you throw these four into Tartarus, the entire sky will fall! Only their presence at the four corners of the earth keeps the wide expanse of Ouranos from crashing down upon us.'

'Maybe.' Zeus grinned. 'But fortunately, Atlas, I have a solution! You're always boasting how strong you are. From now on, you're going to hold the sky up all by yourself!'

'What?'

'Brontes, Arges, Steropes,' Zeus called. 'He's all yours.'

The Elder Cyclopes dragged Atlas to a distant mountaintop where the sky was very close. I don't know how they did it, but they caused the sky to form a new central support pillar – a single funnel cloud, like the bottom point of a spinning top. They chained Atlas to the mountain and forced the entire weight of the sky onto his shoulders.

Now you're thinking, *Why didn't he just refuse to hold it and let the sky fall?*

I did mention the chains, right? He couldn't run away without getting flattened. Also, it's hard to appreciate unless you've done it (which I have), but holding the sky is kind of like being stuck under a loaded barbell during a bench press. All your concentration goes into keeping that thing from crushing you. You can't lift it, because it's too heavy. You can't release it, because it will squash you as it drops. All you can do is hold it in place, sweating and straining and whimpering 'Help!' hoping somebody will walk through the gym, notice you being slowly pressed into a pancake and lift the weight off you. But what if no one does? Imagine being stuck in that situation for *eternity*.

That was Atlas's punishment. All the other Titans who fought in the war got off easy. They were pitched headfirst into Tartarus.

Which leaves us with the million-drachma question: what happened to Kronos?

There are a lot of different stories. Most agree that the Crooked One was dug out of the rubble and brought before Zeus. Most say he was bound in chains like the other Titans and tossed into Tartarus.

According to some later traditions – and I kind of like this version – Zeus took his father's scythe and sliced him up the way Kronos had sliced up Ouranos. Kronos was thrown into Tartarus in teeny-tiny pieces. Supposedly, that's where we get the idea of Father Time with his scythe, being deposed every January first by Baby New Year – though it's difficult to imagine Zeus in a diaper and a party hat.

Some versions claim that Zeus released Kronos from Tartarus many years later – either to live out his retirement in Italy, or to rule the Isles of the Blest in Elysium. Personally, I don't buy that. It doesn't make sense if you believe that Kronos was chopped to bits. And, if you know Zeus, you know he's not exactly the forgive-and-forget type.

Anyway, Kronos was done. The age of the Titans was over.

The Titans who *didn't* fight against the gods were allowed to stick around. Some, like Helios and Selene, kept their jobs. Some even intermarried with the gods.

Zeus named himself the new king of the cosmos, but he was smarter than Kronos. He sat down with his brothers and said, 'Look, I want to be fair about this. How about we throw dice for control of different parts of the world? Highest roll gets first choice.'

Hades frowned. 'I have rotten luck. What parts are we talking about?'

'The sky, the sea and the Underworld,' Zeus offered.

'You mean Tartarus?' Poseidon asked. 'Gross!'

'I mean the *upper* Underworld,' Zeus said. 'You know, the *nice* part nearer to the surface. That's not so bad – big caves, lots of jewels, riverside real estate on the Styx.'

'Huh,' Hades said. 'What about the earth itself? Greece and all the other lands?'

'That will be neutral territory,' Zeus suggested. 'We can all operate on the earth.'

The brothers agreed. Notice how the sisters were not invited to this little dice game? I know. Totally unfair. But that's how it went down.

No surprise, Zeus got the highest roll. He chose the sky for his domain, which made sense because of the lightning bolts and all. Poseidon got the second-highest roll. He chose the sea and became the supreme god of the waters, above Oceanus, who got pushed ever further to the margins of the world, and Pontus, who was mostly asleep in the muck all the time anyway.

Hades got the worst roll, as he expected. He took the Underworld as his domain, but it kind of suited his gloomy personality, so he didn't complain (much).

The Hundred-Handed Ones built Zeus the gleaming palace he'd always dreamed of at the top of Mount Olympus.

Then Zeus sent them back to Tartarus — but this time as jailers to watch over the Titans. The Hundred-Handed Ones didn't really mind. At least now *they* were the ones with the whips.

The Elder Cyclopes went to work for the gods. They constructed a workshop at the bottom of the sea near the island of Lemnos, where there was lots of volcanic heat to power their forges. They made tons of special weapons and other fun collectibles, and had a good health package with a week of paid vacation every year.

As for the gods, Zeus invited them all to live with him on Mount Olympus. Each of them had a throne in the main hall, so, even though Zeus was in charge, it was more like a council than a dictatorship. They called themselves the Olympians.

Well . . . I *say* they were all welcome in Olympus: but Hades, not so much. The guy had always creeped out his siblings. Now that he was lord of the Underworld he seemed to bring doom and darkness with him wherever he went.

'You understand,' Zeus told him privately, 'we can't have an Underworld throne up here on Mount Olympus. It would make the other gods uncomfortable, and the skulls and black stone really wouldn't go with the decor.'

'Oh, sure,' grumbled Hades. 'I see how it is.'

Anyway, that's how things got started with the gods on Mount Olympus. Eventually there would be twelve thrones in the council chamber, and a whole bunch of other gods who *didn't* have thrones.

The Olympians figured that now they could settle down and rule the world in peace.

There was only one problem. Remember that the Earth Mother Gaia was taking a nap all this time? Well, eventually she would wake up. And when she got home, and found out her favourite kids, the Titans, had been thrown into Tartarus, Zeusie was going to have some explaining to do.

But that's a tale for another day.

Now it's time to meet the gods, up close and personal. Just be warned, some of their stories might make you feel like Kronos after a big glass of mustard nectar.

ZEUS

WHY IS ZEUS ALWAYS FIRST?
Seriously, every book about the Greek gods has to start with this guy. Are we doing reverse alphabetical order? I know he's the king of Olympus and all – but, trust me, this dude's ego does *not* need to get any bigger.

You know what? Forget him.

We're going to talk about the gods in the order they were born, women first. Take a backseat, Zeus. We're starting with Hestia.

HESTIA CHOOSES BACHELOR NUMBER ZERO

IN SOME WAYS, Hestia was a lot like her mom, Rhea.

She had an honest smile, warm brown eyes and black hair that framed her face in ringlets. She was gentle and good-natured. She never said a bad word about anybody. If you walked into a party on Mount Olympus, Hestia wouldn't be the first girl who caught your eye. She wasn't flashy or loud or crazy. She was more like the goddess next door – sweet and pretty in an unpretentious way. Usually she kept her hair tucked under a linen shawl. She wore plain, modest dresses and never used make-up.

I said earlier that nobody took her seriously, and it's true the other gods weren't good about taking her advice. Kronos had swallowed Hestia first, so she'd been barfed up last. Because of that, her siblings tended to think of her as the youngest rather than the oldest – the last one to emerge. She was quieter and more peaceful than her siblings, but that didn't mean they didn't *love* her. Like Rhea, Hestia was a hard person not to love.

In one important way, though, Hestia was *not* like Rhea. Her mom was known for being . . . well, a mom. The Great Mother. The Ultimate Mama. *La Madre Grande.*

Hestia wanted nothing to do with being a mom.

She didn't have a problem with *other* people's families. She loved her siblings, and once they started having kids she loved them, too. Her fondest wish was for the whole Olympian family to get along and spend quality time together around the hearth, chatting or having dinner or playing Twister – really any wholesome activity.

Hestia just didn't want to get married herself.

If you think about it, you can see why. Hestia had spent years inside Kronos's gut. She had a very good memory, and could even recall Kronos gulping her down when she was a newborn. She remembered the sound of her mother wailing in despair. Hestia had nightmares that the same thing might happen to her. She didn't want to get married only to find out her husband was actually a baby-swallowing cannibal.

She wasn't being paranoid, either. She had *proof* that Zeus could be as bad as Kronos.

See, after the war with Kronos, Zeus decided it would be a good idea for him to marry a Titan, sort of to show there were no hard feelings. He married one of Oceanus's daughters, a girl named Metis, who was the Titan of good advice and planning – kind of like the Titans' life coach.

Metis was smart about advising others, but apparently she wasn't so bright when it came to her own life. When she was pregnant with her first kid, she told Zeus, 'My husband, I have good news! I foresee that this child will be a girl. But if we have another child together it will be a boy. And – you're going to love this – he will be destined to rule the universe some day! Isn't that awesome?'

Zeus panicked. He thought he was going to end up like Ouranos and Kronos – chopped into little pieces – so he took a page out of Kronos's playbook. He opened his mouth super-wide and created a tornado that sucked Metis right down his throat, compressing her so small that he could swallow her whole.

That kind of freaked out the other Olympians, especially Hestia.

What happened to Metis and her unborn child down there in Zeus's gut? We'll get to that later. But Hestia saw the whole thing, and she said to herself, *Getting married is DANGEROUS!*

Zeus apologized to the Titans and the gods for swallowing Metis. He promised never to do it again. He decided to marry another Titan, but, as you can guess, there weren't a lot of volunteers. Only one agreed: Themis, the Titan of divine law, who happened to be Hestia's favourite aunt.

Themis had sided with the gods in the war. She understood right and wrong, and she knew that the gods would be better rulers than Kronos. (Notice I said *better*, not *good*.)

Like Hestia, Themis was modest and veiled and wasn't interested in marriage, especially after what happened to Metis; but, in the name of peace, she agreed to marry Zeus.

(And, yeah, Themis was technically Zeus's aunt, so feel free to get sick about them getting married. But let's move past that.)

The marriage didn't last long. Themis had two sets of triplets. The first set wasn't so bad – three sisters called the

Horai, who ended up being in charge of the changing seasons.

(You're thinking, *Wait, only three seasons?* But remember this was Greece. I guess they've never had much of a winter.)

The second set of triplets, though – they gave everyone the creeps. They were called the Morai, the Three Fates, and they were *born* old. Right out of the cradle, they grew from three shrivelled babies into three shrivelled old grannies. They liked to sit in the corner and make thread on a magic spinning wheel. Each time they snipped a piece of the line, some mortal down in the world died.

The Olympians quickly realized that the three Fates could not only see the future, they could *control* it. They could bind anyone's life to their magical yarn – literally making a lifeline – and when they snipped off that piece? *Sayonara!* Nobody was sure if they could do the same thing with immortals. But even Zeus was afraid of those girls.

After fathering the Fates, Zeus pulled Themis aside and said, 'You know what? I'm not sure this marriage is going to work out. If we keep having more kids like those Fates, we're all going to be in trouble. What's next – the Three Doomsday Bombs? The Three Little Pigs?'

Themis pretended to be disappointed, but actually she was relieved. She didn't want any more kids, and she definitely didn't want to get sucked down the tornado of Zeus's throat.

'You're right, my lord,' she said. 'I will gladly step aside and let you take another wife.'

Hestia witnessed all this, and she was thinking, I never want that to happen to me. With my luck, I would marry some god and give birth to the Three Stooges. No, the possibility is too horrible.

She decided it was much better to stay single and concentrate on helping her siblings raise *their* families. She could be the cool aunt. The single aunt. The aunt who did not have terrifying shrivelled granny babies.

There was only one problem: some of the guy gods had other ideas. Poseidon kept looking at Hestia and thinking, Hey, she's kind of pretty. Good personality. Easy to get along with. I should marry her.

Yeah, we're back to the whole brother-marrying-sister thing. Let's get it out of our systems – all together, *One, two, three*: 'GROSS!'

A younger Olympian, Apollo, also wanted to marry Hestia. We'll talk more about him later, but it would've been a weird match, since Apollo was one of the flashiest gods. Why he wanted to marry quiet, plain-spoken Hestia, I don't know. Maybe he wanted a wife who would never upstage him.

As it happened, both gods approached Zeus on the same day, asking his permission to marry Hestia. Seems weird that they would ask *Zeus* instead of Hestia but, as you might have noticed, the males weren't real sensitive about stuff like that. Zeus, being the king of the cosmos, had the final say on all marriages.

Meanwhile, Hestia was sitting at the big hearth in the middle of the throne room, not paying much attention. Back then, you needed a central hearth, like an open fire pit, in your main room, because it provided warmth on cold days. It was also where you did your cooking, your water boiling, your chatting, your bread toasting, your marshmallow roasting and your sock drying. Basically, it was the centre of family life.

Hestia always hung out there. She had sort of taken over

responsibility for keeping the home fires burning. It made her feel good, especially when her family gathered around for meals.

Zeus yelled, 'Hey, Hestia! C'mere.'

She approached his throne warily, looking at Poseidon and Apollo, who were both grinning at her, holding bouquets of flowers and boxes of candy. She thought, Uh-oh.

'Great news,' Zeus said. 'Both of these fine gods want to marry you. Because I'm a stand-up king and an all-around thoughtful dude, I will let you pick. Bachelor Number One, Poseidon, likes long walks on the beach and scuba diving. Bachelor Number Two, Apollo, enjoys music and poetry and spends his free time reading prophecies at the Oracle of Delphi. Who do you like better?'

Hestia sobbed in horror, which kind of surprised the bachelors. She threw herself at Zeus's feet and cried, 'Please, my lord. No-o-o! Neither of them!'

Apollo frowned and checked his breath.

Poseidon wondered if he'd forgotten his underarm deodorant again.

Before they could get too angry, Hestia collected herself and tried to explain. 'I have nothing against these gods,' she said. 'But I don't want to marry *anyone*! I want to be single forever.'

Zeus scratched his head. That idea simply did not compute. 'So . . . *never* get married? You don't want kids? You don't want to be a wife?'

'That's correct, my lord,' Hestia said. 'I – I will take care of the hearth for all time. I will tend the flames. I'll prepare the feasts. Whatever I can do to help out the family. Only, promise me I'll never have to get married!'

Apollo and Poseidon were a little miffed, but it was hard to stay mad at Hestia. She was so sweet and earnest and helpful. They forgave her for the same reasons they wanted to marry her in the first place. She was genuinely nice. Among the Olympians, niceness was a rare and valuable commodity.

'I rescind my offer of marriage,' Poseidon said. 'Furthermore, I will protect Hestia's right *not* to marry.'

'Me, too,' Apollo said. 'If that's what she wants, I will honour her wishes.'

Zeus shrugged. 'Well, I still don't get it. But okay. She *does* keep an excellent hearth. Nobody else knows how to toast marshmallows just right – not too soft, not too crispy. Hestia, your wish is granted!'

Hestia breathed a huge sigh of relief.

She became the official goddess of the hearth, which may not seem like a big deal but was exactly what Hestia wanted. Later on, people made up a story about how Hestia used to have a throne on Mount Olympus and gave it up when a newer god named Dionysus came along. It's a good story, but it's not actually in the old myths. Hestia never wanted a throne. She was way too modest for that.

Her hearth became the calm centre of the storm whenever the Olympians argued. Everyone knew the fire was neutral territory. You could go there for a time-out, a cup of nectar or a talk with Hestia. You could catch your breath without getting accosted by anyone – kind of like 'base' in a game of tag.

Hestia looked out for everyone, so everyone looked out for her.

The most famous example? One night Mother Rhea had this big party on Mount Ida to celebrate the anniversary of the

Olympians' victory over Kronos. All the gods and the friendly Titans were invited, along with dozens of nymphs and satyrs. Things got pretty wild – lots of nectar drinking, ambrosia eating and crazy dancing with the Kouretes. The gods even convinced Zeus to tell some of his infamous satyr jokes.

Hestia wasn't used to partying so much. About three in the morning, she got light-headed from the dancing and the nectar and wandered off into the woods. She bumped into a random donkey tied to a tree; probably one of the satyrs had ridden it to the party. For some reason, Hestia found this extremely funny.

'Hello, Mr Donkey!' She giggled. 'I'm going to – *hic!* – I'm going to lie down right here and, uh, take a nap. Watch over me, okay? Okay.'

The goddess fell face first in the grass and started snoring. The donkey wasn't sure what to think about that, but he kept quiet.

A few minutes later, this minor nature god named Priapus came wandering through the woods. You don't hear much about Priapus in the old stories. Frankly, he's not very important. He was a country god who protected vegetable gardens. I know – exciting, right? *O great Priapus, guard my cucumbers with your mighty powers!* If you've ever seen those silly plaster garden gnomes that people put in their yards, that's a holdover from the days when people placed statues of Priapus in their gardens to protect their produce.

Anyway, Priapus was all about parties and flirting with the ladies. He'd had a lot to drink that night. He was roaming the woods looking for some unsuspecting nymph or goddess he could get cuddly with.

When he came to the clearing and saw a lovely goddess passed out in the grass, snoring alluringly in the moonlight, he thought, YES!

He sneaked up to Hestia. He didn't know which goddess she was, but he didn't really care. He was sure that if he just cuddled up next to her, she would be delighted when she woke up, because, hey, who wouldn't want to get romantic with the god of vegetables?

He knelt next to her. She smelled so yummy — like wood smoke and toasted marshmallows. He ran his hand through her dark hair and said, 'Hey, there, baby. What do you say we do some snuggling?'

In the darkness nearby, the donkey apparently thought that sounded like an excellent idea. He brayed, 'HHAWWWWW!'

Priapus yelled, 'Ahhh!!'

Hestia woke with a start, horrified to find a vegetable god leaning over her, his hand in her hair. She screamed, 'HELP!'

Back at the party, the other gods heard her screaming. Immediately they dropped whatever they were doing and ran to help her — because you simply didn't mess with Hestia.

When they found Priapus, all the gods started whaling on him — throwing goblets at his head, punching him, calling him names. Priapus barely got out of there with his life.

Later, he claimed he had no idea he was flirting with Hestia. He thought she was just a nymph or something. Still, Priapus was no longer welcome at the Olympian parties. After that, everyone became even more protective of Hestia.

Now, there's one more part of Hestia's story that's kind of important, but I'm going to have to do some speculating here, because you won't find this in the old myths.

At first, there was only one hearth in the world, and it belonged to the gods. Fire was like their trademarked property. The puny humans didn't know how to make it. They were still cowering in their caves, grunting and picking their noses and hitting each other with clubs.

The Titan Prometheus, who had made those little dudes out of clay, really felt sorry for them. After all, he'd created them to look like immortals. He was pretty sure humans were capable of *acting* like immortals, too. They just needed a little help getting started.

Whenever Prometheus visited Olympus, he watched the gods gather at Hestia's hearth. Fire was the single most important thing that made the palace a home. You could use fire to keep warm. You could cook with it. You could make hot beverages. You could light torches at night. You could play any number of funny practical jokes with the hot coals. If only humans had some fire . . .

Finally Prometheus got up his courage and spoke to Zeus.

'Hey, Lord Zeus,' he said. 'Uh, I thought I should show the humans how to make fire.'

Zeus frowned. 'Humans? You mean those dirty little guys that make funny shrieks when you step on them? Why would they need fire?'

'They could learn to be more like us,' Prometheus said. 'They could build houses, make cities, all sorts of things.'

'That,' Zeus said, 'is the worst idea I've ever heard. Next, you're going to want to arm the cockroaches. Give humans fire, and they're going to take over the world. They'll get all uppity and decide they're as good as immortals. No. I absolutely forbid it.'

But Prometheus couldn't let it go. He kept looking at Hestia sitting next to her hearth. He admired the way she kept the Olympian family together with her sacred fires.

It just wasn't fair, Prometheus decided. Humans deserved the same comfort.

What happened next?

Most versions of the story say that Prometheus stole hot coals from the hearth. He hid them in the hollowed stalk of a fennel plant – though you'd think somebody would notice him sneaking out of the palace with a smouldering plant that smelled like burning liquorice.

None of the stories mention that Hestia helped Prometheus. But the thing is, how could she *not* have known what he was doing? She was always at the hearth. There's no way Prometheus could've stolen fire without Hestia noticing.

Personally, I think she had sympathy for Prometheus and those little humans. Hestia was kind-hearted that way. I think she either helped Prometheus or at least turned a blind eye and let him steal the hot coals.

Whatever the case, Prometheus sneaked out of Olympus with his secret burning liquorice stick and gave it to the humans. It took a while for them to learn how to use the hot flaming stuff without killing themselves, but finally they managed, and the idea spread like . . . well, wildfire.

Usually Zeus didn't pay much attention to what was happening down on the earth. After all, the sky was his domain. But one clear night he stood at the balcony on Mount Olympus and noticed that the world was freckled with lights – in houses, towns, even a few cities. The humans had come out of their caves.

'That little punk,' Zeus grumbled. 'Prometheus armed the cockroaches.'

Next to him, the goddess Hera said, 'Uh, what?'

'Nothing,' Zeus muttered. He yelled to his guards: 'Find Prometheus and get him in here. *NOW!*'

Zeus was not pleased. He didn't like it when someone disobeyed his orders, especially when that someone was a Titan whom Zeus had generously spared after the war. Zeus was *so* displeased he decided to punish Prometheus in a way no one would ever forget. He chained the Titan to a rock on Mount Caucasus at the eastern edge of the world, then summoned a huge eagle, which was Zeus's sacred animal, to peck open Prometheus's belly and feed on his liver.

Oh, sorry. That was a little gross. I hope you weren't on your way to lunch.

Every day, the eagle would rip Prometheus open and chow down. And every night Prometheus would heal up and grow a new liver, just in time for the eagle to show up the next morning.

The other gods and Titans got the message: *Don't disobey Zeus, or bad things will happen to you, most likely involving chains, livers and hungry eagles.*

As for Hestia, no one accused her of anything, but she must have felt bad for Prometheus, because she made sure his sacrifice wasn't in vain. She became the goddess of *all* hearths, across the world. In every mortal home, the central fireplace was sacred to her. If you needed protection, like if someone was chasing you or beating you up, you ran to the nearest hearth and no one could touch you there. Whoever lived in that house was obligated to help if you asked for sanctuary. Families would take their important oaths on the hearth, and whenever they burned a portion of their meal as a sacrifice to the gods, part of that sacrifice went to Hestia.

As towns and cities grew, they operated just like individual homes. Each town had a central hearth that was under Hestia's protection. If you were an ambassador from another city, you always visited the hearth first to proclaim that you had come in peace. If you got in trouble and you made it to the town hearth, no one in that city could harm you. In fact, the citizens were honour-bound to protect you.

It turned out Prometheus was right. Humans *did* start acting like the gods, for better or worse. Eventually, the gods got used to this and even accepted it. The humans built temples for them, burned sweet-smelling sacrifices and chanted about how awesome the Olympians were. That certainly helped.

Still, Zeus didn't forgive Prometheus for disobeying his orders. Eventually Prometheus got freed, but that's another story.

As for Hestia, she was able to maintain peace on Olympus most of the time – but not always.

For instance, one time her sister Demeter got so mad at her brothers she almost caused World War Zero . . .

DEMETER TURNS
INTO GRAINZILLA

O H, YEAH. DEMETER!

Try not to get too excited, because this chapter is all about the goddess of wheat, bread and cereal. Demeter just flat-out *rocks* when it comes to carbohydrates.

I'm not being fair to her, though.

Sure, she was the goddess of agriculture, but she had other things going for her. Among the three eldest goddesses, she was the middle sister, so she combined Hestia's sweet personality with her younger sister Hera's knockout hotness. Demeter had long blonde hair the colour of ripe wheat. She wore a crown of woven corn leaves – not a fashion statement most people can pull off, but she managed. She liked to adorn herself with poppies, which often grow in fields of grain – or so I'm told. I don't go walking in a lot of grain fields.

A dark robe covered her bright green dress, so, whenever she moved, it looked like fresh plant shoots breaking through fertile earth. She smelled like a rainstorm over a field of jasmine.

Since Hestia decided never to get married, Demeter was the first goddess who seriously drew the attention of the guy gods. (Hera was beautiful, too, but her *attitude* . . . well, we'll get to that later.)

Not only was Demeter good-looking but she was also kind-hearted (mostly), she knew how to bake awesome bread and cookies, and she cut a surprisingly warlike figure wherever she went. She rode a golden chariot pulled by twin dragons. At her side gleamed a gold sword.

In fact, one of her Greek names was Demeter Khrysaoros, meaning *the Lady with the Golden Blade*. Sounds like a good title for a martial-arts movie. According to some legends, her blade was actually the scythe of Kronos, which she reforged into the world's most deadly harvesting tool. Mostly she used it for cutting wheat, but if she got angry enough she could fight with it . . .

Anyway, the guy gods all liked her. Zeus, Poseidon and Hades all proposed marriage, but Demeter turned them down flat. She preferred to roam the earth, turning barren plains into fertile fields, encouraging orchards to bear fruit and flowers to bloom.

One day Zeus got persistent. He had just divorced Themis and hadn't remarried yet. He was lonely. For whatever reason, he fixated on Demeter and decided he absolutely *had* to get with her.

He found her in a field of wheat (no surprise). Demeter

yelled at him to go away, but he just kept following her around.

'Come on!' he said. 'Just one kiss. Then maybe another kiss. Then maybe –'

'No!' she shouted. 'You're *so* annoying!'

'I'm the king of the universe,' Zeus said. 'If we got together, you'd be the queen!'

'Not interested.' Demeter was tempted to draw her golden sword, but Zeus *was* the most powerful god, and people who opposed him got into a lot of trouble. (*Cough*, like Prometheus, *cough*.) Also, her golden chariot was parked way at the other end of the field, so she couldn't just hop in and flee.

Zeus kept pestering her. 'Our kids would be powerful and amazing.'

'Go away.'

'Hey, baby. Don't be like that.'

Finally Demeter got so disgusted that she transformed herself into a serpent. She figured she could lose Zeus by hiding in the fields and slithering away.

Bad idea.

Zeus could transform into an animal, too. He changed into a snake and followed her. That was easy, since snakes have a great sense of smell, and, like I said earlier, Demeter had a very distinctive rainstorm-over-jasmine scent.

Demeter slithered into a hole in the dirt. Another pretty terrible idea.

Zeus slithered in after her. The tunnel was narrow, so, once Zeus blocked the entrance, Demeter couldn't get out. She didn't have room to change form.

Zeus trapped her and wouldn't let her go until . . . well, use your imagination.

Months later, Demeter gave birth to her first child – a daughter named Persephone. She was such a cute, sweet baby that Demeter *almost* forgave Zeus for tricking her into reptile hanky-panky. Almost. They didn't get married, and Zeus was a pretty neglectful dad, but still the little girl became the light of Demeter's life.

More about Persephone in a sec . . .

I'd like to say that was the only time Demeter got into a bad situation with a man. Unfortunately, it wasn't.

A few years later, Demeter took a vacation to the beach. She was walking along, enjoying the solitude and the fresh sea air, when Poseidon happened to spot her. Being a sea god, he tended to notice pretty ladies walking along the beach.

He appeared out of the waves in his best green robes, with his trident in his hand and a crown of seashells on his head. (He was sure that the crown made him look irresistible.)

'Hey, girl,' he said, wiggling his eyebrows. 'You must be the riptide, 'cause you sweep me off my feet.'

He'd been practising that pickup line for years. He was glad he'd finally got to use it.

Demeter was not impressed. 'Go away, Poseidon.'

'Sometimes the sea goes away,' Poseidon agreed, 'but it always comes back. What do you say you and me have a romantic dinner at my undersea palace?'

Demeter made a mental note not to park her chariot so far away. She really could've used her two dragons for backup. She decided to change form and get away, but she knew better than to turn into a snake this time.

I need something faster, she thought.

Then she glanced down the beach and saw a herd of wild horses galloping through the surf.

That's perfect! Demeter thought. A horse!

Instantly she became a white mare and raced down the beach. She joined the herd and blended in with the other horses.

Her plan had serious flaws. First, Poseidon could also turn into a horse, and he did – a strong white stallion. He raced after her. Second, Poseidon had *created* horses. He knew all about them and could control them.

Why would a sea god create a land animal like the horse? We'll get to that later. Anyway, Poseidon reached the herd and started pushing his way through, looking for Demeter – or rather sniffing for her sweet, distinctive perfume. She was easy to find.

Demeter's seemingly perfect camouflage in the herd turned out to be a perfect trap. The other horses made way for Poseidon, but they hemmed in Demeter and wouldn't let her move. She got so panicky, afraid of getting trampled, that she couldn't even change shape into something else. Poseidon sidled up to her and whinnied something like *Hey, beautiful. Galloping my way?*

Much to Demeter's horror, Poseidon got a lot cuddlier than she wanted.

These days, Poseidon would be arrested for that kind of behaviour. I mean . . . assuming he wasn't in horse form. I don't think you can arrest a horse. Anyway, back in those days, the world was a rougher, ruder place. Demeter couldn't exactly report Poseidon to King Zeus, because Zeus was just as bad.

Months later, a very embarrassed and angry Demeter gave birth to twins. The weirdest thing? One of the babies was a goddess; the other one was a stallion. I'm not going to even *try* to figure that out. The baby girl was named Despoine, but you don't hear much about her in the myths. When she grew up, her job was looking after Demeter's temple, like the high priestess of corn magic or something. Her baby brother, the stallion, was named Arion. He grew up to be a super-fast immortal steed who helped out Hercules and some other heroes, too. He was a pretty awesome horse, though I'm not sure that Demeter was real proud of having a son who needed new horseshoes every few months and was constantly nuzzling her for apples.

At this point, you'd think Demeter would have sworn off those gross, disgusting men forever and joined Hestia in the Permanently Single Club.

Strangely, a couple of months later, she fell in love with a human prince named Iasion (pronounced 'EYE-son', I think). Just shows you how far humans had come since Prometheus gave them fire. Now they could speak and write. They could brush their teeth and comb their hair. They wore clothes and occasionally took baths. Some of them were even handsome enough to flirt with goddesses.

This dude Iasion (not Jason, that's a different guy) was a hero of Crete. He was handsome and well mannered, and he always looked out for his local farmers, which was a sure way to Demeter's heart. One day Iasion was out inspecting some newly ploughed fields when Demeter happened by in the guise of a mortal maiden. They started talking: *Oh, I love wheat. Me, too! Wheat is the best!* Or something like that; and they fell in love.

They met in the fields several more times. For a few weeks, Demeter was head-over-heels in love. Of course, something had to go wrong. The next time Demeter visited the fields, Zeus happened to be watching from Mount Olympus. He saw Demeter getting cosy with this mortal guy – hugging and kissing and talking about wheat – and Zeus got insanely jealous.

Completely unfair, right? Zeus and Demeter weren't even together. Still, when Zeus saw a mortal hero making time with 'his' girl, he blew his top.

The nice thing about getting mad at mortals – they are mortal. Which means you can kill them.

Demeter was giving Iasion a big kiss when the sky rumbled. The clouds tore open, and lightning flashed. *KER-ZAP!* Suddenly Demeter was alone in the wheat field, her clothes smouldering. A pile of hero ashes lay at her feet.

She wailed and screamed curses at Zeus, but there was nothing she could do. She sulked off to her private apartment on Mount Olympus and stayed there for months. When she finally came out, she was holding the last child she would ever bear – a boy named Pluotos. (Not Pluto. That's *another* different guy.) You don't hear much about Pluotos in the old myths either, but he became a minor god of agricultural wealth. He wandered around Greece, looking for successful farmers and rewarding them for their hard work with bags of cash – kind of like the Old MacDonald Prize Patrol.

At this point, Demeter decided enough was enough. She still had the occasional date, but she never got married, never had another kid, and her relationships with the male gods were always strained.

Her experiences also kind of soured that sweet personality of hers. You might not think a grain goddess could be scary, but *dang*. You should've seen what she did to this one dude, Erisikhthon.

I know. Stupidest name ever. I think it's pronounced 'Err-ISS-ick-thon', but, heck, I'm just guessing. Anyway, this guy was a local prince who thought he was the coolest thing since bronze. He wanted to build himself a huge mansion with lumber from the nearby forests.

The problem? The biggest and nicest trees – the only ones he thought were good enough for his mansion – were in a grove that was sacred to Demeter. These massive oaks and poplars soared over a hundred feet tall, and each one had a nature spirit, a dryad, watching over it. The dryads would dance around, singing songs about Demeter and making flower necklaces, or whatever dryads do in their spare time.

Everybody in the whole country knew the grove was sacred to Demeter, but Eric Whatever-his-name-was – he didn't care. (You know, I think I'll just call him Eric.) So Eric got like fifty of his biggest, strongest friends together. He gave them sharp bronze axes and they headed off to the grove.

As soon as the dryads saw them coming, they shrieked in alarm and called on Demeter to protect them.

They must've had the goddess on speed dial, because she was there in a flash.

Demeter took the form of a human maiden and appeared in the road, right in front of Eric and his army of axe-wielding goons.

'Oh, my!' she said. 'Such big strong men! Where are you going?'

'Out of the way, girl,' Eric grumbled. 'We have some chopping to do.'

'But why are you attacking these poor defenceless trees?'

'I need the lumber!' Eric bellowed. 'I'm going to make the greatest mansion in the world!'

His friends cheered and waved their axes menacingly.

'You should choose other trees,' Demeter said, trying to keep her cool. 'This grove is sacred to Demeter.'

'Bah!' Eric said. 'These are the tallest trees in the land. I need *tall* trees for my great hall. My friends and I intend to feast there every night. We will have such excellent feasts that I will be famous throughout Greece!'

His friends shouted, 'Yum!' and made lip-smacking noises.

'But this is the home of many innocent dryads,' Demeter persisted.

'If the dryads try to stop me,' Eric said, 'I will cut them down too!'

Demeter clenched her jaw. 'And if Demeter tries to stop you?'

Eric laughed. 'Let her try. I'm not afraid of a silly *crop* goddess. Now, stand aside, or I'll chop you up as well, girl.'

He shouldered the goddess aside and marched towards the largest tree – a huge white poplar. As he swung his axe, a blast of hot wind knocked him on his butt.

Demeter grew to a massive height – towering above the trees like Grainzilla in her green-and-black robes, her crown of corn leaves steaming in her golden hair, her scythe blade casting a shadow across the entire group of mortals.

'SO,' the giant Demeter boomed, 'YOU ARE NOT

AFRAID?'

Eric's fifty goons dropped their axes and ran screaming like little girls.

Eric tried to rise, but his knees were jelly. 'I, uh, I just . . . uh –'

'YOU WANTED TO BE FAMOUS FOR FEASTING!' Demeter roared. 'AND YOU *WILL* FEAST, ERISIKHTHON – EVERY NIGHT, A GREAT FEAST AS YOU INTENDED! I AM THE GODDESS OF THE HARVEST, THE MISTRESS OF ALL NOURISHMENT. YOU WILL EAT AND EAT FOR THE REST OF YOUR DAYS, BUT YOUR HUNGER WILL NEVER BE SATISFIED!'

Demeter disappeared in a flash of emerald light.

Poor Eric ran away whimpering, and swearing to the gods that he would never *ever* touch that sacred grove. It didn't matter. That night, when he had finished his dinner, he was just as hungry as when he started. He ate a second dinner, then a third, but he felt no better. He drank, like, a gallon of water, but he couldn't quench his thirst.

Within a few days, the hunger and thirst became unbearable. He only got relief when he slept. Even then, he dreamed about food. When he woke up, he was starving again.

Eric was a rich man, but within a few weeks he had sold most of his possessions just to buy food. He ate constantly, all day every day. Nothing helped. Eventually he lost everything he owned. His friends abandoned him. He got so desperate that he even tried to sell his own daughter into slavery to get money for food. Fortunately, Demeter wasn't cruel enough to let *that* happen. The daughter pleaded for someone to rescue her, and Poseidon came to her aid. Maybe he figured he owed Demeter a favour for the horse-cuddling incident. Maybe he just didn't mind helping out a pretty mortal girl. Anyway, he took the girl under his protection and made her a housekeeper in his underwater palace. As for Erisikhthon, he wasted away and died in agony. Happy ending.

Word got around. The mortals decided that maybe they should take Demeter seriously. Anybody who controls food can bless you – or they can curse you very, very badly.

After that, Demeter figured she'd got her anger out of her system. She decided to relax and enjoy life, and the thing that brought her the most happiness in the world was her eldest daughter, Persephone. Oh, sure, she loved her other kids, but Persephone was her favourite.

'I'm done with drama,' Demeter told herself. 'I'm just going to kick back and enjoy spending time with my wonderful daughter!'

As you can probably guess, that didn't work out so well.

PERSEPHONE MARRIES HER STALKER
(OR, DEMETER, THE SEQUEL)

I HAVE TO BE HONEST. I never understood what made Persephone such a big deal. I mean, for a girl who almost destroyed the universe, she seems kind of *meh*.

Sure, she was pretty. She had her mother's long blonde hair and Zeus's sky-blue eyes. She didn't have a care in the world. She was sure the whole world had been invented just for her pleasure. I guess when your parents are both gods you can come to believe that.

She loved the outdoors. She spent her days roaming the countryside with her nymph and goddess friends, wading in streams, picking flowers in sunlit meadows, eating fresh fruit right off the tree — heck, I'm just making this up, but I'm guessing that's what a teenage goddess would have done before smartphones were invented.

The thing is, Persephone didn't have much else going for

her. She wasn't all that bright. She wasn't brave. She didn't really have any goals or hobbies (other than the flower-picking thing). She was just kind of *there*, enjoying life and being a spoiled, sheltered, overprivileged kid. I guess it's nice work if you can get it, but I didn't grow up that way, so I don't have much sympathy for her.

Still, Demeter *lived* for her daughter, and I can't blame her for being overprotective. Demeter had had enough bad experiences with those sneaky male gods. After all, Persephone had come into the world because of a snake ambush. The kid was lucky she wasn't hatched from an egg.

Of course, since Persephone was declared off-limits, all the male gods noticed her and thought she was incredibly hot. They all wanted to marry her, but they knew Demeter would never allow it. Any time one of them got close, Demeter appeared out of nowhere with her dragon-drawn chariot and her wicked golden sword.

Most of the gods let it go. They decided to find some safer goddess to date.

But one god couldn't get Persephone out of his mind — namely Hades, lord of the Underworld.

Perfect match, right? An old gloomy dude who lives in the world's largest cave filled with the souls of the dead, and he falls in love with a pretty young girl who likes sunlight and flowers and the Great Outdoors. What could possibly go wrong?

Hades knew it was hopeless. Persephone was completely out of his league. Besides, Demeter wouldn't let *any* god get close to her daughter. No way in Tartarus would she let Hades date her.

Hades tried to get over her. But he was lonely down there

in the Underworld with no company except the dead. He kept putting on his helmet of invisibility and sneaking up to the mortal world so he could watch Persephone frolic around. In other words, he was the world's first stalker.

I don't know if you've ever had a crush on somebody that bad, but Hades became obsessed. He kept sketches of Persephone in his pocket. He carved her name on his obsidian dining table with a knife – which took a lot of work. He dreamed about her and had imaginary conversations with her where he admitted his love and she confessed that she had always had a thing for creepy older guys who lived in caves full of dead people.

Hades got so distracted he couldn't even concentrate on his work. His job was to sort out the souls of the dead once they got to the Underworld, but the ghosts started escaping back into the world, or wandering into the wrong spiritual neighbourhoods. The traffic jams at the gates of the Underworld got ridiculous.

Finally Hades couldn't stand it any more. To his credit, he didn't try to trick Persephone or take her by force – at least not at first. He thought, Well, Demeter will never listen to me. Maybe I should talk to Persephone's dad.

It wasn't easy for Hades to visit Mount Olympus. He knew he wasn't welcome there. He certainly didn't want to ask any favours of his annoying little brother Zeus, but he put on a brave face and marched into the Olympian throne room.

He happened to catch Zeus in a good mood. The lord of the skies had just finished all his godly work for the week – scheduling the clouds, organizing the winds and doing whatever else a sky god has to do. Now he was sitting back, drinking some nectar and enjoying the gorgeous day. He was daydreaming about another beautiful lady he was intent on marrying, namely Hera; so, when Hades came to see him, Zeus had a faraway smile on his face.

'Lord Zeus.' Hades bowed.

'Hades!' Zeus cried. 'What's up, man? Long time no see!'

Hades was tempted to remind Zeus that it was 'long time no see' because Zeus had told him he wasn't welcome on Mount Olympus, but he decided he'd better not mention that.

'Uh, actually . . .' Hades tugged nervously at his black robes. 'I need some advice. About a woman.'

Zeus grinned. 'You've come to the right place. The ladies love me!'

'Okay . . .' Hades started to wonder if this was a good idea. 'It's about one particular lady – your daughter, Persephone.'

Zeus's smile wavered. 'Say what, now?'

Hades had been holding in his feelings for so long that he just broke down. He confessed everything, even the stalkerish stuff. He promised he would make Persephone an excellent husband. He would be devoted and give her everything she wanted, if only Zeus would give him permission to marry her.

Zeus stroked his beard. Most days, he would have got angry at such a ridiculous request. He would've brought out his lightning bolts and sent Hades back to the Underworld with his robes on fire and his hair all spiky and smoking. But today Zeus was in a good mood. He was actually sort of touched that Hades had come to him with this problem and been so honest. He felt sorry for his creepy stalker brother, and he *definitely* understood how a guy could get obsessed with a woman.

Sure, Persephone was his daughter, but Zeus had *lots* of

daughters by lots of different ladies. It wasn't like Persephone was his special favourite, or anything. He was inclined to be generous and give her away.

He drummed his fingers on the arm of his throne. 'The problem is Demeter. Uh . . . that *is* Demeter's daughter, right? I forget.'

'Yes, my lord,' Hades said.

'Her favourite daughter,' Zeus remembered. 'The light of her life, whom she never lets out of her sight, et cetera.'

'Yes, my lord.' Hades started to feel uncomfortable. 'Should I talk to Demeter? Perhaps if you broke the ice and made her promise to listen. Or maybe I should declare my love to Persephone?'

'What?' Zeus looked appalled. 'Be honest with women? That never works, bro. You've got to be strong. Take what you want.'

'Uh . . . really?'

'Always works for me,' Zeus said. 'I suggest kidnapping. When nobody is looking, capture Persephone and take her back to your crib. Demeter won't know what happened. By the time she figures it out . . . too late! Persephone will be yours. You'll have plenty of time to convince the young lady to stay with you in the Underworld.'

Hades was starting to have doubts about Zeus's wisdom. 'Um, you're sure this is a good idea?'

'Totally!' Zeus said.

Hades chewed his lip. The whole kidnapping thing seemed a little risky. He wasn't sure if Persephone would actually like being abducted, but he didn't know much about women. Maybe Zeus was right.

(For the record: NO, HE WASN'T.)

'There's one problem, my lord,' Hades said. 'Persephone is never alone. She's either with Demeter or with some nymph or goddess chaperones. How can I abduct her in secret? Even if I use my invisibility helmet, I can't turn *her* invisible or stop her from screaming.'

Zeus's eyes twinkled mischievously. 'Leave that to me. Go get your chariot ready.'

Zeus waited until Demeter was busy doing some agricultural stuff on the far side of the world – like ripening the barley in Libya or something. I'm not sure what.

Anyway, Persephone was left in the care of her nymph chaperones. Usually that worked out fine, but the nymphs weren't really cut out to be bodyguards. They could be easily distracted, and so could Persephone.

As usual, the girls went out into the meadows. They spent the morning exploring the hills and having splash-fights in the river. After a nice lazy lunch, letting their dresses dry in the sunlight, Persephone decided to go pick some flowers.

'Don't wander too far!' one of the nymphs called.

'I won't,' Persephone promised.

She wasn't worried. The world was her playground! Everyone loved her and, besides, what could possibly go wrong while she was picking flowers in a meadow?

The nymphs were sleepy and warm and full from lunch, and so they lay down for a nap.

Persephone roamed the hillside until she'd gathered an entire bouquet from the nearest rose bushes. For some reason, the roses didn't even have thorns. Their intoxicating smell made

Persephone giddy. She traipsed a little further away and spotted a whole field of violets.

'Oh, pretty!'

She wandered through the violets, picking the best ones and dropping the roses, because they now seemed pale in comparison.

Well, you can probably see where this is going, but Persephone was clueless. She didn't realize Zeus was causing these flowers to grow – making each batch more colourful and fragrant than the last, leading Persephone further and further away from her chaperones.

So how could Zeus, a sky god, make flowers grow? Dunno. Best guess: he still had some pull with Gaia the Earth Mother, even though she was asleep. I'm thinking Zeus could occasionally summon her power to make things happen on the earth – maybe not huge things, like creating mountains. But making flowers grow? Not a big deal.

Persephone wandered from flower patch to flower patch, murmuring, 'Ooh, pretty! Ooh, pretty!' as she picked her favourites.

Before she realized it, she was miles away from her sleeping nymph friends. She meandered into a secluded valley filled with hyacinths.

She was reaching down to pick a beautiful red one when the ground rumbled. A chasm opened at her feet, and four black horses pulling a massive chariot thundered into the sunlight. The driver was dressed in dark flowing robes. He wore iron gloves, with a huge sword at his side and a whip in his hand. His face was covered with an elaborate bronze helmet engraved with images of death and torture.

In retrospect, Hades wondered if it was such a good idea to wear his helmet of terror on a first date, but by then it was too late.

Persephone screamed and fell backwards into the grass.

She should have run, but she was in shock. She couldn't even fathom what was happening. Everything had always revolved around her, gone her way. She *couldn't* be in danger. But she was pretty sure she hadn't wished for a demonic-looking guy in a giant black chariot to come and trample her hyacinths.

Truth be told, she'd occasionally had daydreams about some handsome young man sweeping her off her feet. She and the nymphs had spent a lot of time giggling about that.

But this was *not* what she'd envisioned.

Hades took off his helm. His complexion was even paler than usual. He had a bad case of helmet-hair. He was sweating and nervous and blinking like he had something in his eyes.

'I am Hades,' he said in a squeaky voice. 'I love you.'

Persephone screamed again, much louder.

Not knowing what else to do, Hades grabbed her arm, pulled her into the chariot and spurred his horses. His dark ride disappeared into the earth. The chasm closed up behind him.

The only person who actually saw the kidnapping was the Titan Helios, way up in his chick-magnet sun chariot, because he had a great view and could see pretty much everything. But do you think he got on the phone to Olympus to report a kidnapping?

Nope. First, they didn't have phones. Second, Helios didn't like to get involved with godly dramas. He was a Titan, after all. He figured he was lucky just to have a job and not get thrown into Tartarus. Also, this kidnapping wasn't the craziest thing he'd seen while crossing the sky every day. Those gods were always doing wild things. Man, the stories he could tell. Some day he should write a book.

So Helios continued on his way.

As for the nymphs who were supposed to be watching Persephone, they slept right through the abduction. The only person who heard Persephone screaming was the most unlikely person you could imagine.

In a cave on a nearby mountainside, a Titan named Hecate was minding her own business. Hecate was into magic and spooky night-time crossroads and ghosts. She was sort of the first super-fan of Halloween. Normally she only left her cave after dark, so that day she was sitting inside reading spell books or whatever when she heard a girl screaming.

Hecate may have been a dark goddess of magic, but she wasn't evil. She immediately ran to help. By the time she got to the meadow, the action was over.

Hecate's magic was weak in the daytime. She could tell that the earth had opened and somebody had been snatched up in a chariot and dragged underground, but Hecate had no idea who was the kidnapper and who was the kidnappee.

Hecate wasn't sure what to do. It wasn't like she could call 911. Since she didn't know the facts, she decided to go back to her cave and wait until nightfall, when she could cast better spells and hopefully get more information.

Meanwhile, the nymphs woke from their nap and went looking for Persephone, but she had literally vanished off the face of the earth. The nymphs were starting to panic by the time Demeter returned and found out her precious daughter was missing. I'm not sure what Demeter did to punish those nymphs, but it could not have been good.

Anyway, Demeter was freaked. She wandered around shouting for Persephone until her voice got hoarse. She asked everyone she met if they had seen anything.

For *nine days* Demeter didn't change her clothes or take a bath. She didn't eat or sleep. She did nothing but look for Persephone. She must have started searching in the wrong direction, because on the tenth day she finally circled back around and combed the area near Hecate's cave.

Hecate heard Demeter calling for Persephone. Immediately the magic goddess put two and two together. Every night, Hecate had been trying to figure out what the abduction was all about, but her spells weren't telling her anything. Some strong magic was at work, covering up the kidnapping. Hecate had a feeling a powerful god was behind it – or maybe more than one.

Hecate ran down to meet Demeter. She told the grain goddess about the screaming she'd heard, and her belief that some unknown god had kidnapped Persephone.

The distraught mom didn't take the news well. She shrieked so loudly that all the plants within a five-mile radius withered and died. For hundreds of miles in each direction, every ear of corn on the Greek mainland exploded into popcorn.

'I will find whoever has taken her!' Demeter wailed. 'I will murder him! Then I will murder him again!'

At this point, most folks would've backed away from the crazy lady, but Hecate felt bad for her.

'I'll help you search tonight,' she told Demeter. 'I've got torches, and I'm really good at seeing in the dark.'

They searched from dusk until dawn but had no luck.

Hecate went back to her cave to rest, promising to help again after nightfall, but Demeter couldn't stop.

She stumbled on alone until evening fell and she came to a kingdom called Eleusis. At this point, even the immortal goddess was getting exhausted. She decided to visit the town, maybe rest her feet for a few minutes and mingle with the locals. Perhaps they had seen something or heard some news.

Demeter disguised herself as an old mortal woman. She made her way to the town's central hearth, because that's where strangers normally went when they wanted to ask the locals for assistance. A crowd had gathered in the square. A lady with fine robes and a golden crown was making some kind of speech. Being an intelligent goddess, Demeter thought, She must be the queen.

It turned out Queen Metaneira was there with her family and her household guards, offering sacrifices to the gods in celebration of the birth of her newest son, Demophoon. (Or maybe she was there to apologize to the gods for giving her son such a dumb name.) Anyway, when Demeter walked up, Queen Metaneira was just offering a prayer to Demeter. Even in Demeter's desperate state of mind, that must've been sort of a rush, hearing somebody praying to her when they didn't know she was in the crowd.

If it were me, I'd wait until the queen said, 'O great Demeter —'

Then I'd jump out with a bunch of explosions and fireworks and say, 'YOU CALLED?'

Probably a good thing nobody has made me a god.

At any rate, Demeter figured this was a good omen. She

waited for the queen to finish blessing her new baby, who was very cute. As the crowd broke up, Demeter made her way towards the queen, but Metaneira noticed her first.

'Old woman!' called the queen.

Demeter blinked. She looked around, wondering who Metaneira was talking to. Then she remembered she was in disguise.

'Oh, right! Yes, my queen!' Demeter said in her best old-lady voice.

The queen studied Demeter's face and her ragged clothes. Even in disguise, Demeter must have looked weary. After ten days, she didn't smell nearly as jasmine sweet as usual.

'I do not know you,' the queen decided. Her family and retainers gathered around.

Demeter wondered if she was going to have to turn into a hundred-foot-tall grain monster and scare them away, but the queen only smiled. 'Welcome to Eleusis! We always greet strangers, because you never know when one of them might be a god in disguise, eh?'

The queen's guards chuckled. They were probably thinking, Yeah, right. This old lady, a goddess.

Demeter bowed. 'Very wise, my queen. Very wise indeed.'

'Do you need a place to stay?' the queen asked. 'Do you require food? How may we help you?'

Wow, Demeter thought. She's *serious*.

After days of anxiety, running frantically around Greece looking for her daughter, Demeter was dumbstruck to receive such kindness. These puny mortals didn't know her from any ordinary beggar – yet the queen herself took time to be nice to her, nicer in fact than most of Demeter's fellow gods would have been.

Demeter felt so tired and emotionally spent that she burst into tears. 'My daughter,' she sobbed. 'My daughter has been stolen from me.'

The queen gasped. 'What? This is an outrage!'

A handsome young man stepped forward and took Demeter's hands. 'Old woman, I am Triptolemus, the firstborn son of the queen. I pledge that I will help you find your daughter, however I can!'

Queen Metaneira nodded in agreement. 'But come, dear guest. You are clearly exhausted. It won't help your daughter if you kill yourself with weariness and hunger while trying to find her. Please stay in my palace tonight. Tell us your story. Rest and eat. In the morning, we will decide how best to help you.'

Demeter wanted to decline. She wanted to keep going. Since she was immortal, she obviously wasn't in danger of dying. But she *was* tired. These people were nice. And after ten days on the road her filthy clothes were starting to sprout types of mould and fungus even the *plant* goddess didn't recognize.

She thanked the queen and accepted her hospitality.

After taking a nice hot bath and putting on some new clothes, Demeter felt much better. She joined the royal family for dinner and told them of her troubles, though she left out some minor details, such as being a goddess. She explained that her daughter had disappeared while on a day trip in the meadow with her friends. A woman who lived nearby had heard screaming, so it was clear her daughter had been kidnapped, but Demeter had no idea who had taken her or where she might be.

The royal family brainstormed some helpful suggestions: offering a reward, putting Persephone's face on milk cartons, stapling MISSING posters around town. Finally Triptolemus had the winning idea.

'I will send riders in all four directions,' he said. 'We will gather news and spread word of this abduction. Stay with us and rest a few days, honoured guest. I know you are anxious, but this is the quickest way to search the countryside. When my riders return, we will know more.'

Again, Demeter wanted to protest. She was worried sick about her daughter, but she couldn't think of a better idea, and she was grateful for this family's hospitality. Also, she *could* use a few days' rest.

Since her initial panic after the abduction, Demeter's mood had started to shift to cold determination. In her heart, she knew Persephone was still out there – captured, but unharmed. Her motherly instincts told her so. No matter how long it took, Demeter would find her. And when she got her hands on the kidnapper . . . oh, her vengeance would be terrible. She would cover him in fertilizer, cause barley to sprout from all his pores and laugh at his terrified screams as he transformed into the world's largest Chia Pet.

Demeter smiled at Prince Triptolemus. 'Thank you for your kindness. I accept your offer.'

'Excellent!'

'Goo,' said the newborn child Demophoon, gurgling contentedly in the queen's arms.

Demeter gazed at the baby boy. Her heart filled with warmth and nostalgia. It seemed like just last century Persephone had been that small!

'Let me repay your kindness,' Demeter told the queen. 'I'm an excellent nursemaid, and I know what it's like being a new mom. You could use some sleep! Let me take care of your baby tonight. I promise to keep him safe. I'll bless him with special charms against evil so he'll grow up to be a strong, handsome hero!'

I've never been a mom, but I think I'd be pretty suspicious if some old lady off the street offered to watch my baby for the night. As you can probably tell, though, Queen Metaneira was a kind-hearted, trusting person. She felt terrible for this old woman who had just lost her daughter. Also, it was true that Metaneira hadn't been sleeping much since the baby came along.

'I would be honoured,' the queen said, handing Demeter to Demophoon.

That night, the goddess rocked the baby by the fire. She sang him nursery songs from Mount Olympus, like 'The Itsy-Bitsy Satyr' and 'I'm a Little Cyclops'. She fed Demophoon nectar, the drink of the gods, mixed with his regular milk. She whispered powerful blessings to keep him safe.

I will make you immortal, little one, Demeter thought. *It's the least I can do for your kind mother. I will make you so strong no one will ever abduct you the way my poor daughter was abducted.*

When the child dozed off, Demeter placed him in the blazing fireplace.

You're probably thinking, *Ah! She roasted the little dude?*

No, it's cool. The kid was fine.

Demeter's magic protected him, so the flames only felt warm and pleasant. As Demophoon slept, the fire began burning away his mortal essence, starting the process that would turn him into a god.

In the morning, Queen Metaneira couldn't believe how much her baby had grown. He'd put on several pounds overnight. His eyes were brighter and his grip was stronger.

'What did you feed him?' the queen asked in amazement.

Demeter chuckled. 'Oh, nothing special, but I did promise to look out for him. He's going to be a fine young man!'

At breakfast, Triptolemus announced that his riders had already left. He expected news in the next day or two. Demeter was anxious. She was half-tempted to keep travelling on her own, but she agreed to wait for the riders to return.

That night, Demeter again took charge of the baby Demophoon. She fed him more ambrosia and laid him down to sleep in the fire. In the morning, she was pleased to see that he was immortalizing nicely.

'One more night ought to do it,' she decided.

When she gave the child back to the queen at breakfast, Metaneira wasn't so thrilled. Her boy suddenly looked like a four-month-old rather than a newborn. She wondered what kind of magic Demeter was using, and whether it had passed the safety test for babies. Maybe the old lady was slipping some kind of growth hormone into Demophoon's milk. In a few more days, the kid might have six-pack abs and hairy armpits.

Still, the queen was too polite to yell at her guest or throw accusations with no proof. She kept her doubts to herself. Secretly she hoped the riders would come back today, and the old lady would be on her way.

Unfortunately, the riders didn't return.

'I'm sure they'll be back in the morning,' Triptolemus promised. 'Then we should have more information.'

Demeter agreed to stay one more night. This time, when

dinner was finished, she took the baby from the queen without even asking, just assuming it was okay. Metaneira's heart hammered in her rib cage. She watched Demeter carry Demophoon back to her guest room, and the queen tried to convince herself everything was fine. The old lady was harmless. She would *not* turn her newborn son into a 'roid-raging monster overnight.

But the queen couldn't sleep.

She worried that she was going to miss her baby's entire childhood. She would wake up in the morning and see this big bulky three-year-old with facial hair running towards her, shouting in a deep voice, 'Hey, Mom! What up?'

Finally Metaneira couldn't stand it any more. She crept down the hall to Demeter's room to check on the baby.

The bedroom door was open just a crack. Firelight glowed at the sill. Metaneira heard the old woman singing a lullaby inside, but the baby wasn't making a sound. Hopefully that was good. He was sleeping peacefully. But what if he was in danger?

Without knocking, she opened the door . . . then screamed at the top of her lungs. The old lady was sitting calmly in a rocking chair, watching baby Demophoon burn in the fire!

Metaneira charged to the fireplace. She snatched the baby out of the flames, heedless of how much it burned her hands and arms. The baby started wailing, unhappy about waking up from a nice warm nap.

Metaneira wheeled on Demeter, ready to chew her face off, but the old lady yelled at her *first*.

'What are you THINKING?' Demeter shouted, rising from her chair with her fists clenched. 'Why did you do that? You've ruined everything!'

Metaneira was stunned speechless. Meanwhile, Prince

Triptolemus and several guards stumbled into the room to investigate the screaming.

'What's wrong?' Triptolemus demanded.

'Arrest this woman!' Metaneira shrieked, clutching her baby in her blistered arms. 'She tried to kill Demophoon! He was burning in the fireplace!'

The guards surged forward, but Triptolemus yelled, 'WAIT!'

The guards hesitated.

Triptolemus frowned at his mother, then at the old woman. He was smart enough to realize something wasn't right here. The baby was crying, but otherwise he seemed fine. He didn't look burned. The blanket wasn't even singed. The old woman looked more exasperated than guilty or scared.

'What is the meaning of this?' he asked their guest.

'The meaning,' growled Demeter, 'is that your mother just *ruined* things for the baby.'

The old woman began to glow. Her disguise burned away and she stood before them as a golden-haired goddess, her robes shimmering with green light, her scythe sword glinting at her side.

The guards dropped their weapons and retreated. Maybe they'd heard the story of Eric.

The queen gasped. As a pious woman, she knew how to spot her gods. 'Demeter!'

'Yes,' said the goddess. 'I was *trying* to do you a favour, you silly woman. A few more hours in the fire, and your baby boy would have been immortal! He would've grown into a fine young god and brought you eternal honour. Now you've ruined the magic. He will simply be human — a great hero, yes, strong and tall, but doomed to a mortal life. He will only be Demophoon, when he could have been Fully Phoon! Phoon the Great!'

Metaneira gulped. She wasn't sure if she should apologize, or thank the goddess, or what. She was so relieved to have her baby back safely, unburned and without hairy pits, that she didn't really care whether he was immortal. A great hero sounded good enough for her. Still, she didn't think she should say that to the goddess.

'I – I should have trusted you,' Metaneira murmured. 'Please, great Demeter, punish me for my lack of faith, but do not harm my family.'

Demeter waved her comment aside. 'Don't be silly. I won't punish you. I'm just annoyed. You've been helpful in my search, and –'

'Oh!' Triptolemus raised his hand like he had a burning question.

'Yes?' Demeter asked.

'That reminds me,' Triptolemus said. 'One of my riders just returned with news.'

'About my daughter?' Demeter completely forgot her annoyance and grabbed the prince's shoulders. 'Have you found her?'

Triptolemus wasn't used to being shaken by an immortal goddess, but he tried to keep his cool. 'Uh, not exactly, my lady. However, the rider says he met someone who met someone who met a guy in a tavern far to the east. This guy claimed he was the Titan of the sun, Helios. He was trying to impress the women with his stories, apparently.'

Demeter narrowed her eyes. 'Flirting with random women

in a tavern? That sounds like Helios. Well, it sounds like most of the gods, actually. What did he say?'

'Apparently he was telling a story about your daughter Persephone. He claimed that he saw the abduction and he knew who did it. But, er, he didn't name the culprit.'

'Of course!' Demeter got so excited that grass started to sprout on Triptolemus's shirt. 'Oh, sorry . . . but this is excellent news! I should've thought to visit Helios sooner. He sees everything!'

She kissed Triptolemus on the cheek. 'Thank you, my dear boy. I will not forget your help. Once I reclaim my daughter, I will reward you handsomely.'

Triptolemus tried to smile but failed. He was worried Demeter was going to make him sleep in a burning fireplace. 'That's okay. Really.'

'No, I insist. But now I must fly!'

Demeter turned into a turtle dove, which was one of her sacred birds, and flew out the window, leaving behind the very confused royal family of Eleusis.

Helios knew he was in trouble as soon as Demeter burst into his throne room. The sun Titan always liked to relax in the last hours of the night, before he had to saddle his fiery horses and get to work.

He was kicking back, thinking about all the crazy stuff he'd seen during his ride the day before. He really *should* write a book. Then suddenly the bronze doors of his audience chamber flew open, and Demeter rode her dragon-drawn chariot right up the steps of his throne. The dragons snarled and bared their fangs, drooling all over Helios's golden shoes.

'Uh, hi?' he said nervously.

'Where is my daughter?' Demeter's voice was calm and deadly serious.

Helios winced. He didn't want to get involved in godly disagreements. They didn't pay him enough for that. But he decided that right now was *not* the time to withhold information.

'Hades took her,' he said. He told her everything he'd seen.

Demeter held back a scream. She didn't want to cause another popcorn epidemic. But *Hades*? Of all the disgusting, horrible male gods who might have taken her precious daughter, Hades was the most disgusting and horrible of all.

'And *why* didn't you tell me this sooner?' Her voice was as sharp as her scythe.

'Well, um —'

'Never mind!' she snapped. 'I'll deal with you later. When Zeus hears how Hades has dishonoured our daughter, he'll be furious!'

She rode out of the sun palace and made straight for Mount Olympus.

As you can guess, her conversation with Zeus didn't go quite the way she planned. She marched into the throne room and yelled, 'Zeus! You won't believe what happened.'

She told him the whole story and demanded he do something.

Strangely, Zeus did *not* seem furious. He wouldn't meet Demeter's eyes. He kept picking at the end of his lightning bolt. Sweat trickled down the side of his face.

A cold feeling came over Demeter — a kind of anger that was much deeper than anything she'd felt before.

'Zeus, what did you do?'

'Well . . .' Zeus shrugged sheepishly. 'Hades might have mentioned that he wanted to marry Persephone.'

Demeter's fingernails dug into her palms until her hands were dripping golden ichor. 'And?'

'And it's a good match! Hades is powerful. He's handsome . . . or, um, well, he's *powerful*.'

'I want my daughter back,' Demeter said. 'NOW.'

Zeus squirmed on his throne. 'Look, babe —'

'Do NOT call me babe.'

'I can't go back on my word. It's done. She's down in the Underworld. They're married. End of story.'

'No,' Demeter said. '*Not* the end of the story. Until I have my daughter back, *nothing* will grow on the earth. Crops will die. People will starve. Every single living creature will share my pain until *you* do the right thing and return Persephone!'

Demeter thundered out of the room. (Thundering was usually Zeus's job, but she was beyond mad.) She went back to Eleusis, the one kingdom where people had helped her. She allowed the crops there to continue growing, but on the rest of the earth everything withered and died just as she'd threatened.

Zeus told himself, *She's just throwing a tantrum. Give her a few days and she'll get over it.*

Weeks passed. Then months. Humans starved by the thousands. And when humans starved they couldn't make burnt offerings to the gods. They couldn't build new temples. All they could do was cry out in agony, praying to the gods twenty-four/seven, *Help us! We're starving!* Which gave Zeus a *huge* headache.

Also, the gods were reduced to eating ambrosia and nectar,

which got old quickly. Without grain, they couldn't have any bread or those awesome fresh-baked brownies that Hera sometimes made.

Finally Zeus relented. He summoned his main messenger, a god named Hermes, and said, 'Hey, Hermes, go down to the Underworld. Tell Hades he's got to send Persephone back right away or we'll never have any peace – or brownies.'

'On it, boss.' Hermes zoomed down to the Underworld.

Meanwhile, Persephone had been in the palace of Hades this whole time, and she was learning the hard way that the world did *not* revolve around her.

No matter how many times she stamped her feet, held her breath or screamed for her mother, she couldn't get what she wanted.

She threw some epic tantrums. She tore up her bed (which made it hard to sleep); she kicked the walls (which hurt her foot); and when Hades's ghostly servants brought her meals she smashed the plates and refused to eat anything, even though she was starving.

The 'not eating' thing was important. See, in Greek times, eating food in another person's house was like signing a contract. It meant you accepted your place as their guest. They had to treat you properly, but you also had to behave properly. Basically, it meant you and your host were on friendly terms.

Persephone didn't want to sign that contract. Not at all.

The first few days, she refused to leave her room. Hades didn't force her to, though he tried to talk to her a few times.

'Look,' he said, 'your dad agreed to the marriage. I'm sorry about the whole kidnapping thing – which by the way was *his* idea – but, honestly, I *love* you. You're amazing and beautiful and I promise –'

'Get out!' She threw whatever she could grab – which happened to be a pillow. The pillow bounced off Hades's chest.

Hades looked sad and left her alone.

Around the fourth day, Persephone got bored and left her room. No one stopped her. She quickly realized why. Outside the king's palace, there was no place to go. She was stuck in the Underworld, with nothing in any direction except grey gloomy plains filled with dead people, and no sky above except dark mist.

Even if she ran away from the palace, she didn't want to walk through those fields full of dead souls, and she had no idea how to get back to the upper world.

The most infuriating thing? Hades *refused* to get mad at her, no matter how many plates she smashed or sheets she tore up, or how many horrible names she called him – though honestly she didn't know that many insults. She'd lived a happy, sheltered life, and calling Hades *Stupid Head* didn't quite seem forceful enough.

Hades took her abuse and told her he was sorry that she was angry.

'I do love you,' he promised. 'You are the brightest thing in the entire Underworld. With you here, I will never miss the sunlight again. You are warmer than the sun by far.'

'You're a stupid head!' she screamed.

After he left, she realized that what he'd said was sort of sweet – but only in a creepy, pathetic way, of course.

The days passed. The more Persephone wandered through

the palace, the more amazed she became. The mansion was *huge*. Hades had entire rooms made of gold and silver. Every day, his servants set out new bouquets of flowers made from precious jewels: a dozen ruby roses on diamond stems, platinum and gold sunflowers with emerald-studded leaves. Even on Mount Olympus, Persephone had never seen such dazzling wealth.

She started to realize that as creepy and horrible as Hades was, he had tremendous power. He controlled thousands of souls. He commanded horrifying monsters and creatures of the darkness. He had access to all the wealth under the earth, making him the richest god in the world. No matter what Persephone destroyed, he could instantly replace it with something even better.

Still, she hated the place. Of course she did! She missed the sun and the meadows and the fresh flowers. The Underworld was so clammy she could never get warm. The constant gloom gave her a serious case of seasonal affective disorder.

Then one day she stumbled across Hades's throne room. He was sitting at the far end, on a throne sculpted from thousands of bones, talking to a shimmering ghost. Persephone guessed it was a soul newly arrived from the mortal world, as it seemed to be giving Hades the latest news.

'Thank you,' Hades told the spirit. 'But I will never give in! I don't care *how* many mortals die!'

Persephone marched up to the dais. 'What are you talking about, you horrible person? Who are you killing now?'

Hades looked stunned. He waved at the ghost and it disappeared.

'I – I don't want to tell you,' Hades said. 'It would bring you pain.'

Which only made her want to know more. 'What's going on?'

Hades took a deep breath. 'Your mother is angry. She knows now that I took you for my wife.'

'Ha!' Persephone's heart soared. 'Oh, you're in so much trouble. She's on her way down here right now with an army of angry nymphs and grain spirits, isn't she?'

'No,' Hades said.

Persephone blinked. 'No?'

'She will not cross into the Underworld,' Hades said. 'She *hates* it here. She hates me.'

'Of course she does!' Persephone said, though she was a little disappointed. She'd been counting on her mom to rescue her. Surely Demeter would come get her personally, whether or not she hated the Underworld. 'But . . . I'm confused. What were you saying about mortals dying?'

Hades grimaced. 'Your mother is trying to force Zeus into getting you back. Demeter is starving the entire world, letting thousands of people die until you are returned to her.'

Persephone almost fell over. Her mother was doing *what*?

Demeter had always been so gentle and kind. Persephone couldn't imagine her mom letting a corn plant die, much less thousands of people. But something told her that Hades wasn't lying.

Persephone's eyes stung. She wasn't sure if she was sad or angry or just sick to her stomach. Thousands of mortals were dying because of *her*?

'You must return me,' Persephone said. 'Immediately.'

Hades clenched his jaw. For the first time he didn't look

mopey or weak. He met her gaze. His dark eyes flared with purple fire.

'You are my very existence now,' Hades said. 'You are more precious to me than all the jewels under the earth. I'm sorry you do not love me, but I will be a good husband to you. I'll do everything I can to make you happy. I will *not* return you. If I must, I will counter Demeter's attack. I will open the gates of the Underworld and let the dead flood back into the world rather than release you!'

Persephone didn't know what to do with that information. Her heart felt like it was compressing into a tiny jewel, as bright and hard as a diamond.

She turned and fled. She ran down a corridor she'd never explored before, opened a doorway, and stepped out into . . . a garden.

She couldn't breathe. It was the most incredible place she had ever seen. Ghostly warm lights floated overhead – perhaps the souls of particularly sunny dead people? She wasn't sure, but the garden was warmer and brighter than anywhere else in the Underworld. Beautiful subterranean flowers glowed in the dark. Orchards of carefully pruned trees bore sweet-smelling blooms and neon-bright fruit.

The paths were sculpted with rubies and topaz. White birch trees soared into the air like frozen ghosts. A brook wended through the middle of the garden. On a nearby table sat a silver tray with a frosted decanter of nectar, along with Persephone's favourite cookies and fresh fruits.

She couldn't understand what she was seeing. All the flowers and trees she loved best from the upper world were here in this garden, somehow blooming and flourishing in the darkness.

'What . . . ?' She couldn't form a sentence. 'How –'

'Do you like it?' Hades spoke just behind her. He'd followed her outside, and for once his voice didn't make her cringe.

She turned and saw a tiny smile on his face. He didn't look so horrible when he smiled.

'You – you did this for me?'

He shrugged. 'I'm sorry it wasn't ready sooner. I gathered the best gardeners in the Underworld. Askalaphos! Where are you?'

A thin young man appeared from the bushes. He had gardening shears in his hand. He was obviously one of the dead, judging from his papery skin and the yellowish tinge in his eyes, but he managed a smile. He somehow looked more alert than the other zombies Persephone had met.

'Just pruning the roses, my lord,' said Askalaphos. 'My lady, a pleasure to meet you.'

Persephone knew she should say something, like *hello*, but she was too stunned.

Just then a winged gargoyle flew into the garden. It whispered something in Hades's ear, and the god's face grew stern. 'A visitor,' he said. 'Excuse me, my dear.'

When he was gone, Askalaphos gestured to the patio table. 'My lady, would you like something to eat?'

'No,' Persephone said automatically. Despite everything, she knew she shouldn't accept the hospitality of a god who had kidnapped her.

'Suit yourself,' said the gardener. 'I just picked these ripe pomegranates, though. They're amazing.'

He pulled one from his overalls and set it on the table, then cut the fruit into three parts with his knife. Hundreds of juicy purple-red seeds glistened inside.

Now personally I'm not a big pomegranate fan, but Persephone loved them. They reminded her of her happiest moments above ground, frolicking in the meadows with her nymph friends.

She looked at the luscious fruit, and her stomach howled in protest. It had been days since she'd eaten anything. She was immortal, so she couldn't die, but she *felt* like she was starving.

A little bite won't hurt, she told herself.

She sat down, put one seed in her mouth and couldn't believe how good it tasted. Before she knew it, she had eaten a third of the fruit. She probably would've eaten more if Hades hadn't returned with his visitor – the god Hermes.

'My love!' Hades called, and his voice sounded like he'd been weeping.

Persephone shot to her feet. She hid her sticky purple fingers behind her and hoped she didn't have juice running down her chin. 'Mmm-hmm?' she mumbled, working a few half-chewed seeds around in her mouth.

'This is Hermes.' Hades's face looked broken with despair. 'He – he has come to take you back.'

Persephone swallowed. 'But . . . you said –'

'Zeus commands it.' Hades sounded so sad that Persephone forgot this was good news. 'I would gladly fight any god for your sake, but even I cannot fight against the entire Olympian council. I am . . . I am forced to give you up.'

Persephone should have been shouting with joy. This was what she wanted! So why did she feel so bad about it? She couldn't stand the look of devastation on Hades's face. He'd made this garden just for her. He'd treated her well . . . at least after the initial kidnapping, and that had been *Zeus's* idea. Hades had been ready to open the gates of the dead for her sake.

Hermes didn't seem bothered by any of that. 'Well, excellent!' He grinned at Persephone. 'Ready to go? Just some regulation questions I have to ask first — you know, customs stuff for crossing the border. Have you come into contact with any live animals?'

Persephone frowned. 'No.'

'Visited any farms?' Hermes inquired. 'Are you carrying more than ten thousand drachmas in foreign currency?'

'Uh . . . no.'

'Last question,' Hermes said. 'Have you eaten any food in the Underworld?' He held up his hands in apology. 'I know it's a stupid question. I mean, obviously you're smarter than that. If you ate any food in the Underworld, you'd have to stay here forever!'

Persephone cleared her throat. 'Uh . . .'

I don't know if she would've lied or not, but, before she could answer, the gardener Askalaphos said, 'Show them your hands, my lady.'

Persephone blushed. She held out her hands, which were stained purple. 'One third of a pomegranate,' she said. 'That's all.'

'Oh,' Hermes said. 'Whoops.'

'She can stay!' Hades danced in a circle, grinning from ear to ear, then seemed to realize he didn't look very dignified. 'Er, I mean, she *must* stay. I'm — I'm sorry, my dear, if that makes you sad. But I can't pretend I'm not delighted. This is wonderful news.'

Persephone's emotions were so jumbled that she wasn't sure *how* she felt.

Hermes scratched his head. 'This complicates things. I've got to report for new orders. Back soon.'

He flew to Mount Olympus and told the other gods his news.

When Demeter heard the problem, she flew into a rage. Somehow she managed to send a powerful curse straight through the ground, into that Underworld garden in Hades's mansion. She zapped the gardener Askalaphos into a gecko because he'd told on Persephone.

Why a gecko? I have no idea. I guess, off the top of her head, a zombie gecko was the worst curse she could think of.

Demeter threatened to let the world keep starving unless she got her daughter back. Hades sent a new message via Hermes, warning that the dead would rise in a zombie apocalypse unless Persephone stayed with him. Zeus was getting a splitting headache, imagining his beautiful world being ripped apart, until Hestia came up with a solution.

'Let Persephone divide her time,' suggested the hearth goddess. 'She ate one third of the pomegranate. Let her spend a third of the year with Hades, and two-thirds with Demeter.'

Amazingly, all the gods agreed. Hades was happy to have his wife, even for just a third of the year. Demeter was overjoyed, though she never got over being mad at Hades. Whenever Persephone was in the Underworld, Demeter turned cold and angry and wouldn't let the plants grow.

According to the old stories, that's why there are three distinct seasons in Greece, and during the colder months of autumn crops don't grow.

As for Persephone, the whole experience kind of forced her to grow up. She fell in love with Hades and made a place for herself in the Underworld, though she still enjoyed spending time in the mortal world with her mom and her old friends. The magic Titan Hecate, who had helped Demeter search, went to the Underworld and became one of Persephone's attendants. That was cool with Hecate. The Underworld was much darker, and a better place to work magic than a draughty cave.

Demeter even remembered her promise to Triptolemus, the prince of Eleusis. She gave him his own serpent-wheeled chariot and made him the god of farming. She told him to travel the world and teach people about agriculture. It doesn't sound like a very flashy job, but I guess Triptolemus liked it better than being thrown in a bed of fire.

After that, Demeter really *did* settle down. She didn't throw any more tantrums, which was good, because once her sister Hera got started Hera's temper would make Demeter's anger look *tame*.

HERA GETS A LITTLE CUCKOO

L ET'S START WITH THE GOOD NEWS. Hera was hot. I
mean totally knockout gorgeous.

She had long liquorice-black hair. Her face was regal
and unapproachably beautiful, like the face of a supermodel
on a fashion runway. The Greeks described her eyes as 'oxlike'.
Believe it or not, that was a compliment. It meant she had large,
soft brown eyes that you could get lost in. I guess the Greeks
spent a lot of time staring at oxen.

Anyway, in the early days of Mount Olympus, all the male
gods and Titans were falling over themselves for Hera. Which
brings us to the bad news. Hera had a short temper and massive
attitude. Whenever a guy approached her, she would cut him
down so fast – pointing out his faults, trash-talking him like
a pro – that the guy would leave in tears and never try flirting
with her again.

Mother Rhea decided Hera would do well at a boarding school for girls, where she could grow up a little and learn to be less abrasive. Unfortunately, nobody had invented boarding schools for girls yet.

Rhea did the next best thing. She sent Hera off to live with her Uncle Oceanus and Aunt Tethys at the bottom of the furthest sea.

For a while, Hera was off the radar screen. She spent some happy years with Oceanus and Tethys, who had a pretty solid marriage compared to the other immortals. Hera decided she wanted a marriage like that. She would hold out for the right guy. She wouldn't marry just any old god who came along, unless he could prove he would be a good and faithful husband.

She'd heard about her sister Demeter's troubles. Poseidon, Zeus and Hades were all complete jerks. Hestia had been smart to stay single.

Hera wasn't about to be a bachelorette forever, though. She wanted a husband, kids, a house in the suburbs – the whole package. She would just have to be careful about *which* husband she chose.

After a few years, she moved back to Mount Olympus and got her own set of apartments in the palace. Her nasty temper was more under control, but the guy gods still found her hard to flirt with. If they got too fresh, she would shut them down *fast*.

Kiss Hera? I don't think so, loser. Not unless you show her a wedding ring and a financial statement proving you can support a family.

Eventually most of the gods and Titans decided Hera

was too much work, even though she was absolutely the most beautiful goddess in creation. (Well, so far, anyway.)

One god saw her as a challenge, though.

Zeus didn't like to take no for an answer. You may have noticed that.

He would slide in next to her at the dinner table and tell his best jokes. He would sing for her at the hearth. He would see her walking down the hall, and he'd suddenly bust into a Kouretes dance number just to get her to smile.

Secretly she enjoyed the attention. Zeus was funny when he wanted to be. He was handsome with his dark hair and blue eyes, and he liked to walk around without his shirt on, casually flexing his muscles and showing off his abs. He was in good shape, no doubt about it. And, yes, he was the king of the universe, so most women might consider him a good match.

But not Hera. She knew all about Zeus's womanizing. He'd already been married *at least* twice. He'd had a child with Demeter. There were rumours of many other affairs with goddesses, Titans and even mortals.

Hera was *not* going to be another conquest. She wasn't a trophy. She knew that if she ever gave in to Zeus he would lose interest in her immediately, stop being so charming and go off to flirt with other women. Hera couldn't stand that idea.

One night at dinner he told a particularly funny joke – something about a donkey, a god and a Cyclops walking into a temple – and Hera couldn't help laughing. She had tears in her eyes and couldn't breathe.

She gazed across the table and met Zeus's gaze a moment too long. She cleared her throat and looked away, but Zeus had glimpsed her feelings.

'You like me,' he said. 'You know you do.'

'I certainly do *not*,' she said. 'You're a fool, a womanizer, a villain and a liar!'

'Exactly!' Zeus said. 'Those are my best qualities!'

She tried hard not to laugh. She'd never met a guy who was so immune to her insults. Zeus was almost as stubborn as she was.

'When will you give up?' she demanded. 'I'm *not* interested.'

'I'll never give up,' he said. 'And you *are* interested. You and I . . . king and queen of the cosmos. Imagine it! We'd be an unbeatable couple. Clearly, you are the most beautiful goddess in creation. And I, of course, am devilishly handsome.'

He flexed his muscles. He was a ridiculous show-off, but Hera had to admit he was buff.

She shook her head. 'How can I convince you that you're wasting your time?'

'You can't. I love you.'

She snorted. 'You love anything in a dress.'

'This is different. You're the right goddess. I know it. You do, too. Just say *I love you*. You can do it. You'll feel better if you're honest.'

'Never,' she said. 'I will never tell you that. *Ever*.'

'Oh, sounds like a challenge!' Zeus grinned. 'If I can get you to admit you love me, will you marry me?'

Hera rolled her eyes. 'Sure, Zeus. Since that will never happen, I can safely say that if I ever admitted to . . . you know, what you said . . . then sure I'd marry you. Which I can only promise because IT WILL NEVER HAPPEN!'

Zeus winked. 'Challenge accepted.'

He left the dinner table, and Hera began wondering if she'd somehow made a mistake.

Hera had almost forgotten about the conversation by a few nights later. Strangely, Zeus hadn't mentioned it again. In fact, he hadn't paid much attention to her at all since that night – which should have filled her with relief, but somehow it bummed her out.

Forget him, she told herself. *He finally got the message. He's probably accosting some other poor goddess.*

She tried to convince herself this was good news. She wasn't jealous. That would be ridiculous.

During the night, a huge thunderstorm raged over Mount Olympus – which probably should've made Hera suspicious, since Zeus was the god of the sky and all – but she was too busy covering her windows to keep out the rain.

She ran to her bedroom and was just closing the last shutters when a small bird fluttered in and collapsed, exhausted, on her floor.

'Yikes!' Hera stepped back in alarm. 'How did *you* get here?'

The bird flapped helplessly on the marble tiles. Its chest heaved, its whole body shivering from the cold. Hera knelt down and saw that it was a cuckoo.

Have you ever seen an *actual* cuckoo bird (not the carved ones that pop out of old clocks)? I haven't. I had to look it up. It's a weird-looking little guy. It's got a sort of Mohawk thing going on with its head feathers, which don't match its sleek brown-and-white wings or its long tail. Basically, it looks like its head got zapped in some mad scientist's device, so I can see why *cuckoo* became another word for *crazy*.

Anyway, Hera knelt down and scooped up the bird. She could feel its heart beating against her palm. One of its wings was bent the wrong way. Hera didn't understand how such a small bird could have flown all the way up to Mount Olympus. Usually only eagles flew that high, since the airspace around Olympus was restricted.

On the other hand, Hera knew that storms had powerful winds. Possibly the poor bird just got swept away.

'It's a miracle you're alive,' Hera told the bird. 'Don't worry, little guy. I'll take care of you.'

She made a nest of blankets at the foot of her bed and gently set the bird inside. She dried its wings and fed it a few drops of nectar, which seemed to help. The cuckoo puffed up its feathers. It closed its eyes and started to make whistling, snoring noises, like soft notes played on a flute. Hera found the sound pleasing.

'I'll just keep him overnight,' she said to herself. (She'd decided it was a boy.) 'If he's better in the morning, I'll send him on his way.'

In the morning, the cuckoo made no attempt to fly away. He sat contentedly on Hera's finger, eating pieces of seed and nut out of her hand. Hera had never had a pet before, and it made her smile.

'You're a good friend, aren't you?' she murmured to the bird.

'Coo,' said the cuckoo.

Hera's heart warmed as she looked into his trusting orange eyes. 'Should I keep you?'

'Coo.' The cuckoo rubbed his beak on her finger in an unmistakably affectionate way.

Hera laughed in delight. 'All right, then. Yes. I love you, too.'

Instantly the cuckoo hopped to the floor. It began to grow. At first Hera was afraid she'd fed him too much nectar and the bird was going to explode, which would have been both distressing and messy. Instead, the bird took on the form of a god. Suddenly Zeus was standing before her in his glowing white robes, his golden crown gleaming in his black hair, which was still mussed up in a cuckoo-style hairdo.

'Sweet words, my lady,' Zeus said. '*I love you, too.* Now, I believe you and I had a deal.'

Hera was so stunned that she couldn't respond. Anger overwhelmed her. But she also felt a creeping admiration for what an incredible no-good scoundrel Zeus was. She wasn't sure whether she should hit him or laugh at him or just kiss him. He *was* awfully cute.

'On one condition,' she said tightly.

'Name it.'

'If I marry you,' she said, 'you will be a good, *faithful* husband. No more playing around. No more affairs or chasing after pretty mortals. I will not be made a laughing stock.'

Zeus counted on his fingers. 'That seems like more than one condition. But never mind! I accept!'

Hera should have made him promise on the River Styx, which is the most serious oath the gods can make. She didn't, though. She agreed to marry him.

After that, the cuckoo became one of her sacred animals. You'll usually see pictures of Hera holding a staff topped with either a cuckoo or a lotus flower, which was her sacred plant. In case you're curious, her other sacred animal was the cow, because it was such a motherly animal. Personally, if somebody told me, 'Wow, babe, you remind me of a heifer,' I would not take it as a compliment, but it didn't seem to bother Hera. Whatever clunks your cowbell, I suppose.

Zeus and Hera announced the happy news, and the gods began preparing for the biggest wedding in the history of weddings.

You have to pity Hermes the messenger god, who had to deliver the wedding invitations. Every god, Titan, mortal, nymph, satyr and animal in the world was invited to join the party. I hope the snails got their invites early. It must've taken them forever to get there.

Different people will tell you different stories about where the wedding was held. We'll go with the island of Crete, because it makes sense. That was where Zeus hid on Mount Ida when he was a baby, so the place had good karma.

I'm still trying to figure out the logistics, though . . . So, you invite a wild rabbit living in Italy to a party on the island of Crete. What's it supposed to do, swim there? Its little tux would get wet.

Anyway, everybody who was invited showed up, except for one really stupid nymph named Chelone. She lived in Arcadia on the Greek mainland, in this hut by a river, and she just threw her invitation away.

'Meh,' she said. 'Stupid wedding. I'd rather stay home.'

When Hermes discovered she was a no-show, he got mad.

(I guess it was also his job to check the guest list.) He flew back to Chelone's place and found her bathing in the river.

'What's the deal?' he demanded. 'You're not even dressed. The wedding is on!'

'Uh . . .' Chelone said. 'I, um . . . I'm a little slow. I'll be there!'

'Really? That's the story you're going with?'

'Okay, no,' she admitted. 'I just wanted to stay home.'

Hermes got a dark look in his eyes. 'Fine.'

He marched over to Chelone's hut and picked up the entire building, Superman-style. 'You want to stay home? Stay home *forever*.'

He threw the house right on top of her, but, instead of dying, Chelone changed form. The house shrank over her back, melting into a shell, and Chelone became the world's first tortoise, an animal that's always slow and carries its house on its back. That's why *chelone* means *tortoise* in Greek. Hey, you never know. You might need that info on *Jeopardy!* some day.

The rest of the world was smart and went to the party. The bride and groom entered the sacred grove in a golden chariot driven by Eos, the Titan of the dawn, so rosy red light spread over the crowd as Zeus and Hera approached, signalling the dawning of a new day. The Three Fates officiated at the ceremony, which would have made me nervous. Those creepy old ladies could control the future and snip your lifeline, so you'd have to take your vows pretty seriously.

Hera and Zeus became man and wife, king and queen of the universe.

Everybody gave them amazing presents, but the last one

was Hera's favourite. The earth rumbled, and a sapling burst from the ground – a young apple tree bearing solid gold fruit. There was no card attached, but Hera knew it was a gift from her grandmother Gaia, who was still asleep, but who must have sensed a party going on.

Hera ordered the apple tree taken to the furthest western corner of the earth, where it was replanted in a beautiful garden right at the feet of the Titan Atlas, who was still holding up the sky. She sent an immortal dragon named Ladon to guard the tree, along with a group of Atlas's daughters called the Hesperides, the nymphs of the evening sky.

Why Hera planted her apple tree way out there instead of keeping it on Mount Olympus, I don't know. Maybe she just wanted to make it harder for heroes to steal her apples later on. If so, her plan worked . . . mostly.

Zeus and Hera stayed happily married for three hundred years, which isn't a long time for gods but is better than your average Hollywood marriage. They had three kids together: a boy, Ares, who was what you'd call a problem child; a girl, Hebe, who became the goddess of eternal youth; and another girl, Eileithyia, who became the goddess of childbirth. Kind of bad planning – having the goddess of childbirth *last*, after you've had two kids. It's almost like Hera thought, Wow, this childbearing stuff? This hurts! We should have a goddess for this.

After their third kid was born, Zeus started to get the three-hundred-year itch. He remembered the good old days when he was a single guy, ambushing goddesses in snake pits and fun stuff like that. He started looking at other women and flirting again.

He'd promised to be a good husband, and he *had* been . . . for a while. But when you're immortal those vows about 'as long as you both shall live' take on a whole new meaning.

The more he flirted, the more upset and suspicious Hera got.

What she hated most were all the kids Zeus had by other women. They just kept popping up like weeds. Zeus claimed they were all from previous relationships, but that excuse didn't really cut it. Some of these kids were mortal, and they definitely didn't look over three hundred years old. Every time one of them showed up, Hera imagined the other gods snickering behind her back, whispering about what a fool she'd been to trust Zeus.

Finally she blew her lid.

She shouted at Zeus, 'You keep having kids without me! You think that's funny? You think I appreciate you going back on your promise?'

Zeus frowned. 'Is that a trick question?'

'See how you like it!' Hera cried. 'I'm going to have a kid without you, without *any* man! I'll have a baby all by myself!'

Zeus scratched his head. 'Uh, honey, I don't think it works that way.'

'Bah!' Hera marched out of the throne room.

I don't know how she did it. Since her wedding with Zeus, Hera had become the goddess of marriage and motherhood, so I suppose she had certain powers. Anyway, out of sheer force of will, some very effective breathing exercises, possibly some Eastern meditation and a proper diet, Hera got pregnant magically, with absolutely no help.

That was the good news.

The bad news? When the baby arrived, he looked like he could've *used* some help. His head was misshapen. His whole body was covered with patches of curly black hair. He had a large chest and bulky arms, but his legs were shrivelled and bent, one slightly longer than the other. Instead of crying, he made grunting noises like he really needed to use the bathroom.

He was the ugliest kid Hera had ever seen. Even though he was her own baby, she felt no motherly connection at all – no love, just embarrassment.

Personally, I'm not surprised things turned out badly. I mean, you have a baby for revenge? That's a pretty messed-up reason, but it wasn't the kid's fault.

Hera said to herself, *I can't show this baby to the other gods. I'll be ridiculed.* She went to the open window of her bedroom and looked down the side of Mount Olympus. It sure was a long way down.

Who would ever know if the kid disappeared? She could always claim that she'd never been pregnant. False alarm.

Before she could rethink this pretty terrible idea, she tossed the baby out the window.

I know. *Totally* cold. Like a kid is something you can just throw away. But Hera was complicated that way. One day she was the perfect mother. The next day she was throwing babies out the window.

Oh, but the kid wasn't gone. His name was Hephaestus, and we'll see what happened to him later on.

In the meantime, Hera had other problems to deal with.

The first time a mortal hero visited Mount Olympus, it was a big deal. His name was Ixion, and apparently he was the first human to figure out that you could kill other humans in battle. *Congratulations! You win a prize!*

The gods were so impressed he'd learned to fight other humans with an actual sword instead of just chucking rocks and grunting at them that they invited Ixion to a feast on Mount Olympus.

You'd think the guy would be on his best behaviour. Nope.

He had too much to eat and drink. All the praise went to his head. He started thinking the gods were actually his friends, his peers, his comrades. Big mistake. No matter how nicely the gods treat you, they *never* see you as their equal. Remember, to them we are gerbils who have fire, cockroaches who can use weapons. We're kind of entertaining. Occasionally we're useful, if the gods need to kill small things down on earth. But BFFs? No.

All evening, Ixion kept making eyes at Hera, since she was the most beautiful lady at the table. Zeus was too busy partying to notice, much less care. Finally Hera got really uncomfortable and excused herself.

Ixion figured that was his cue to follow her. The guy had learned how to kill people, but apparently he had a lot to learn about goddesses. After she'd left, Ixion waited at the table for a few minutes, then he announced to the gods, 'Hey, all this drink is going right through me. Where's the bathroom? Uh, do gods even *have* bathrooms?'

'Down the hall,' Zeus said. 'First door on the right. They're marked *mortals* and *gods*. Just be sure you use the correct one.'

Ixion headed off in the direction Hera had gone. He found her standing on a balcony, looking at the clouds.

'Hey, beautiful,' he said.

She flinched. She probably would have turned him into some form of snail – something very slimy – but she was too stunned that this mortal had dared to speak to her.

Ixion took her silence as shyness. 'Yeah, I know you've been checking me out. I think you're awesome, too. How about a kiss?'

He put his arm around her and tried to kiss her. Hera was so panicked that all she could do was push him away and run. She lost him in the corridors of the palace, locked herself in her room and waited until her pulse returned to normal.

Why hadn't she incinerated him? Or at least changed him into a slug?

She'd been too shocked. Also, maybe, she was a little confused by the flirting. It had been several hundred years since she'd had to deal with that. Once she'd got married, she'd put other men out of her mind completely.

Whatever Hera's faults, she was *not* a cheater. She didn't have an unfaithful bone in her immortal body. She truly and honestly believed that marriage was forever, for better or worse, which was why Zeus's little adventures drove her into a rage.

Once she had calmed down, she started to plot her revenge. She could punish Ixion herself, sure. But why not tell Zeus instead? Let *him* be the jealous one for a change. Maybe if he had to defend her honour he would start taking his marriage vows more seriously.

Hera composed herself and returned to the dinner table. Ixion sat there chatting away, as if nothing had happened – the little weasel. Hera gave him a smile, just to show she wasn't rattled. Then she leaned over to Zeus and whispered, 'My lord, may I speak with you in private?'

Zeus frowned. 'Am I in trouble?'

'Not yet,' she said sweetly.

She led him down the hall and explained what had happened.

Zeus scowled. He stroked his beard thoughtfully.

Hera had been hoping he would march right back into the dining room and blast Ixion to ashes, but he didn't.

'Did you *hear* me?' Hera asked. 'Why aren't you getting angry?'

'Oh, I heard you.' Zeus cleared his throat. 'It's just . . . well, he's a guest in my house. He's eaten our food. I can't incinerate him without good reason.'

'*WITHOUT GOOD REASON?*' she cried. 'He made a pass at your *wife!*'

'Yes, yes. And that's very serious. Still, I need indisputable proof.'

'My word is not good enough?' Hera was about to throw Zeus off the balcony and take care of Ixion herself, but Zeus raised his hands to placate her.

'I have a plan,' he said. 'We'll see if Ixion really intended to dishonour you, or if he just made a drunken, stupid mistake. Once we have proof, none of the other gods will object to my punishing this mortal, even though he is my guest. Trust me. If he's guilty, his punishment will be spectacular.'

Hera clenched her fists. 'Do what you have to do.'

Zeus reached over the railing and summoned down a cloud. It condensed and churned before him in a small white tornado, shaping itself into a humanoid figure. It became an exact replica of Hera, only pale and cold.

I take that back. It was an exact replica of Hera.

Fake Hera looked at Real Hera. 'Hello.'

'That is creepy,' said Real Hera.

'Just wait here,' Zeus told Real Hera.

He took Fake Hera back to the party.

Ixion picked up right where he'd left off, flirting with Fake Hera. To his delight, Fake Hera flirted back. She gestured for him to follow her down the hall. One thing led to another.

In the morning, the bleary-eyed gods stumbled into the dining hall for breakfast. They were surprised to find that Ixion had stayed overnight and, when they asked why, Ixion told them that the Queen of Heaven had invited him to stay in her apartment – wink, wink, wink.

'I have her wrapped around my little finger,' he bragged. 'She said I was *much* handsomer than Zeus. She's going to make me immortal just so she can be with me forever.'

He went on boasting about how cool he was and how much Hera wanted to leave Zeus and marry him. Meanwhile, Zeus himself entered the dining hall and walked up quietly behind Ixion.

Finally Ixion realized that all the gods at the table had gone silent.

He faltered. 'He's right behind me, isn't he?'

'Why, yes!' Zeus said cheerfully. 'And if you're going to steal another man's wife you really shouldn't brag about it in his own house. Also, you should make sure it's *actually* the man's wife you stole, and not a cloud dummy.'

Ixion gulped. 'I guess I'm in trouble.'

'Just a bit!' Zeus agreed.

None of the other gods objected to Zeus's punishing his guest. Zeus called for a spare chariot wheel and strapped Ixion to the spokes, stretching his limbs so tight they were about to snap. Then he set the wheel on fire and threw it into the sky like a Frisbee. Ixion became immortal, all right, but only so he could suffer eternal agony. He's still up there in orbit, spinning and burning and screaming, 'Hera! I thought you liked me!'

The strangest part of the story? Fake Hera actually had a baby. How does a cloud have a baby? I have no clue, but their son was a guy named Centaurus, who apparently fell in love with a horse — again, no clue. Their kids became the race of centaurs, who are half human, half horse.

Like I told you at the beginning, I couldn't make up stuff this weird.

Hera hoped Zeus would be a more attentive husband after the Ixion incident, but she was disappointed. Instead, Zeus seemed to think he'd successfully defended Hera's honour, so now he deserved some playtime.

If I tried to tell you all the times Hera took revenge on Zeus's girlfriends, we'd be here for a century. It sort of became Hera's full-time job.

But one particular mortal girl *really* got under her skin. Semele was a princess of the Greek city of Thebes and, though no one dared to say it aloud, everyone knew she was the most beautiful mortal of her generation — as beautiful as a goddess, perhaps even more beautiful than Hera herself.

Zeus started taking a lot of 'shopping trips' down to Thebes. Hera was suspicious, of course, but Zeus was clever.

Hera could never catch him and Semele together. Then one day she was hovering over Thebes as a golden cloud when she happened to spot Zeus (in disguise as a mortal, but Hera could still recognize him) exiting a house in the best part of town.

A moment later, Semele appeared at the door and waved after him. The girl only stood there for a second, but one thing was obvious: she was *immensely* pregnant.

Hera snarled and muttered to herself, but she couldn't simply kill the girl outright. Even though Zeus was a no-good scumbag, he was a very *powerful* no-good scumbag. If he found out that Hera had killed one of his girlfriends, he could inflict all sorts of pain and suffering on her. She would have to work through trickery.

Hera floated down to Thebes in her golden cloud and took the form of an old woman. She knocked on Semele's door, thinking she would pretend to be a beggar or perhaps a travelling saleslady.

Semele opened the door and gasped. 'Beroe, is that you?'

Hera had no idea what the girl was talking about, but she played along. 'Why, yes, my dear! It is I, Beroe, your, um –'

'My nursemaid from childhood!'

'Exactly!'

'Oh, you have aged so!'

'Thanks,' Hera muttered.

'But I would still know you anywhere. Please, come in!'

Hera got a tour of the house. She was outraged to find it was just as nice, if not better, than her own apartment on Mount Olympus.

She asked innocently how Semele came by such an amazing mansion, which seemed elaborate even for a princess.

'Oh, it's my boyfriend,' Semele said, beaming with pride. 'He's so awesome; he gives me *anything* I want. Look at this necklace he just brought me.'

She showed Hera a jade, gold and ruby pendant that was much nicer than anything Zeus had ever given Hera.

'How lovely.' Hera resisted the urge to punch the princess in her perfect teeth. 'So, who is this guy? Is he local?'

'Oh . . . I'm not supposed to say.'

'But I'm your old nursemaid, Beryl!' Hera said.

'Beroe,' Semele said.

'That's what I meant! Surely you can tell me.'

Semele was bursting with excitement. She'd been dying to tell someone, so she didn't take much convincing.

'Well . . . it's Zeus,' she confessed. 'The lord of the sky. The king of creation.'

Hera stared at her, feigning disbelief. Then she sighed in sympathy. 'Oh, my poor girl. My poor, poor girl.'

Semele blinked. That wasn't the reaction she'd been expecting. 'But . . . I'm dating the king of the universe!'

Hera snorted. 'So he says. How many guys have used *that* line before? Like, every one of them! How do you know he's *actually* a god, and not just some rich old creep *pretending* to be a god?'

Semele's face reddened. 'But he *said* he was Zeus. And he seems very . . . godly.'

'Has he done anything to prove it?'

'Uh, well, no.'

Hera pretended to think about the problem. 'This is the father of your child. You should be sure. You said he would do anything for you?'

'Yes! He promised!'

'Get him to swear,' Hera advised. 'Then ask him to appear before you the way he appears before his wife Hera – in his true godly form. That's the only way you'll know for sure.'

Semele pondered this. 'Sounds dangerous.'

'Not if he truly loves you! Are you not as good as Hera?'

'Of course.'

'And as beautiful?'

'More beautiful. Zeus told me so.'

Hera clenched her jaw so hard that she cracked an immortal tooth. 'There you go, then. If Hera can handle Zeus's godly form, then surely you can too! I hope he really is Zeus, my dear. Honestly! But you must be sure. Your child's future is on the line. When is he coming back?'

'Very soon, actually.'

'Well, look at the time!' Hera said. 'Wonderful catching up, but I should go. I have . . . old-lady things to do.'

Hera left. An hour later, Zeus returned to Semele's house.

'Hey, babe,' he said as he walked in.

Immediately he noticed something was wrong. Semele didn't run up and hug him and kiss him as usual. She was sulking on her couch with her arms crossed across her pregnant belly.

'Uh . . . what's up?' Zeus asked.

Semele pouted. 'You said you'd do anything for me.'

'And I will! You want another necklace?'

'No,' she said. 'I want a different favour. Only one thing will make me happy.'

Zeus chuckled. Maybe Semele wanted a dress this time, or a pair of those new things the humans had just invented . . . what were they called . . . shoes?

'Anything you want,' Zeus said.

'Promise?'

He spread his arms magnanimously. 'I swear on the River Styx. Ask me any favour, and it's yours.'

'Good.' She allowed herself a smile. 'I want you to appear before me in your true godly form, the way you appear to Hera.'

Zeus sucked in his breath. 'Oh . . . bad idea, babe. Ask me something else.'

'No!' Semele struggled to her feet. 'You said *anything*. I want proof that you're really a god. I'm just as good as Hera! I want to see you the way *she* sees you.'

'But a god's true form . . . that's not for mortals to look on. Especially pregnant mortals. Especially pregnant mortals who would like to live longer than a few seconds.'

'I can handle it,' she said. 'I *know* I can.'

Zeus was not so sure about that. He'd never actually tried appearing to a mortal in his pure godly form before, but he imagined that for the mortal it would be like looking at the sun without protective eyewear, or looking at an actor first thing in the morning pre-make-up. *Dangerous.*

On the other hand, Zeus had sworn on the River Styx, and he couldn't back out of that. Also, Semele was a feisty girl. She was the daughter of the famous hero Cadmus. If she thought she could handle seeing a god's true form, maybe she could.

'Okay, ready?' Zeus asked.

'Ready.'

Zeus's mortal disguise burned away. He appeared in all his glory as a swirling pillar of fire and lightning, like a supernova, in Semele's living room. The furniture went up in flames. The door blew off its hinges. The window shutters exploded.

Semele couldn't handle it. She vaporized, leaving an after-image scorch mark on the living-room wall. However, the baby inside her *did* survive, probably because he was part god. The poor little guy was suddenly hovering in midair where his nice cosy mother used to be. Zeus took physical form just in time to catch him before he hit the floor.

Of course Zeus was in shock over Semele's death, but he realized that the most important thing right now was the baby. The little dude wasn't fully grown yet. He obviously needed a few more months to develop before he was ready to be born.

Zeus had to think quickly. He pulled out his lightning bolt and made an incision in his own right thigh. Must've hurt like crazy, but Zeus stuffed the baby into his thigh just like he was putting him in the pocket of a pair of cargo pants. Then he sewed his skin shut.

Guys . . . do not try this at home. It won't work.

But I guess gods are different. Somehow the kid stayed alive in there and kept growing until he was ready to be born.

No word on whether the other gods said, 'Hey, Zeus, why is your right thigh so huge, dude? You should really get that looked at.'

When the baby was ready, Zeus cut him out; and the kid became the god Dionysus. We'll get to his story later on. His birth is the *least* strange thing about him.

Anyway, Hera got her revenge on Semele, and I wish I could tell you it was the harshest thing she ever did.

Unfortunately, she was just getting warmed up.

Another one of Zeus's girlfriends was this lady named Aigina. Apparently, Aigina had heard the story about Semele, because she was not anxious to become Zeus's special friend, even though he constantly flirted with her and showered her with gifts. Finally, Zeus convinced her to fly away with him to a secret island.

'No one will ever know,' he promised.

'What about Hera?' Aigina asked.

'Especially not her.' Zeus turned into a giant eagle and flew her to an island that now bears her name: Aigina.

Zeus *almost* got away with it. Hera didn't find out about the affair until years later, after Aigina had passed away. By then, Aigina and Zeus's son was the king of the island where he'd been born. I don't know how Hera found out, but, once she did, she was outraged that she couldn't punish Aigina personally.

'How *dare* she die so that I can't kill her!' Hera growled. 'Well, I'll just take out my anger on her son.'

His name was King Aeacus. (I think he needs a few more vowels in his name. No idea how to pronounce it, so I'm going with 'Eye-AH-cuss'.) Anyway, King Aeacus happened to be on the verge of war. He was getting his armies together to defend his kingdom.

Hera summoned a massive poisonous snake and dropped it into the headwaters of the island's only river. The venom spread through the water supply, and soon most of the population of the entire island was dead.

Hey, that's fair, right? Zeus sleeps with a mortal woman, so Hera finds the woman's son and kills everyone in his kingdom. No, that's not psychotic at all.

As you can imagine, Aeacus panicked. He went to his palace garden, where he could see the blue sky. He fell on his knees and prayed to Zeus, 'Hey, Dad, I'm about to get invaded here, and your wife just pretty much killed every man in my army and most of the civilians.'

Zeus's voice rumbled from the heavens: 'Bummer. How can I help?'

Aeacus thought about that. He looked down at his flower-beds and saw ants marching around, thousands of the little dudes, tireless and industrious like . . . like an army.

'You know what would be cool?' Aeacus asked. 'If you could turn these ants into an army for me.'

'Done!' Zeus thundered.

Immediately the entire colony of ants grew into men — thousands of hardened warriors in gleaming red-and-black armour, already drilled to march in rows and fight with perfect discipline. They feared no enemy. They were incredibly strong and tough. They were called the Myrmidones, and they became the most famous elite fighting unit in Greece, like the Navy SEALs or the Green Berets of the ancient world. Later on, they would have a famous commander named Achilles. Maybe you've heard of him, or at least his heel.

The last thing about Hera — and I really don't get this — is how quickly she could change from being somebody's enemy to his friend, or vice versa. Take Poseidon, for instance.

At first, they didn't get along. In fact, they both had their eye on the same Greek kingdom, called Argos. See, it was a big deal back then to be the patron god of this city or that city. Like, it was a huge honour if you could claim to be the god of New York City. If you were the god of Scranton, Pennsylvania . . . not so much. (Okay, sorry, everybody in Scranton. But you get the idea.)

I guess Argos was a nice place, because both Hera and Poseidon wanted to be its patron. The king decided to go for Hera. Probably he didn't want his population dying off from snake poison.

Hera was delighted. Poseidon wasn't. He flooded the entire kingdom and, when Hera complained, Poseidon said, 'Fine. I'll take back the water. I'll take back *all* of it.' The sea receded, and all the springs and rivers in the whole country went dry.

Hera complained again. The two of them were on the verge of an epic smackdown. Finally Poseidon relented and let some of the water come back, but Argos is still a very dry place. Many of the rivers have no water unless it rains. Hera became the patron of Argos, which was helpful later on for a dude named Jason, who led a crew of heroes called the Argonauts. But that's another story.

My point is that Hera changed her tune shortly afterwards. She and Poseidon had a sit-down and decided that Zeus was getting out of control as a leader. They plotted the first-ever Olympian rebellion.

But we'll get to that when we talk about Poseidon.

Now we have to visit the Underworld and see how it's going with our favourite creepy stalker death god, Hades.

HADES DOES HOME IMPROVEMENT

I FEEL FOR THE GUY.

No, seriously.

Hades might be a creep, but there's no doubt he got the short end of the universe. Despite being Rhea's eldest son, he was always counted as the youngest, since the gods went by the order they got barfed from Kronos's gut.

If that wasn't bad enough, when the gods rolled dice to divide up the world, Hades got the least desirable part – the Underworld.

Of course, Hades was kind of a gloomy dude to begin with, so you could argue that he was destined to hang out underground. He was always brooding and dressed in black. His dark hair covered his eyes like one of those emo dudes from Japanese manga. Once he became lord of the Underworld, all the colour drained out of his complexion, because he was leaving the mortal world behind.

Even if the other gods *wanted* to keep in touch with him (which they didn't), the Underworld had really bad phone service and zero Wi-Fi. When Hades was down there, he had no idea what was going on in the world above. His only news came from the spirits of the recently dead, who would fill him in on the latest gossip.

In fact, in Ancient Greek times, whenever you invoked the name of Hades, you had to bang your fist against the ground, because that was the only way to get his attention. Kind of like *Hey, I'm talking to you!*

Why would you *want* to get Hades's attention? I'm not sure.

Eventually the entire Underworld would be called *Hades* after the god Hades, which made things confusing, but the Underworld had actually been around much longer than the god. Its original name was Erebos and, when Hades took over, the place was a real fixer-upper.

Let's start with the plumbing. Five different rivers flowed into the Underworld, and you wouldn't want to use any of them for taking a bath or brushing your teeth. The *least* dangerous was the Cocytus, the River of Wailing, which looked tame enough. Its dark-blue waters wound peacefully through the plains of Erebos, with plenty of nice-looking spots on the riverbank for a picnic, but if you got too close you would hear the cries of tortured souls churning in the current.

See, the Cocytus was fed by the tears of the damned. Just being near it would send you into a state of depression. If you actually *touched* the water . . . well, trust me, you didn't want to do that. No amount of cute puppy videos on the Internet would ever lift your spirits again.

The second river was the Phlegethon, the River of Fire. It roared through the Underworld caverns like a torrent of burning gasoline, cutting channels through the black volcanic rock, lighting everything blood-red, filling the air with smoke and fumes until finally the river plummeted as a fiery waterfall into the deeper abyss of Tartarus, which was like the basement of the basement.

So, yeah . . . when Hades turned on the hot water in his shower, he got a face full of burning Phlegethon. No wonder the guy was always in a bad mood.

The crazy thing was Phlegethon water wouldn't kill you, even if you were mortal. Sure, it would burn like radioactive chili peppers sautéed in acid. It would make you *wish* you were dead. But the river was actually designed to keep its victims alive so that they could suffer forever — hooray! Many damned souls had to swim through it for all eternity, or be stuck in the fiery water up to their necks.

According to some legends, the Phlegethon could eventually burn away your sins and let you go free if you were really, really sorry for the things you'd done. If you want to test that theory, go ahead and jump in. Me, I think I'll pass.

River number three, the Acheron, was the River of Pain. If you guessed it was painful, you win a cookie! The Acheron started in the mortal world, near a temple of the dead in Epirus. Maybe that's why ghosts were drawn to it and filled the river with their own pain and suffering. The Acheron meandered along until it plunged underground and tumbled into Erebos. There it widened into a dark, steamy, swampy expanse that caused pain to anyone unlucky enough to touch its waters or even *hear* its current. After a while, the Acheron split into two smaller rivers – the Cocytus and the Styx – that flowed in opposite directions until they both spilled into Tartarus.

River number four was my least personal favourite: the Lethe, River of Forgetfulness. (I've had some bad experiences with amnesia. Long story.) Anyway, the Lethe looked harmless. In most places it was a gentle span of milky-white water that rolled over a shallow bed of stones, softly gurgling in a way that made your eyes feel heavy. You would think you could wade across this river, no problem. My advice? Don't.

A single drop of Lethe water would wipe your short-term memory. You wouldn't remember anything that happened in the last week. Take a full drink, or wade into those waters, and your mind would be completely erased. You wouldn't remember your own name, or where you came from, or even that the New York Yankees are *obviously* better than the Boston Red Sox. I know – terrifying, right?

For some spirits of the dead, however, the Lethe was actually a blessing. Crowds of ghosts were always gathered at the banks, drinking from the river so that they could forget their former lives, because you can't miss what you don't remember. Occasionally spirits were even allowed to reincarnate – to be reborn in the mortal world for another life. If you took that chance, you *had* to drink from the Lethe first so that you wouldn't remember your old life. Because, seriously – who would want to go through twelve boring years of school again if you remembered doing it before?

Poppies grew all along the banks of the Lethe, which is why poppy juice has the power to put people to sleep and dull their pain. (We call that *opium*, children. And don't do drugs, because DRUGS ARE BAD. Okay, I had to put that in there.) At one point, the Lethe curved around the entrance of a dark cave where the god Hypnos lived – the god of sleep. What was it like inside? No one has ever described it, probably because anyone stupid enough to go in fell asleep and never came out again.

The fifth river of the Underworld was the Styx, the River of Hate. It was definitely the most famous river, but the name alone sort of dampened any chance for tourism. '*Hey, kids, we're going to the River of Hate for spring break!*' '*Yay!*'

The Styx flowed through the deepest, darkest parts of the Underworld. Some legends claimed it was created by the water Titan, Tethys, and was fed by salty springs from the bottom of the ocean.

The Styx circled Erebos like a moat, so you pretty much *had* to cross it to get into the Underworld. (Some stories say the Acheron was the river you had to cross, but, since the Styx was a branch of the Acheron, I guess both versions are correct.)

The current was dark and sluggish, always shrouded in foul-smelling mist, and the water was corrosive to mortal flesh. Mix sulphuric acid with sewage and a splash of liquid hatred, and you've got the Styx.

So you're wondering, *Why would anybody want to get into the Underworld?* I don't know. But ever since humans were created, whenever they died, their souls just sort of instinctively drifted down to Erebos, like lemmings jumping off a cliff, or tourists flocking to Times Square. You could tell them all you wanted that it was a stupid idea, but they just kept doing it.

The problem was that the souls had no reliable way to cross the River Styx. A few managed to swim it. Others tried, only to dissolve in the water. Many just wandered along the mortal side of the river, wailing and pointing at the other side, like, *I wanna go that way!*

Finally, one industrious daimon named Charon decided to go into business. What's a daimon? It's not a devil-type demon with a pitchfork and a tail and red skin. Daimons were immortal spirits, kind of like lesser gods. Some looked like monsters or mortals. Some were good. Some were bad. Some just kind of hung around.

This dude Charon was a son of Nyx, the goddess of night. Charon could take different forms, but most of the time he appeared as an ugly old man in tattered robes, with a greasy beard and a cone-shaped hat. If it was me and I could change shape, I would walk around looking like Brad Pitt, but I guess Charon didn't care about impressing the ghosts.

At any rate, one day Charon realized that all these mortal souls were clamouring to get to Erebos, so Charon built himself a boat and started ferrying people across.

Not for free, of course. He accepted gold, silver and most major credit cards. Since the Underworld had no regulations, Charon just charged whatever he wanted to. If he liked you, he might let you across for a couple of coins. If he didn't like you, he'd demand a fortune. If you were unlucky enough to be buried without any money – oh, well! You'd have to wander around on the mortal side of the Styx forever. Some of the dead even drifted back to the mortal world to haunt the living as ghosts.

Even if you got across the Styx, you'd find Erebos in

complete chaos. The ghosts were *supposed* to divide into different groups according to how good they'd been in their lives. If they were real scum suckers, they went to the Fields of Punishment to enjoy special torture for eternity. If they were good, they went to Elysium, which was like Paradise, Las Vegas and Disneyland rolled into one. If the spirits hadn't been particularly good or bad in life but had just sort of existed (which was most people), they were forced to wander forever in the Fields of Asphodel, which wasn't a horrible place – just incredibly, mind-numbingly boring.

That's how spirits got sorted, in theory. Unfortunately, before Hades took over, nobody was policing the Underworld. It was kind of like a school day when all your teachers are sick and you have nothing but subs who don't know the rules, so naturally the kids take total advantage. Doomed souls from Punishment sneaked into Asphodel and no one stopped them. The spirits from Asphodel crashed the party in Elysium. And some really dumb but noble spirits bound for Elysium took a wrong turn, ended up in Punishment, and either couldn't get out or were too nice to complain about it.

To make matters worse, even the spirits who went where they were supposed to go didn't always deserve to be there, because, before Hades took over, you were judged for the afterlife while you were still alive.

How did that system work? I have no idea. Apparently a panel of three living judges interviewed you right before you died and decided if you deserved the Fields of Punishment, Elysium or Asphodel. Don't ask me how the judges knew you were about to die. Maybe they guessed. Maybe the gods told them. Maybe the judges just yelled at random people, 'Hey, you! Get over here! It's your turn to croak!'

Anyway, the judges listened to your testimony and decided your eternal fate. Guess what happened. People lied. They bribed the judges. They showed up in their best clothes, smiled and flattered and acted nice so the judges would think they *were* nice. They brought in witnesses to say, 'Oh, yeah. This guy lived a *totally* awesome life. He hardly ever tortured anybody.' Stuff like that.

A lot of evil people managed to charm their way into Elysium, and a lot of good people who didn't kiss up to the judges landed in the Fields of Punishment.

You get the idea . . . the Underworld was a mess. When Hades took over, he looked around and said, 'Nuh-uh! This ain't gonna work!'

So he went to Olympus and explained the situation to Zeus. Having to get Zeus's approval for what he planned to do kind of rankled Hades, but he knew he'd need to get the Big Guy's thumbs-up for any major changes to the afterlife, especially since humans were involved. The gods considered humans shared property.

Zeus listened and frowned thoughtfully. 'So what do you propose?'

'Well,' Hades said, 'we could keep the panel of three judges, but –'

'The audience could vote!' Zeus guessed. 'At the end of each season, the winning mortal could be crowned Elysian Idol!'

'Uh, no,' Hades said. 'Actually, I was thinking the judges could be spirits of the dead rather than living people. And each mortal soul would only be judged once it enters the Underworld.'

'So . . . not a competition format? Hmm, too bad.'

Hades tried to keep his cool. 'See, if the judges are spirits under my control, they'll be impossible to influence. The souls who come before the court will be stripped of everything but their essence. They can't rely on good looks or fancy clothes. They can't bribe the judges or call character witnesses. All their good and bad deeds will be laid bare, because the judges can literally see right through them. Lying will be impossible.'

'I like it,' Zeus said. 'Who will you pick for judges?'

'Probably three deceased mortals who were kings in the upper world,' Hades said. 'Kings are used to passing judgement.'

'Good,' Zeus agreed. 'As long as the kings are all *my* sons. Agreed?'

Hades gritted his teeth. He didn't like his brother getting involved in everything, but since almost every Greek king was a son of Zeus, there would still be plenty of kings to choose from. 'Agreed.'

Zeus nodded. 'How will you make sure the judgements are enforced, and the souls go where they're supposed to?'

Hades smiled coldly. 'Oh, don't worry. I've got that covered.'

When he got back to Erebos, Hades appointed three former kings, all demigod sons of Zeus, as his dead-celebrity judges: Minos, Aiakos and Rhadamanthys.

Then he rounded up the three Furies – those spirits of vengeance who had been formed from the blood of Ouranos ages before. Hades hired them to be his enforcers, which was a good call, since nobody wanted to cross a demonic grandmother with bad breath and a whip.

Like most daimons, the Furies could take different shapes, but usually they appeared as ugly old ladies with long stringy hair, black tattered robes and giant bat wings. Their fiery whips could cause excruciating pain to the living or the dead, and they could fly invisibly, so you never knew when they would swoop down on you.

Hades used them to keep the dead in line. Sometimes he let the Furies go nuts and design new tortures for the worst of the doomed souls. He could even send the Furies after living people if they committed a truly horrific crime – like killing a family member, desecrating a temple or singing Journey songs on karaoke night.

Hades's next Underworld improvement: he made it a lot easier for spirits of the dead to find their way to Erebos. He convinced Hermes, the messenger god, to keep a lookout for lost souls on the mortal side of the Styx. If Hermes saw any ghosts who looked confused, he would steer them in the right direction and provide them with a handy full-colour map, compliments of the Underworld Chamber of Commerce.

Once the souls of the dead made it to the River Styx, the daimon Charon would ferry them across for a standard fee of one silver coin. Hades had convinced him (read: *threatened* him) to charge everyone the same price.

Hades also spread the word to the mortals up above that they'd better take their funeral rites seriously, or they wouldn't be allowed into the Underworld. When you died, your family was supposed to make offerings to the gods. They had to give you a decent burial and place a coin under your tongue so you could pay Charon. If you didn't have a coin, you'd end up haunting the mortal world as a ghost forever, which was both pointless and boring.

How did Hades spread the word among the mortals? He had this army of black-winged nasties called *oneiroi*, or dream daimons, who visited mortals while they slept, delivering visions or nightmares.

Ever had one of those dreams where you wake up startled because you felt like you were falling? That's the *oneiroi* messing with you. They probably picked you up and dropped you, just to be mean. Next time it happens, smack your fist on the floor and yell, 'Hades, tell your stupid daimons to knock it off!'

Another upgrade Hades made: he tightened security at the gates of Erebos. He went down to the Tartarus Humane Society and adopted the biggest, baddest dog you can imagine – a monster named Cerberus, who was sort of a cross between a pit bull, a rottweiler and a rabid woolly mammoth. Cerberus had three heads, so if you were a mortal hero trying to sneak into Hades's realm, or a dead person trying to sneak out, you had three times the chance of getting spotted and devoured. In addition to razor-sharp fangs and claws, Cerberus supposedly had a mane made out of snakes and a serpent for a tail. I can't vouch for that. I only met Cerberus once. It was dark, and I was mostly focused on not whimpering or wetting my pants.

Anyway, once the departed spirits got inside the gates, they were sorted out by the three dead-celebrity judges and ushered to their proper places. Like I said earlier, most people hadn't really done much with their lives, good or bad, so they ended up in the Fields of Asphodel. There they existed as wispy shadows that could only chitter like bats and float around aimlessly, trying to remember who they were and what they were doing – sort of like teachers during first period, before they've had enough coffee.

If you had led a good life, you went to Elysium, which was about as nice as you could get in the dark Underworld. You got a mansion of your own, free food and drinks, and pretty much five-star service for whatever you needed. You could hang out with the other lucky good people and chill for eternity. If Elysium got boring, you could choose to drink from the River Lethe and be reborn in a new mortal life.

A few souls were *so* good that they managed to live three virtuous lives in a row. If that was you, you could retire to the Isles of the Blest, which were Caribbean-type private islands in a lake in the middle of Elysium. Not many people were that lucky or that virtuous. It was sort of like winning the Good Person Powerball Lottery.

If you'd lived an evil life, you got the special naughty treatment – boiling in oil forever, having your skin flayed, getting chased by hungry demons over a field of broken glass, or sliding down a giant razor blade into a pool of lemon juice. You know, the usual. Most of the punishments weren't very creative, but if you managed to *really* annoy Hades, he could always come up with new and interesting ways to torture your immortal soul.

A couple of examples?

Tantalus. That dude was *messed up*. He was a Greek king – a son of Zeus, no surprise – who got invited to share ambrosia and nectar on Mount Olympus with the gods. Big honour, right? But Tantalus got greedy.

'Wow,' he said after dinner, patting his belly. 'That's good stuff! Could I get a doggie bag to share with my friends back home?'

'Holy me!' Zeus swore. 'Absolutely not! This ambrosia and nectar is rare and magical stuff. You can't go sharing it with just anybody.'

'Oh . . .' Tantalus forced a smile. 'Of course. I see how it is. Well . . . next time, dinner at my place, huh?'

Tantalus should've let it go. He should've remembered what happened to Prometheus when he tried to take stuff from the gods and share it with mortals. But Tantalus was angry. He felt insulted. The gods didn't trust him. They didn't want him to become famous as the mortal who brought ambrosia to earth.

The more he thought about it, the angrier he got. He invited the gods to a feast at *his* palace, but to get back at them, he decided he would serve them the most insulting meal he could think of. He just wasn't sure *what*.

He was standing in his kitchen, staring at the empty cooking pots, when his son Pelops walked in.

'What's for dinner, Dad?' Pelops asked.

Tantalus had never liked his son. I don't know why. Maybe Tantalus knew the kid would take over his kingdom some day. Greek kings were always paranoid about stuff like that. Anyway, Tantalus gave his son an evil smile and pulled out a butcher's knife. 'Funny you should ask.'

That night, the gods gathered at Tantalus's palace for dinner and got served a pot of yummy stew.

'What is this meat?' Demeter said, taking the first bite. 'Tastes like chicken.'

Tantalus had meant to wait until all the gods had eaten,

but he couldn't hold in the crazy giggles. 'Oh . . . just a family recipe.'

Zeus frowned and put down his spoon. 'Tantalus . . . what have you done?'

Hera pushed her bowl away. 'And where is your son Pelops?'

'Actually,' Tantalus said, 'that's him in the stew. Surprise, you idiots! Ha, ha! Ha, ha!'

Honestly, I don't know what he was expecting. Did he think the gods would chuckle and slap him on the back? *Oh, Tantalus, you old kidder. Good one!*

The Olympians were horrified. After all, they still had post-traumatic stress from getting swallowed by their father, Kronos. Zeus pulled out a lightning bolt, blasted Tantalus to ashes, and turned the king's soul over to Hades.

'Make a special punishment for this one,' Zeus said. 'Something involving food, please.'

Hades was happy to oblige. He sank Tantalus up to his waist in a pool of fresh water, his feet stuck in the riverbed like in cement. Over Tantalus's head hung the branches of a magical tree that grew all sorts of luscious fragrant fruits.

Tantalus's punishment was just to stand there forever.

Well, he thought, this isn't so bad.

Then he got hungry. He tried to grab an apple, but the branches rose just out of reach. He tried for a mango. No luck. He tried jumping, but his feet were stuck. He tried pretending to be asleep so he could launch a surprise attack on the peaches. Again, no luck. Each time, Tantalus was *sure* he would score a piece of fruit, but he never could.

When he got thirsty, he scooped up water, but by the

time his hands reached his mouth the water had magically evaporated and his hands were completely dry. He bent down, hoping to gulp straight from the lake, but the entire surface of the water shrank away from him. No matter what he tried, he couldn't get a single drop. He just got hungrier and thirstier, even though food and water were so close — *tantalizingly* close, which is a word that comes from his name. Next time you want something really badly but it's just out of reach, you've been tantalized.

What's the moral of the story? I dunno. Maybe: *Don't chop up your son and feed him to your dinner guests.* Seems kind of obvious to me, but whatever.

Another guy who got a special punishment was Sisyphus. With a name like *Sissy-Fuss* you have to figure the guy had issues, but at least he didn't make his kids into stew. Sisyphus's problem was that he didn't want to die.

I can relate to that. I wake up every morning and think, *You know what would be good today? Not dying.*

But Sisyphus took things too far. One day Death showed up at his house. And by Death, I mean Thanatos, the god of death, the Grim Reaperino, who was one of Hades's main lieutenants.

Sisyphus opened the door and found a big guy with black feathery wings looming over him.

'Good afternoon.' Thanatos consulted his notepad. 'I have a delivery for Sisyphus — one painful death, requires a signature. Are you Sisyphus?'

Sisyphus tried to hide his panic. 'Um . . . Why, yes! Come in! Just let me get a pen.'

As Thanatos ducked under the low doorway, Sisyphus grabbed the nearest heavy object he could find – a stone pestle he used to grind his flour – and smacked the god of death over the head.

Thanatos passed out cold. Sisyphus tied him up, gagged him and stuffed him under the bed. When Mrs Sisyphus came home, she was like, 'Why is there a giant black wing sticking out from under the bed?'

Sisyphus explained what had happened. His wife wasn't pleased.

'This is going to get us both into trouble,' she said. 'You should have just died.'

'I love you, too,' Sisyphus muttered. 'It'll be fine. You'll see.'

It wasn't fine. Without Thanatos on the job, people stopped dying. At first, nobody objected. If you were supposed to die and you didn't, why would you complain?

Then a big battle happened between two Greek cities, and Ares, the god of war, got suspicious. He hovered over the battlefield like he always did, ready for an exciting day of carnage. When the two armies clashed, no soldiers fell. They just kept whaling on each other, hacking each other to bits. Things got messy, with plenty of blood and gore, but no one died.

'Where's Death?' Ares screamed. 'This is no fun without Death!'

He flew from the battlefield and started asking all around the world: 'Excuse me, have you seen Death? Big guy with black feathery wings? Likes to reap souls?'

Finally somebody mentioned that they'd seen a guy like that heading towards old man Sisyphus's house.

Ares broke down Sisyphus's front door. He pushed the old dude aside and spotted Thanatos's left wing sticking out from under the bed. Ares pulled out the god of death, brushed off the dust bunnies and cut his bonds. Then both gods glared at Sisyphus.

Sisyphus backed into the corner. 'Um, look, guys, I can explain –'

BOOM!

Ares and Thanatos vaporized him with a double blast of godly wrath.

Once Sisyphus's soul found its way to the Underworld, Sisyphus somehow managed to get an audience with Hades himself.

The old man bowed before the god's throne. 'Lord Hades, I know I did a bad thing. I'm ready to face my punishment. But my wife! She didn't do the proper funeral rites for me! How can I enjoy eternal damnation knowing that the missus didn't honour the gods with sacrifices as you have commanded? Please, just allow me to return to the world long enough to scold my wife. I'll come straight back.'

Hades frowned. Of course he was suspicious, but he'd always been under the impression that spirits couldn't lie. (He was wrong.) Also, Sisyphus's story filled him with outrage. Hades hated it when people didn't take funeral rites seriously. And sacrifices to the gods? Those were even *more* important!

'Fine,' Hades said. 'Go scold your wife, but don't take too long. When you get back, I'll have a special punishment ready for you.'

'I can't wait!' Sisyphus said.

So his spirit returned to the world. He found his vaporized

remains and somehow got them back together into a regular body. You can imagine his wife's surprise when Sisyphus walked in the front door, alive as ever. 'Honey, I'm home!'

After his wife woke up from fainting, Sisyphus told her the story of how he cleverly escaped death yet again.

His wife was not amused. 'You can't cheat Hades forever,' she warned. 'You're asking for trouble.'

'I've already been condemned to the Fields of Punishment,' Sisyphus said. 'What do I have to lose? Besides, Hades is busy. He sees thousands of souls every day. He won't even know I'm gone.'

For years, Sisyphus's plan actually worked. He kept a low profile. He stayed at home most of the time and, when he had to go out, he wore a fake beard. Hades *was* busy. He forgot all about Sisyphus, until one day Thanatos happened to ask, 'Hey, what'd you ever do to that creep who stuffed me under his bed?'

'Oh . . .' Hades frowned. 'Whoops.'

This time, Hades sent the messenger god Hermes to look for Sisyphus. Hermes wore a helmet, so he couldn't get whacked over the head so easily. The messenger god dragged Sisyphus back to the Underworld and threw him at the foot of Hades's throne.

Hades smiled coldly. 'Lie to *me*, will you? Oh, I have something *very* special for you!'

He took Sisyphus to the middle of the Fields of Punishment, to a barren hill five hundred feet high with sides that sloped at forty-five degrees, just perfect for skateboarding. At the bottom of the hill sat a big round boulder the size of a compact car.

'Here you are,' Hades said. 'As soon as you manage to push this rock to the top of that hill, you can go. Your punishment will be over.'

Sisyphus sighed with relief. He'd been expecting much worse. Sure, the boulder looked heavy. Pushing it up the hill would suck, but at least it wouldn't be impossible.

'Thank you, Lord Hades,' Sisyphus said. 'You are merciful.'

'Right.' Hades's dark eyes glinted. 'Merciful.'

The god disappeared in a cloud of gloom, and Sisyphus got to work.

Unfortunately, he soon found out his job *was* impossible. Pushing the rock took every bit of his strength, and as soon as Sisyphus got close to the top of the hill he lost control. No matter what he tried, the boulder would roll back to the bottom. Or it would run over him and *then* roll to the bottom.

If Sisyphus stopped to rest, one of the Furies came along and whipped him until he got moving again. Sisyphus was doomed to roll his rock uphill for eternity, never reaching the top.

Another happy ending! Ares, the god of war, got to watch people die again. Mrs Sisyphus got some peace and quiet. And Thanatos, the god of death, decided not to ring anyone's doorbell and require a signature any more. From then on, he just sneaked around invisibly and took his victims' souls without warning. So, if you were planning on living forever by tying up the god of death and stuffing him under your bed, you're out of luck.

So that's how Hades got the Underworld organized. He built his dark palace on the edge of the Fields of Asphodel, and once he married Persephone he more or less settled down and was about as happy as an Underworld god can be.

He started raising a herd of black cattle so that he could have fresh steak and milk, and he appointed a daimon named Menoetes to look after the cows. Hades also planted an orchard of magical pomegranate trees to honour his wife.

The Olympian gods rarely visited – except for Hermes, who had to deliver messages and souls – but if you happened to be in Hades's throne room on any given day you might find Thanatos hanging out, or the Furies, or the three dead-celebrity judges. The best deceased artists and musicians from Elysium were often summoned to the palace to entertain the king.

Were Persephone and Hades a happy couple? Hard to say. The old stories aren't even clear about whether they had any children. Apparently Persephone had a daughter named Melinoe, who was the daimon in charge of ghosts and nightmares, but Hades may or may not have been the father. Some stories say the father was actually Zeus *disguised* as Hades, which gets us into a whole new level of gross.

A few poems mention Makaria, the daughter of Hades and Persephone. She was the goddess of blessed peaceful deaths, as opposed to painful, terrible, horrifying deaths, but there aren't really any stories about her.

At any rate, Hades wasn't always faithful to Persephone. He's a god. What did you expect?

One time Hades was visiting the Titan Oceanus at the bottom of the sea. What he was doing there, I have no idea. Maybe he was checking on the salty springs that fed the River Styx. Anyway, while he was roaming around, he happened to meet a beautiful ocean nymph named Leuke, one of Oceanus's daughters. She was tall and pale and lovely, and apparently she made a big impression. At the end of the visit, Hades abducted her and took her back to the Underworld.

It was just a fling, a momentary madness, but you can guess how Persephone reacted when she found out her husband had brought a souvenir girl home with him.

'She goes or I go,' Persephone snarled. 'And don't just send her back to the ocean. She stole my husband! She must die!'

'Um . . . okay,' Hades said. 'I mean, yes! Of course, dear! What was I thinking?'

Hades ran down to the Fields of Asphodel, where Leuke was waiting for him.

'Well?' Leuke demanded. 'You abducted me and brought me here. What do you plan to do with me?'

'Actually, it's not going to work out,' Hades said. 'My wife doesn't approve.'

'What a shocker,' Leuke muttered. 'Fine. Take me home!'

'I can't,' Hades said. 'Persephone wants you dead.'

Leuke turned even paler. 'That – that isn't right! You stole *me*!'

'It's okay,' Hades assured her. 'I have an idea. Instead of killing you, I'll just change you into something – like a plant. Then you'll live forever, and I can always remember you.'

'That's a horrible idea!'

'Maybe a tree,' Hades mused.

'No!'

'A tall, pale, white tree,' Hades decided. 'A tree as beautiful as you are.'

'I –'

POOF.

Leuke became the first poplar tree, and Hades hugged her trunk. 'Thanks for understanding. I will always remember you.'

The poplar quickly multiplied, until the Fields of Asphodel were dotted with them – a little bit of beauty in the gloomy fields of Asphodel. The poplar became one of Hades's sacred trees and tended to grow especially thick along the banks of the Underworld rivers, maybe because Leuke remembered that she had come from the sea and was trying to grow her way back there. Good luck with that, Leuke.

After his failed romance with the poplar girl, Hades became depressed. One day he decided to take a long stroll along the River Cocytus, the River of Wailing, which is an odd place to walk if you're trying to cheer yourself up.

Hades happened to see a lovely young woman in a pale-green dress sitting by the water. Her fragrance wafted towards him on the subterranean breeze – a sweet, subtle perfume unlike anything he'd ever smelled.

He walked over and stared at her in amazement. Hades tended to surprise people, being so dark and stealthy and all; so, when the girl finally noticed him, she flinched in alarm.

'What do you want?' she demanded.

'Uh . . .' Hades found it hard to think. The woman's eyes were pale green like her dress. 'I'm Hades. You smell good. Who are you?'

The girl wrinkled her nose. 'I'm Minthe, of course. Daughter of the River Cocytus.'

Hades frowned. 'The Underworld rivers have naiads? I never knew that.'

'Well, maybe we're not proud of it,' Minthe muttered. 'It's

not easy being the nature spirit for a wailing river, you know. I'd much rather be in the upper world, where I could enjoy the sunlight and the fresh breeze.'

'I'll take you there,' Hades blurted. 'Just give me a kiss, and I'll take you to the upper world.'

Minthe knitted her eyebrows. 'Why would you?'

'I love you,' Hades said foolishly, but he didn't meet many beautiful women. Also, it was springtime. Persephone had gone to visit her mother in the mortal world, and Hades was lonely.

Minthe stood. She wasn't sure what to think of this dark god, but a trip to the upper world sounded good. She said, 'All right.'

She kissed him. Hades put his arms around her, and together they dissolved into shadows.

They appeared on the side of a hill near the Greek town of Pylos. Minthe gasped when she saw the blue sky and the sun, the green hills marching on forever.

She smiled and threw her arms around Hades, and for about twenty seconds they were very much in love. Minthe's fragrance was intoxicating.

Then something changed. Hades tensed. Maybe the fresh air cleared his mind.

'What am I doing?' he wailed, pushing Minthe aside. 'It's springtime. My wife will be around here somewhere, making plants grow and whatnot. She'll find us!'

'Who cares?' Minthe asked. 'You said you loved me.'

'I – I –' Hades gulped.

Minthe's green eyes were gorgeous. She was very pretty and she smelled good, but now Hades realized their love was hopeless. He remembered the murderous look in Persephone's eyes when she'd heard about Leuke.

'I've got to get back to Erebos,' Hades said. 'Enjoy the upper world.'

'You're coming back, right?' Minthe demanded.

'Um . . .' Hades chickened out and dissolved into shadows.

Minthe should've forgotten him. She'd made it to the mortal world! She could've found a new river to bind her life force to. She could've lived forever in the beautiful forests and hills of Greece.

But nope. Too easy!

Being dumped on the hillside made her angry. It dawned on her that she'd wrapped the god Hades around her little finger without even trying. She really *must* be beautiful. And she did smell great. She deserved to be a queen.

'Hades loves *me!*' she shouted to the wind. 'He's going to come back and get me and make *me* the queen of the Underworld! I am more beautiful than Persephone, and more wonderful, and I smell better, and –'

The hillside rumbled. Grass and flowers swirled into a massive funnel cloud of petals. The goddess Persephone appeared as a fifty-foot-tall colossus.

At that point, Minthe realized she'd made a mistake.

'YOU, PRETTIER THAN ME?' Persephone boomed. 'YEAH, RIGHT! YOU DO SMELL GOOD, THOUGH. PERHAPS I CAN FIND A USE FOR YOU AMONG THE PLANTS!'

Persephone raised her giant sandalled foot and squashed Minthe flat. When she smeared her foot across the hillside, tiny green plants sprang up. Their leaves smelled wonderful whenever they were crushed. Persephone decided to call them *mint* plants, and the hill near Pylos where they first grew is still called Mount Minthe.

So next time you have mint chocolate-chip ice cream, you can thank Persephone, though it can be a little hard to eat the stuff when you realize it's made from smashed river nymph.

After that, Hades didn't have many affairs. He mostly stayed in his palace and minded his own business.

Mortal heroes didn't always leave *him* alone, though. They kept popping down, demanding things. One hero wanted his dog, Cerberus. Another hero wanted Hades to return his dead sweetheart to life. Another hero even tried to abduct Persephone. Maybe I'll tell you those stories another time, but all this gloomy Underworld stuff is making me claustrophobic.

I need some fresh sea air. Let's pop over to the Mediterranean and I'll introduce you to my dad – the one and only Poseidon.

POSEIDON GETS SALTY

I'M BIASED.

But if you're going to have a Greek god for a parent you couldn't do better than Poseidon. Sure, I've had my problems with him. He's not the most attentive dad. But, hey, none of the Greek gods is.

At least Poseidon has awesome powers and a laid-back attitude (most of the time).

He's amazingly cool, considering how hard it was for him as a young god. He was the middle boy. He was always being compared to his brothers, like, *Wow, you're almost as handsome as Zeus! You're almost as powerful as Zeus!* Or sometimes, *You're not as much of a loser as Hades!*

That can really grate on a guy after a few centuries.

Back when Zeus, Poseidon and Hades threw dice to divide up the world, Poseidon got the *second*-best roll. He had to accept his brother Zeus's becoming lord of the universe and telling him what to do for all eternity, but Poseidon didn't complain. He'd won the sea. That was fine with him. He liked the beach. He liked swimming. He liked seafood.

True, Poseidon wasn't as flashy or powerful as Zeus. He didn't have lightning bolts, which were like the nuclear arsenal of Mount Olympus. But Poseidon *did* have his magical trident. He could stir up hurricanes, summon tidal waves and make a *mean* smoothie. Since the seas wrapped around the earth, Poseidon could also cause earthquakes. If he was in a bad mood, he could level whole cities or make islands sink beneath the waves.

The Greeks called him the Earthshaker, and they went to a lot of trouble to keep him happy, because no matter whether you were on land or at sea you *didn't* want Poseidon mad at you.

Fortunately, Poseidon was usually calm. His mood reflected the Mediterranean Sea, where he lived, and most of the time the Mediterranean was smooth sailing. Poseidon would let the ships travel where they wanted. He'd bless fishermen with good catches. He'd chill on the beach, sip his umbrella drink from a coconut shell and not sweat the small stuff.

On nice days, Poseidon would ride his golden chariot across the waves, pulled by a team of white hippocampi, which were horses with golden manes, bronze hooves and fish tails. Everywhere he went, the sea creatures would come out to play around his chariot, so you'd see sharks and killer whales and giant squids all frolicking together, gurgling, 'Hooray, Poseidon is in the house!' or whatever.

But sometimes the sea got angry, and Poseidon was the same way. When that happened, he was a totally different dude.

If you were a ship's captain and you forgot to sacrifice to

Poseidon before you set sail, you were a major-league derp. Poseidon liked at least one bull sacrificed in his honour per ship. Don't ask me why. Maybe at one point Poseidon had told the Greeks, *Just pour me a Red Bull and we'll call it even*, and the Greeks thought he wanted an actual red bull.

If you forgot to sacrifice, there was a good chance your ship would get smashed on the rocks, or eaten by a sea monster, or captured by pirates with bad personal hygiene.

Even if you never travelled by sea, that didn't mean you were safe. If your town somehow offended Poseidon . . . well, say hello to Hurricane Derp.

Still, Poseidon kept it together most of the time. He tried to follow Zeus's orders, though Zeus annoyed him constantly. Whenever those two started arguing, the other gods buckled their seat belts, because a fight between the sky and the sea could rip the world apart.

Mother Rhea must've sensed the tension early on. Shortly after the gods took over the world, she suggested that Poseidon get out of Olympus and explore his new domain. She sent him to live on the ocean floor with a tribe of aquatic weirdos called the *telkhines*.

This was a strange suggestion, since the telkhines were twisted little dudes. They'd once been land dwellers, until they did something to anger Zeus; so he tossed the worst ones into Tartarus and exiled the rest to the bottom of the sea.

What did they do? Not sure, but the telkhines were known for sorcery and crafting dangerous stuff. They could summon sleet, rain or even snow (which you don't get much in Greece) and call down sulphurous rain that destroyed plants and burned flesh, which was kind of cool in a gross, smelly way.

Some stories say that the telkhines invented metalworking, and even made Kronos's scythe at Gaia's request. Could be true. They were greedy and would do anything for the right price.

After Zeus threw them into the ocean, their forms changed so that they looked like a cross between dogs, seals and humans, with canine faces, stunted little legs and half-flipper hands that were nimble enough for metalwork but still made great ping-pong paddles.

When Poseidon came to live with them, the telkhines showed him around and taught him the ways of the ocean: *These are fish! This is coral!* One especially nasty trick they taught him was how to use his trident as a lever. Poseidon learned how to wedge the trident's points under the base of an island and flip it so that the whole landmass disappeared under the sea. In combat, he could do this with mountains on dry land. A couple of times he flipped mountains right on top of his enemies, crushing them flat. See, I told you he was a boss.

Eventually, Poseidon got tired of the telkhines and decided to build his own palace. *(Good move, Dad.)*

He went to the bottom of the Aegean Sea and used his earthshaking, wave-making powers to raise a big mansion made of pearl, sea stone and abalone shell. His gardens were full of exotic sea plants, with luminescent jellyfish drifting around like Christmas lights. He had great white sharks for guard dogs and mermen for servants; and his doorways were huge, because every once in a while the whales and sea monsters would float through to pay their respects.

If you ask me, Poseidon's crib was *way* cooler than Hades's or Zeus's, and when Poseidon was sitting on his polished coral throne he felt pretty good about himself. The entire sea was under his control. The fish adored him. All the sailors in the Mediterranean made offerings to him and prayed for safe passage. Everybody seemed to love him.

So Poseidon thought, Hey, I should go up top and offer to be the patron for one of the mortal cities!

Like I mentioned earlier, this was a big deal for gods. The more mortals who prayed to you, the stronger you got. If you could get a whole city dedicated to you – with statues and temples, and souvenir T-shirts in all the tourist shops – that was the ultimate in bragging rights.

Poseidon decided to try for the capital of Attica on the Greek mainland, which was one of the biggest and most important cities in Greece. Hey, go big or go home, right?

He showed up at the city's acropolis, which was the main fortress on the top of the tallest hill. The earth shook. Poseidon appeared in a swirling column of salt and mist. He struck his trident against the nearest rock, splitting it open and creating a geyser of salt water.

'Behold!' he shouted to the crowds. 'I am Poseidon, here to become patron of your city!'

Pretty good entrance. Unfortunately, Athena, the goddess of wisdom, had shown up a few seconds before with the exact same offer. She was standing nearby in her grey robes, her battle helmet tucked under her arm, conducting negotiations with the city elders.

'Ah,' Poseidon muttered. 'Awkward.'

The city elders gaped at the sea god with his glowing trident, and at the massive geyser of salt water that now spouted from the hilltop.

'Lord Poseidon!' one said. 'Oh . . . um . . .'

The poor mortals looked back and forth between the two gods. I can't blame them for being nervous. You never want to be forced to choose between gods. No matter which you pick, the other one is likely to stomp you as if you were a cockroach.

Poseidon wasn't sure what to do either. How dare this upstart goddess Athena, this second-generation Olympian, steal his idea? He was tempted to chase her off with his trident, but, before he could, Athena cried, 'I know how we can settle this peacefully!'

Typical. Athena *always* had some sneaky idea. Poseidon wasn't interested in peace at the moment, but the mortals all looked very relieved, and he didn't want to act like a bad sport in front of his future followers.

'Well?' he grumbled. 'What is your plan?'

'A contest,' Athena said. 'You and I will each create one gift for the city. The elders will judge between them. Whichever god gives the city the most *valuable* gift will be its patron. The other god will accept the elders' judgement and leave in peace. Agreed?'

Thousands of mortal eyes turned to Poseidon. He still wanted to smack Athena into the sea, but she had put him on the spot. He couldn't exactly say no.

'Yeah,' he grunted. 'Okay.'

Athena gestured to him courteously. 'Gentlemen first.'

Poseidon frowned. What would be a valuable gift for these mortals? A box of pearls? Some pet jellyfish? Perhaps a stable of trained whales they could ride? Hmm. Parking the whales downtown might be a problem.

Perhaps another form of animal . . . something strong and fast, but adapted to land-dwelling humans?

Poseidon gazed at the waves breaking on the beach far below. As the whitecaps raced and crashed, he got an idea. He began to smile.

'Watch this,' he said.

He pointed his trident, and the waves began to take shape. When they reached the shore, they became majestic animals with four long legs and flowing manes. They ran straight onto the beach, whinnying and prancing.

'I call them *horses!*' Poseidon shouted. 'They are fast and strong. You can ride them anywhere. They carry heavy stuff, pull ploughs or wagons. You can even ride them into war and trample your enemies. Plus, they just look really cool.'

The mortals murmured and clapped politely. Horses were obviously a valuable gift, though a few of the townspeople looked disappointed, like maybe they'd been hoping for pet jellyfish.

Everyone turned to Athena.

The goddess raised her hand. A sickly-looking shrub broke through the nearby rocks. It had grey-green leaves and green knobby fruits the size of warts.

Poseidon couldn't help laughing. 'What the spume is that?'

'It's an olive tree,' Athena said.

The mortals shifted uneasily. The olive tree didn't look very impressive, but nobody wanted to say that to Athena.

Poseidon chuckled. 'Okay, well, nice try. I guess we know who won *this* contest!'

'Not so fast,' Athena said. 'The olive tree may not look like much, but you can grow it with very little effort. It will spread across the countryside until olives are the most important food in Greece.'

'Those knobby green things?' Poseidon protested. 'They're tiny!'

'But they will grow by the thousands,' Athena said. 'And they're tasty on pizza! The mortals of this city will export olives across the world and become rich! You can use olive oil for cooking and lighting lamps. You can even add perfume to the oil and use it for bathing, or moisturizing or cleaning those hard-to-get-out stains on your kitchen counters.'

She turned to the crowd of mortals. 'How much would you pay for it now? But don't answer! It's my gift to you, free of charge. And if you order today you'll also get my patronage for your city, which includes tons of wisdom, advice about warfare and all sorts of helpful crafts. You will be the richest and most important city in Greece! All I ask is that you name your city after me and build me a temple, which can be done in three easy instalments.'

Poseidon's confidence started to crumble. 'But wait . . . my horses . . .'

The mortals were no longer listening. They were much more interested in making money and, while the countryside around their city was great for growing olives, it was too hilly and rocky for horses to be much use.

It was kind of ironic. The people of the city would eventually become famous sea traders, exporting their olive oil; but they turned down the sea god Poseidon's patronage. He might've done better if he'd offered them trained whales.

So Athena won the contest, and that's why the city is named Athens, after her, when it could have been named something cool like Poseidonopolis.

Poseidon stormed off, literally. He forgot his promise not to take revenge and almost destroyed the lower part of the city with a huge flood, until finally the Athenians agreed to build a temple on the acropolis honouring both Athena *and* Poseidon.

The temple is still there. If you go, you can see the marks left by Poseidon's trident where he struck the rock to make the saltwater spring. There are probably still olive trees around, too. But I doubt you'll see any horses.

After that, Poseidon got a little obsessed with finding a city to sponsor, but he didn't have any luck. He fought with Hera for the city of Argos. Hera won. He fought with Zeus for the island of Aegina. Zeus won. He fought with Helios for the city of Corinth and almost won, but Zeus said, 'No, you guys split it. Helios, you can have the main city and the acropolis. Poseidon – you see that little skinny strip of land next to the city? You can have that.'

Poseidon just kept getting shafted – or lightning-bolted, or olive-treed. The more times it happened, the crankier he got.

This was bad, because when Poseidon got touchy he was more likely to punish whoever he thought was insulting him.

For instance, he was very proud of these fifty sea spirits called the Nereids, whose beauty was known throughout the world. They had long, flowing hair as dark as midnight, sea-green eyes and gossamer white dresses that billowed around them in the water. Everyone knew they were absolute knockouts, and having them in *his* domain was something that delighted Poseidon, kind of like living in a town with a championship football team.

Anyway, this mortal queen named Cassiopeia down in North Africa – she started bragging about how she was *way* more beautiful than the Nereids.

Poseidon had no patience for that nonsense. He summoned up a flesh-eating, blood-drinking sea serpent about a thousand feet long, with a mouth that could swallow a mountain, and he sent it to terrorize the coast of Africa. The monster raged up and down, devouring ships, making waves that sank villages, and bellowing so loudly no one could get any sleep.

Finally, to stop the attacks, Cassiopeia agreed to sacrifice her own daughter, Andromeda, to the sea monster. Like, *Oh, yeah, my bad. I shouldn't have bragged. Here, you can kill my innocent daughter!*

In case you're worried, my dad didn't actually let that happen. He allowed a hero to rescue Andromeda and kill the sea monster (which is a whole other story), but, even after Cassiopeia died, Poseidon never forgot her insult. He put her in the night sky as a constellation and, because she had lied about being more beautiful than the Nereids, she always appeared to be spinning backwards.

She's a stupid-looking constellation, too.

After that, the Nereids were grateful to Poseidon for upholding their honour. Maybe that was his plan all along. You can't beat having fifty beautiful women thinking you're awesome.

Most of the Nereids would've been happy to marry Poseidon, but one Nereid avoided him, because she was shy and didn't ever want to get hitched. Naturally, *she* was the one who caught Poseidon's eye.

Her name was Amphitrite, and her idea of paradise was

living a quiet life at the bottom of the sea with no gods calling her up for dates or trying their cheesy pickup lines on her when she went to the underwater mall.

Unfortunately, Amphitrite was gorgeous. The more she tried to avoid the gods, the more they pursued her. Her black hair was pinned back in a net of pearls and silk. Her eyes were as dark as mocha. She had a kind smile and a beautiful laugh. Usually she dressed in a simple white gown, her only piece of jewellery a circlet of polished red crab claws across her brow — which doesn't strike me as very attractive, but I guess it was fashionable among the Nereids.

Poseidon tried everything to win her heart: saltwater taffy, a serenade of whale songs, a bouquet of sea cucumbers, a Portuguese man-of-war festooned with pretty red ribbons. Amphitrite refused all his advances. Whenever he got too close, she blushed and swam away.

Finally she got so spooked that she fled for good. Poseidon searched for her everywhere, with no luck. He began to think that he'd never see her again. His heart sank deeper than a navy submersible. He moped around his palace, crying like a humpback whale, confusing all the sea mammals and giving the giant squids migraines.

Eventually the sea creatures elected this god named Delphin to go talk to Poseidon and see what was wrong. Delphin was the immortal king of dolphins and a good friend of the sea god's. What did Delphin look like? A dolphin. Duh.

So Delphin swam into the throne room and chattered in Dolphinese: 'What's up, P-man? Why the face?'

'Oh, it's Amphitrite.' Poseidon heaved a sigh. 'I love her, but she ran away!'

'Huh.' Delphin thought that was a pretty stupid reason to mope around. 'You do realize there are forty-nine other Nereids, right?'

'I don't care!' Poseidon sobbed. 'I want Amphitrite!'

'Yeah, well, that's a bummer,' Delphin said. 'Look, your moaning and groaning is messing up everybody's sonar. Just this morning two blue whales got in a head-on collision and backed up the Aegean morning commute for miles. So how about I find this lady Amphitrite and convince her to marry you?'

Poseidon's tears dried immediately, which was impressive since he was underwater. 'You could do that for me?'

'I'm a dolphin,' Delphin chattered. 'I have a huge brain. Back soon.'

It took Delphin a while, but he finally located Amphitrite at the western edge of the Mediterranean, near where the Titan Atlas held up the sky.

Amphitrite sat on a coral ledge, watching the sunset filter through the deep water and make rosy streaks in the seaweed forests. A sea bass lay in her open palm, all blissed out, because Amphitrite really had a way with fish. Normally I don't think of sea bass as cuddly, but they *loved* her.

Delphin could see why Poseidon liked her. She radiated a sort of kindness and gentleness that you don't see in a lot of immortals. Usually with gods, the longer they lived, the more they acted like spoiled children. Delphin wasn't sure why, but that whole thing about getting wiser as you got older? Not so much.

Delphin floated up to Amphitrite. 'Hey, what's up?'

Amphitrite didn't try to flee. She had never felt threatened by Delphin, maybe because of his dolphin smile.

'Oh, Poseidon keeps bothering me.' Amphitrite sighed. 'He wants me to marry him.'

The sea bass swam in a lazy circle around Amphitrite's hand, then settled back into her palm. Delphin had to resist the urge to snap up the fish. Sea bass were tasty.

'Poseidon's not a bad guy,' Delphin offered. 'You could do a lot worse.'

'But I don't want to get married to anyone!' Amphitrite protested. 'It's too much trouble, and it's scary. I've heard stories about the gods, the way they treat their wives . . .'

'Most of the gods are jerks,' Delphin agreed. 'And they have a lot of girlfriends even after they get married –'

'Gah!' Amphitrite said. 'I wouldn't care about *that*. I'm not the jealous type. I just don't want to be mistreated. I want to be my own person, do my own thing, without some *man* lording over me!'

'Oh, is that all?' Delphin chittered with relief. 'Because Poseidon is easygoing. I can't guarantee he'd be faithful to you forever, but he would totally treat you well and let you do whatever you wanted. I can talk to him, make him promise. If he breaks his word, he'll have to deal with Mr Dolphin.'

Delphin flexed his flippers, which he thought made him look intimidating.

'You would do that for me?' Amphitrite asked.

'Sure!' Delphin said. 'And the best thing: if you married Poseidon, none of the *other* gods could flirt with you or pester you any more. They'd have to leave you alone, because Poseidon is so powerful. You could have kids, too. Kids are awesome. Even better than sea bass.'

'Really?' Amphitrite studied the sea bass flopping around

in her hand, as if she had trouble believing anything could be better than that. 'Well . . . I suppose if you talked to Poseidon first, and he promised . . .'

'Trust me,' Delphin said. 'The dolphin god's got your back!'

So Delphin returned to Poseidon and explained the deal. Poseidon was overjoyed. He agreed immediately. His marriage to Amphitrite was the biggest party ever held under the ocean. Gods, sea monsters, all forty-nine of Amphitrite's Nereid sisters . . . everybody was on the guest list. Whales swam overhead, spitting glowing clouds of krill that spelled out CONGRATULATIONS, POSEIDON + AMPHITRITE, which was no easy task since whales can't spell very well. The dolphins put on an acrobatics show. The jellyfish glowed above the palace courtyards as the sea nymphs and merpeople danced the night away.

Poseidon and Amphitrite made a good couple. They were happy together and had three godly children. The first was Triton, who looked like a merman but had two fish tails instead of one. He served as Poseidon's herald. Whenever Poseidon was on the move, Triton swam in front, blowing his conch horn to clear the way, like, *The boss is coming! Everybody look busy!*

Poseidon and Amphitrite's second kid was Rhode, a sea nymph who became the patron goddess of the island Rhodes (named after her, of course). She ended up marrying the sun Titan Helios.

Their third kid, a daughter named Kymopoleia, was big and clumsy and loud, and just never got as much love as her siblings. I always felt sorry for her. Her name meant *the Wave Ranger*, which makes her sound like a sports utility vehicle, but she looked more like a monster truck. Eventually she found happiness. She became the goddess of violent sea storms and married Briares, one of the Hundred-Handed Ones, who was also big and loud and didn't mind a monster-truck wife.

As the years went by, Amphitrite discovered that Delphin was right. She *did* love her children even more than sea bass, and most of the time Poseidon was a very good husband. He did have a lot of affairs with nymphs and mortals and whatnot, but strangely that didn't bother Amphitrite so much. As long as Poseidon didn't try to *own* her and tell her what to do, and as long as he was good to their three children, Amphitrite was cool.

She was even nice to Poseidon's demigod children, unlike some other goddesses I could name. (*Cough*, Hera, *cough*.) One time the hero Theseus came to visit, and Amphitrite treated him like an honoured guest. She even gave him a purple cloak to wear, which was a sign of kingship.

She's been pretty cool to me, too. She doesn't freak out when I leave my dirty laundry in the guest room. She makes cookies for me. She's never tried to kill me that I know of. Pretty much all you could ask of an immortal stepmom.

As for Poseidon, it's a good thing he had an easygoing wife, because he had so many girlfriends and kids from other relationships . . . I mean, you think Zeus was busy? Poseidon holds the record for the most demigod children.

If I tried to tell you about all the ladies he dated, we'd need an extra three hundred pages with a separate index and table of contents. We'd call it *Poseidon's Little Black Book*. But it would be too weird for me to talk about *all* my dad's girlfriends, so I'm just going to hit the highlights.

First was a Greek princess named Koroneis. She had feathery black hair and always wore dark dresses like she was going to a funeral, but for some reason Poseidon thought she was incredibly hot. One day he was following her along the beach, trying to flirt with her, when she got scared and ran off. Poseidon didn't want her to get away like Amphitrite had, so he started running after her. 'Hey, come back! I just want a kiss! I won't kill you!'

Which is probably not the thing to say if you're chasing a girl.

Koroneis panicked and screamed, 'Help! Somebody help!'

She ran towards the city gates, but they were too far away. She knew she'd never make it. She scanned the horizon and happened to focus on the glittering roof of the temple of Athena in the distance.

Since Athena was the first Olympian she thought of, Koroneis yelled, 'Athena, save me! I don't care how you do it!'

Which, again, is probably not a wise thing to say.

Way up on Mount Olympus, Athena heard Koroneis yelling her name. Gods have *incredibly* good hearing when it comes to their own names. The goddess spotted this poor helpless girl being chased by Poseidon, and Athena got angry.

'I don't think so, Barnacle Beard,' she muttered.

She snapped her fingers, and down on the beach Koroneis instantly turned into a bird with pitch-black feathers – the first crow, which is why *koronis* means *crow* in Greek. The crow flew away and left Poseidon on the beach, heartbroken and lonely with a black feather stuck in his hair.

Of course, Poseidon realized that Athena was responsible for changing Koroneis into a crow. He already resented Athena because of their contest over Athens. Now he was starting to hate her.

He decided to look for any opportunity to insult Athena. It didn't take him long. Pretty soon he became obsessed with another beautiful girl named Medusa.

Unlike Koroneis, Medusa was flattered that the sea god liked her.

They had a nice candlelight dinner together and a walk on the beach. Finally Poseidon said, 'Hey, why don't we go somewhere more private?'

Medusa blushed. 'Oh . . . I don't know. My sisters warned me about sea gods like you!'

'Aw, c'mon!' Poseidon said. 'I know a quiet spot. You'll love it.'

Medusa should've said no, but Poseidon could be pretty charming when he wanted to be.

He took her into town, straight to the temple of Athena. It was closed for the night, but Poseidon opened the doors easily.

'Are you sure this is a good idea?' Medusa whispered.

'Sure,' Poseidon said. 'We'll have the place to ourselves.'

Now, I'm not going to excuse Poseidon's behaviour. He knew very well that Athena would get angry. He was using Medusa to get revenge. He lost sight of the fact that *Hey, maybe Athena will take her anger out on this poor mortal girl. . . .*

Poseidon and Medusa made themselves comfortable and got romantic at the foot of Athena's statue, which was a huge insult to Athena — kind of like somebody leaving a burning bag of dog poo on your porch, ringing the doorbell and running away. Not that I have ever personally done anything like that, of course.

Athena looked down from Olympus and saw what was going on. She wanted to hurl. 'That is the most disgusting thing I have ever seen,' she grumbled. 'I think I'll show Poseidon something even *more* disgusting.'

She conjured up the most awful and creative curse she could think of – and Athena could be pretty creative.

Down in the temple, Medusa grew brass bat wings and brass talons. Her hair turned into a nest of writhing poisonous snakes. Her face twisted into something so horrible that one glance would turn anyone who saw her to stone.

Poseidon's eyes were closed. He was leaning in for another kiss, his lips all puckered up, when he heard a weird hissing noise.

'Baby, did you spring a leak?' he teased.

Then he opened his eyes. He jumped back faster than a breaching whale. 'Holy . . . What the . . . OH GODS! I *kissed that* . . . AHHH! MOUTHWASH! MOUTHWASH!'

Since he was immortal, he didn't turn to stone, but he screamed a bunch of other stuff I can't put into writing and got out of there fast, without even an apology to poor Medusa.

Medusa quickly realized what she looked like. She covered her head with her shawl and slunk away. Eventually she ended up living in a cave far from civilization, with just her two sisters for company. Together, the three of them were called the Gorgons. Over the years, just from being close to her, Medusa's two sisters transformed into monsters as ugly as she was. They couldn't turn people to stone, but the gods decided to make them immortal – maybe out of pity, maybe as a curse – so the sisters could take care of Medusa forever without getting petrified. The Gorgons caused all kinds of grief to heroes over the years, but that's another story. Eventually the face of Medusa became one of Athena's symbols, as if to say: *THIS IS WHAT HAPPENS IF YOU MESS WITH ME.*

Not all of Poseidon's relationships worked out so badly. He dated one girl named Eurynome who was really nice. By the way, her name is pronounced 'your enemy', and I don't know how Poseidon could say that without laughing. *Oh, your enemy, give me a kiss! My girlfriend is your enemy! I'm going out with your enemy!* Anyway, they had a kid together named Bellerophon, who became a great hero.

Another one of Poseidon's girlfriends, Aethra, gave birth to an even greater hero named Theseus. So don't start thinking all the important heroes were Zeus's kids. That's just Zeus's PR machine at work.

My favourite thing about Poseidon? If he really liked you, he could grant you shape-shifting powers. He did that for one of his girlfriends, Mestra, so she could turn into any animal she wanted. He also gave that power to one of his demigod grandsons, Periclymenus, who could fight as a snake or a bear or even a swarm of bees.

Me, I can't change shape. *Thanks a lot, Dad.*

On the other hand, some of Poseidon's kids didn't turn out too well. Maybe it depended on what kind of mood he was in, or what he'd had for dinner, but sometimes Poseidon sired actual monsters. One of his sons was a man-eating Cyclops named Polyphemus. Another was an ugly giant named Antaeus, who liked to break people in half. And you think *your* brothers are bad.

Another time, Poseidon fell in love with a princess named

Theophane, who was so beautiful that every guy in her kingdom wanted to marry her. They just wouldn't leave her alone. They followed her down the street. They broke into the palace, demanding to see her. They even tried following her into the bathroom. She was like a superstar surrounded by paparazzi. No peace or privacy *ever*.

Finally it got so bad that she prayed to Poseidon, who had been trying to date her, too. 'If you can get me away from my other suitors,' Theophane said, 'I'll be your girlfriend. Just get me out of here!'

The earth rumbled. A deep voice said, 'NO PROBLEM. TONIGHT, GO TO THE SHEEP PENS.'

That didn't sound like much of a plan to Theophane, but when darkness fell she put a veil over her face and tried to sneak out of the palace. Immediately she was spotted. Sixty guys swarmed her with bouquets of flowers, shouting, 'Marry me! Marry me!'

Theophane ran for the sheep pens. She dodged a mob of guys with boxes of chocolates, then twelve dudes with guitars trying to serenade her.

By the time she reached the sheep pens, over a hundred suitors were at her heels. Theophane was so desperate she dived straight into the pens.

POOF!

Instantly she turned into a ewe – a female sheep – and was lost in the herd.

The mob of love-struck guys stopped and looked around, baffled. They searched the pens but couldn't find Theophane anywhere. Eventually they gave up and went back to stake out the palace, figuring Theophane would return there sooner or later.

'Thank the gods!' bleated Theophane.

'You're welcome,' said a big ram, right next to her.

Theophane gulped. (Can ewes gulp?) 'Poseidon?'

The ram winked. 'You like my new wool coat? Because I like *ewe*. Get it? *Ewe*?'

Theophane started to feel queasy. 'I suppose I have to be your girlfriend now?'

'A deal's a deal,' Poseidon said.

They had some quality time together as sheep, which I'm not going to go into, or I'll get queasy myself. A few months later, the ewe Theophane gave birth to a magical ram named Krysomallos, who for some reason had wool made of gold.

Eventually, Krysomallos would be skinned for his fleece, which became known as the Golden Fleece, which means I am related to a sheepskin rug.

This is why you don't want to think too hard about who you're related to in the Greek myths. It'll drive you crazy.

Last story about Poseidon, and it's a tearjerker: how he almost took over the universe and ended up as a minimum-wage bricklayer.

Happened like this: Hera got it into her head that the gods should have a rebellion against Zeus.

I can't blame her, really. Zeus could be a total diaper wipe. She decided that the universe would be in much better shape if it were run by the whole Olympian council like a democracy, so she gathered some of the other gods – Poseidon, Athena and

Apollo, the god of archery – and she told them her plan.

'We tie Zeus up,' Hera said.

Poseidon frowned. 'That's your plan?'

'Hey, I sleep in the same room with him,' Hera said. 'When he's in a deep sleep, snoring really loudly, I'll call you guys in. We bind him tight. Then we force him to give up his throne so we can rule the cosmos together, as a council of equals.'

The others looked uncertain, but they all had reasons to dislike Zeus. He was erratic and quick to anger, and his weakness for pretty women had caused them all headaches.

Besides, each of the gods was secretly thinking, Hey, I could rule the universe better than Zeus. Once he's gone, I could take over!

Poseidon was definitely tempted. Why not? With his big brother tied up, he would be the strongest god in the world.

'A council of equals,' Poseidon said. 'Sure. I like it.'

'Right . . .' Athena glanced suspiciously at Poseidon. 'A council.'

'Great,' Hera said. 'Get some strong rope – the magical self-adjusting kind.'

'Where can you buy that?' Apollo wondered. 'Home Depot?'

'I've got some,' Athena said.

'Of course you have,' Poseidon muttered.

'Enough!' Hera snapped. 'Tonight, the three of you hide in the hallway and wait for my signal. When Zeus is asleep, I will call like a cuckoo.'

Poseidon wasn't sure what a cuckoo sounded like, but he figured he'd know it when he heard it.

That night, Hera made sure Zeus ate a heavy dinner and

drank only decaffeinated nectar. When he was fast asleep, she called for the others. They rushed in and tied up the king of the gods.

'Hrmmph?' Zeus snorted. 'Wh-what is this?'

He began to struggle. He tried to reach his lightning bolts, but his arms were tied fast. His bolts were on the dresser on the other side of the room.

'TREASON!' he roared. 'LET ME GO!'

He thrashed and tried to change form to get free of the rope, but the rope tightened every time he attempted to shape-shift. He yelled at the other gods and called them all sorts of unflattering names.

'WHAT DO YOU WANT?' he demanded.

Even completely bound, Zeus was scary. The gods backed away from the bed.

At last Poseidon mustered his courage. 'Zeus, you're a bad leader. We want you to abdicate, so we can all rule the cosmos as a council of equals.'

'What?!' Zeus shouted. 'NEVER!'

Hera sighed in exasperation. 'Fine! We don't need you! We'll convene the council ourselves and leave you here to rot.'

'You traitorous little –'

'Let's go,' Hera told the others. 'We'll check on him in a few days and see if he's come to his senses.'

Poseidon wasn't sure it was a good idea leaving Zeus unguarded, but he also didn't want to stay in the room with a screaming lightning god.

The gods adjourned to the throne room and held their very first (and very last) meeting of the People's Republic of Olympus.

They quickly found that voting on everything was messy. It took a long time. Just deciding on a design for the new Olympian flag took hours!

Meanwhile, a Nereid named Thetis was strolling down the hall near Zeus's bedroom. What was a sea nymph doing on Olympus? Maybe she was just spending the night, or visiting friends.

She had no idea what was going on with the rebellion, but when she heard Zeus yelling for help she burst into his bedroom, saw him tied up and said, 'Uh . . . is this a bad time?'

'Thetis, thank the Fates!' Zeus cried. 'Get me out of here!'

He quickly told her what the other gods had done. 'Please,' he pleaded. 'You're a sensible sea nymph. Let me out, and I'll really owe you one.'

Thetis gulped. If Poseidon was part of the rebellion . . . well, he was the lord of the sea, and thus her boss. But Zeus was lord of *everything*. No matter what she did, she was going to make a powerful enemy.

'If I let you out,' Thetis said, 'promise me you'll be merciful to the other gods.'

'MERCIFUL?'

'Just don't throw them into Tartarus, or chop them into tiny pieces, okay?'

Zeus fumed, but he reluctantly promised to be *merciful*.

Thetis grabbed some scissors from the dresser and tried to cut the ropes, but she had no luck. The magical bonds were too strong.

'Blast them with my lightning!' Zeus said. 'Wait . . . I'm *in* the ropes. On second thought, don't blast them.'

'Hang on,' Thetis said. 'I know somebody who might be able to help.'

She turned into a cloud of salty water vapour and sped to the sea, where she found Briares the Hundred-Handed One. Briares owed Zeus for letting him out of Tartarus, so he was happy to help. Somehow, Thetis managed to smuggle the big dude into Olympus without the gods noticing, and with his hundred dexterous hands Briares quickly untied the magical ropes.

Zeus sprang out of bed, grabbed his lightning bolts and marched into the throne room, where the other gods were still trying to design their new flag.

BOOM!

Zeus floored further discussion, along with all the other gods.

When he was done blowing things up and using the Olympians for target practice, he punished the rebels for their treason.

He kept his promise to Thetis. He didn't chop the gods into tiny pieces or throw them into Tartarus. But he tied Hera up and suspended her on a rope over the abyss of Chaos, so she could contemplate what it would be like to drop into nothingness and be dissolved. Every day, Zeus would visit her with his lightning bolt in hand and say, 'Yep, today might be a good day to blast that rope and watch you fall!'

That's the sort of loving relationship they had.

Hera eventually got free, but we'll get to that story later.

As for Athena, she got off with no punishment. Totally unfair, right? But Athena was a quick talker. She probably convinced Zeus that she'd had nothing to do with the plot, and she was just biding her time before she could set Zeus free. Like an idiot, Zeus believed her.

Apollo and Poseidon got the worst punishments. They were temporarily stripped of their immortal powers.

I didn't even know Zeus could *do* stuff like that, but apparently he could. To teach the two former gods a lesson, Zeus made them work as labourers for the king of Troy, a dude named Laomedon. Apollo became his shepherd and watched the royal flocks. Poseidon had to single-handedly build new walls around the city.

'Are you kidding me?' Poseidon protested. 'That'll take years!'

King Laomedon smiled. 'Yes, well . . . I promise to reward you for your hard work, but you'd better get started!'

Actually, Laomedon had no intention of paying Poseidon. He didn't like the sea god. He just wanted to get as much free work as possible out of Poseidon for as long as possible.

Since Poseidon didn't have a choice, he set to work.

Even without his godly powers, Poseidon was still pretty awesome. He was stronger than any mortal and could carry five or six massive blocks of stone at a time. The project took him years, but he finally constructed the mightiest walls any mortal city had ever had, making Troy nearly invincible.

At last, tired and sore and irritated, Poseidon marched into King Laomedon's throne room.

'Finished,' Poseidon announced.

'With what?' Laomedon looked up from the book he was reading. It had been so many years that he'd totally forgotten about Poseidon. 'Oh, right! The walls! Yes, they look great. You can go now.'

Poseidon blinked. 'But — my reward.'

'That *is* your reward. You can go. I'll let Zeus know you fulfilled your oath, and he'll make you a god again. What better reward could there be?'

Poseidon growled. 'I made your city the strongest on earth. I built walls that will withstand any army. You promised me compensation, and now you won't pay?'

'Are you still here?' Laomedon asked.

Poseidon stormed out of the throne room.

Zeus made him a god again, but Poseidon never forgot how Laomedon had insulted him. He couldn't destroy Troy outright; Zeus forbade it. But Poseidon *did* send a sea monster to terrorize the Trojans. He also made a special point of sinking Trojan ships whenever he got the chance. And when a little event called the Trojan War came along . . . well, Poseidon was *not* on the side of Troy.

And that's my dad, folks: a calm, easygoing dude most of the time. But if you made him angry he had a long, long memory.

The only god who held longer grudges . . . yeah, you guessed it. Old Thunderpants himself. I suppose we've put him off long enough. It's time to talk about Zeus.

ZEUS KILLS EVERYONE

Y OU WANT SCARY?

Think about this: Zeus was the god of law and order. The guy who threw random lightning bolts when he got angry and couldn't keep his own wedding vows — *this* was the guy in charge of making sure kings acted wisely, councils of elders were respected, oaths were kept and strangers were given hospitality.

That would be like making me the god of homework and good grades.

I guess Zeus wasn't *all* bad. Sometimes he would show up at mortals' homes disguised as a wanderer to see whether folks would let him in and offer him food. If you treated the visitor kindly, good for you! That was your duty as a Greek citizen. If you slammed the door in his face . . . well, Zeus would be back later with his lightning bolts.

Just knowing that every traveller or homeless person might be Zeus in disguise kept the Greeks on their toes.

Same with kings. Zeus was the god of kingly power, so he watched over mortal rulers to make sure they didn't abuse their position. Obviously, a lot of kings got away with terrible things (probably because Zeus was busy chasing some girl and didn't notice), but there was always a chance that if you did something really evil or stupid Zeus would bring down the godly thunder and lightning and blast you right off your throne.

Example? Salmoneus. That dude should've won the grand prize for being an idiot. He was one of seven brothers, all princes of a Greek kingdom called Thessaly. Since there were so many princes hanging around the palace with nothing to do except play video games and wait to inherit the kingdom, their father the king said, 'You guys, get out of here! Get some exercise, for once! Why don't you all go start new kingdoms or something? Stop loafing and get a job!'

The seven princes didn't really feel like founding new kingdoms. That was hard work. But their dad insisted, and so did his heavily armed guards. The princes each took a group of settlers and struck out into the wilderness of southern Greece.

Prince Salmoneus was pretty full of himself. He named his new kingdom Salmonea. He put his settlers to work building a capital city, but he got annoyed because the people wanted to build temples to the gods before they started a palace for *him*.

'Your Majesty,' they said, 'we *have* to honour the gods first. Otherwise they'll get angry!'

The new king grumbled. He didn't really believe in the gods. He was pretty sure those stories were a bunch of rubbish the priests had made up to keep people in line.

That night Salmoneus sat in his partially built palace, watching his citizens working late, putting the final touches on the temple to Zeus, with its gold roof and marble floors. He could smell all kinds of tasty food being burned on the ceremonial fires.

'They don't bring tasty food to *me*,' Salmoneus muttered to himself. 'They're so afraid of the gods, but they're not afraid of their own king? They wouldn't treat me this way if *I* were a god . . .'

Salmoneus suddenly got an evil idea. He remembered the games he and his brothers used to play back in Thessaly when they were kids. They would dress up and pretend to be heroes and gods. Salmoneus was always the best actor.

He called in his most trusted advisor and said, 'Trusted advisor, we have work to do. We need props and costumes.'

His advisor frowned. 'Are we putting on a play, Your Majesty?'

Salmoneus grinned. 'Sort of . . .'

A few days later, Salmoneus was ready. He donned his costume, got in his newly decorated chariot and rode into the streets of his capital.

'Behold!' he screamed at the top of his lungs. 'I am Zeus!'

A farmer was so startled that he dropped a basket of olives. A lady fell off her donkey. Many other citizens screamed and ran away, because they were afraid of getting trampled by the king's horses.

Salmoneus looked pretty impressive. He wore white robes lined with gold. A golden wreath glinted in his hair. Since the eagle was Zeus's sacred bird, Salmoneus had painted eagles on the sides of his chariot. Mounted behind him, concealed under a tarp, were two brass kettledrums. When he raised his hand, his advisor (who was hiding under the tarp and not feeling very comfortable) would pound on the drums and make a sound like muffled thunder.

Salmoneus rode through the streets, screaming, 'I am Zeus! Bring me tasty food!' Finally he stopped at the steps of the new temple to Zeus and turned the chariot towards the assembled crowd. 'You will worship me!' he commanded. 'For I am a god.'

One of his braver subjects called out, 'You look like Salmoneus.'

'Yes!' Salmoneus agreed. 'But I am also Zeus! I have decided to inhabit the body of your king. You will worship him as you worship me. This temple will be my palace. You will bring me all your offerings. But don't burn them any more. That's a waste. I'll just eat them.'

A few of his more timid subjects started to obey, placing food baskets on the ground near the chariot.

One man called out, 'Why do you have chickens painted on your chariot?'

'They're eagles!' Salmoneus yelled.

'They look like chickens,' the man insisted.

'Silence, mortal!' Salmoneus kicked his advisor under the blanket. The advisor started pounding his kettledrums.

'See?' Salmoneus said. 'I can summon thunder!'

A lady in the back said, 'Who's under the blanket behind you?'

'No one!' Salmoneus yelled, a bead of sweat trickling down his neck. This wasn't going as well as he'd hoped, so he decided to use his props.

He pulled a torch from his bucket o' flaming torches ($99.99 at Walmart) and tossed one towards the lady in the crowd.

The people cried and shuffled away from the torch, but it landed harmlessly on the pavement.

'There!' Salmoneus roared. 'I have cast a lightning bolt at you! Do not test me, or I shall strike you down!'

'That's a torch!' somebody yelled.

'You asked for it, mortal!' Salmoneus started lobbing torches into the crowd and kicking his advisor under the tarp to bang on his drums, but soon the novelty wore off and the crowd got angry.

'Boo!' someone yelled.

'Impostor!' yelled another. 'False ZEUS!'

'Real ZEUS!' Salmoneus yelled back. 'I am ZEUS!'

'YOU'RE NOT ZEUS!' yelled the crowd.

So many people were yelling the name *Zeus* that the big guy himself up on Mount Olympus took notice. He looked down and saw a mortal king in a bad costume, riding around on a chariot painted with chickens, lobbing torches and calling them lightning bolts.

The god of the sky wasn't sure whether to laugh or rage.

He decided on raging.

Storm clouds gathered over the new city of Salmonea. Real thunder shook the buildings. The sky god's voice boomed from on high: *I AM ZEUS.*

A jagged bolt of lightning split the sky, blasting Salmoneus and his poor advisor into grease spots. When the smoke cleared, there was nothing left but a burning chariot wheel and a half-melted kettledrum.

The mortals of Salmonea cheered. They would've thrown a party in Zeus's honour for getting rid of their idiot king, but Zeus wasn't finished.

His voice bellowed from the sky: *SOME OF YOU BROUGHT HIM OFFERINGS. SOME OF YOU ACTUALLY BELIEVED THAT FOOL!*

'No!' the mortals yelled, grovelling and cowering. 'Please!'

I CANNOT ALLOW THIS CITY TO EXIST, Zeus rumbled. *I MUST MAKE YOU AN EXAMPLE SO THAT THIS NEVER HAPPENS AGAIN. LIGHTNING BOLTS INCOMING IN FIVE, FOUR, THREE . . .*

The mortals broke ranks and ran, but Zeus didn't give them much time. Some people made it out of Salmonea alive, but, when the lightning bolts started coming down, most of the mortals were blown to bits or buried under the rubble.

Zeus wiped the city of Salmonea off the map. No one dared to repopulate the area for another generation, all because of one guy with a bad Zeus costume, a chicken chariot and a bucket o' torches.

Overkill. Literally. But it wasn't the worst punishment Zeus ever doled out. One time he decided to destroy the entire human race.

I don't even know why. Apparently humans were behaving badly. Maybe they weren't making the proper sacrifices, or they didn't believe in the gods, or they were cursing a lot and driving over the speed limit.

Whatever. Zeus got angry and decided to destroy the entire race. I mean, *Come on.* How bad could the humans have been? I'm sure they weren't doing anything humans haven't always done. But Zeus decided enough was enough. He acted like one of those teachers who lets you get away with stuff all semester and then one day, for no apparent reason, decides to crack down way too hard. Like, 'All right, that's it! Everybody is getting detention right now! The whole class!'

Like, *Dude, please.* There are options between *nothing* and *going nuclear.*

Anyway, Zeus called the gods together and broke the news.

'Humans are disgusting!' he cried. 'I'm going to destroy them.'

The throne room was silent. Finally Demeter said, 'All of them?'

'Sure,' Zeus said.

'How?' asked Ares. The god of war had an eager gleam in his eyes. 'Fire? Lightning? We could get a bunch of chain saws and –'

'Bug bombs,' Zeus said. 'We set a few of those babies off, leave the world for a few days, and –'

'No one has invented bug bombs yet,' Hera pointed out.

'Oh, right.' Zeus frowned. 'Then a flood. I'll open the skies and unleash torrents of rain until all the humans drown!'

Poseidon grunted. 'Floods are *my* department.'

'You can help,' Zeus offered.

'But without humans,' Hestia asked from the hearth, 'who will worship you, my lord? Who will build your temples and burn your sacrifices?'

'We'll think of something,' Zeus said. 'This isn't the *first* race of humans, after all. We can always make more.'

According to the old stories, this was technically true. The humans back in Kronos's time had been called the golden race.

Supposedly they'd all died out and been replaced by the silver race. The ones in the early days of Mount Olympus were called the bronze race. What made those humans different from us? There are a lot of stories, but the main thing was: they died off, and we haven't . . . yet.

'Besides,' Zeus continued, 'a flood is good. We need to give the earth a proper power-washing once in a while to get all the grime off the pavements.'

Reluctantly, the gods agreed to his plan, but many of them had favourite humans, so they secretly sent warnings in the form of dreams or omens. Because of this, a few people survived. The most famous were the king and queen of Thessaly in northern Greece: a guy named Deucalion and his wife, Pyrrha.

Deucalion was human, but his dad was the Titan Prometheus – the dude who'd brought men fire and was now chained up on a mountain far away, getting his liver pecked out by an eagle.

I'm not sure how Prometheus managed to have a mortal kid with all the other stuff he had going on. You can't exactly join a dating service when you're chained to a rock being tortured. Whatever the case, Prometheus somehow heard about Zeus's plan, and he still had a lot of love for humanity. He especially didn't want his own son Deucalion to drown, because Deucalion was a good guy. He was always respectful to the gods and treated his subjects well.

So Prometheus warned him in a dream: *FLOOD COMING! GATHER SUPPLIES IN THE BIGGEST CHEST YOU CAN FIND! HURRY!*

Deucalion woke up in a cold sweat. He told his wife about the dream, and she remembered a huge oak chest they kept up in the attic. They grabbed some food and water from the kitchen and ran upstairs, warning all their servants along the way: 'Get your families. There's a flood coming! Seek higher ground!' because Deucalion and Pyrrha were nice people that way. Unfortunately, most of the servants didn't listen. The king and the queen were getting old, so the servants figured they'd gone senile.

Deucalion and Pyrrha emptied all the old clothes and knickknacks out of the chest to make room for their provisions. The rain started to fall. Within minutes, the sky was nothing but sheets of grey water. Lightning flashed. Thunder shook the earth. In less than an hour, the whole kingdom of Thessaly was swallowed by the flood. Decalion and Pyrrha closed their chest full of supplies, lashed themselves to the lid and floated right out the attic window.

It wasn't a comfortable ride, shooting up and down forty-foot swells while the storm raged, chunks of debris swirled past and the entire world was drowning. The king and queen got salt water up their noses, like, a million times. But the wooden chest acted like a life preserver and kept them from going under.

After what seemed like forever, the rain stopped. The clouds broke and the sun came out. The flood slowly receded, and Deucalion and Pyrrha landed their chest on the slopes of Mount Parnassus.

At this point, some of you may be thinking, *Hey, a guy escapes a big flood and floats to safety while the rest of the wicked human race drowns. Wasn't there another story like that? Some dude named Noah?*

Yeah, well, every ancient culture seems to have a flood story. I guess it was a pretty massive disaster. Different people remembered it different ways. Maybe Noah and Deucalion passed each other on the sea, and Deucalion was like, 'An ark! Two animals of every kind! Why didn't *we* think of that?'

And his wife Pyrrha would be like, 'Because they wouldn't fit in this chest, ya moron!'

But I'm just guessing.

Finally the waters sank back into the sea, and the land started to dry out.

Deucalion looked around at the empty hills of Greece and said, 'Great. What do we do now?'

'First,' Pyrrha said, 'we make a sacrifice to Zeus and ask him never to do this again.'

Deucalion agreed that that was a good idea, because another flood would really suck.

They sacrificed all their remaining food, along with the chest, in a big fire and pleaded with Zeus to spare them from any more power-washings.

Up on Olympus, Zeus was pleased. He was surprised that anyone had survived, but, since the first thing Deucalion and Pyrrha did was honour *him*, he was cool with that.

NO MORE FLOODS, he voice boomed from above. *BECAUSE YOU ARE PIOUS PEOPLE AND I LIKE YOU, YOU MAY ASK ANY FAVOUR, AND I WILL GRANT IT.*

Deucalion grovelled appropriately. 'Thank you, Lord Zeus! We beg you, tell us how to repopulate the earth! My wife and I are too old to have kids, and we don't want to be the last humans alive. Let the humans come back, and this time they'll behave. I promise!'

The sky rumbled. *GO TO THE ORACLE AT DELPHI. THEY WILL ADVISE YOU.*

It was a long distance, but Deucalion and Pyrrha walked

all the way to the Oracle. As it happened, the people of Delphi had been warned about the flood by a bunch of howling wolves. Which god sent the wolves, I don't know, but the people had climbed the tallest mountain near Delphi and survived the flood, so now they were back in business, dispensing prophecies and whatnot.

Deucalion and Pyrrha went into the cave of the Oracle, where an old lady sat on a three-legged stool, shrouded in green mist.

'O Oracle,' Deucalion said. 'Please, tell us how to repopulate the earth. And I don't mean by having kids, because we're too old for that nonsense!'

The Oracle's voice was like the hissing of snakes: *When you leave this place, cover your heads and throw the bones of your mother behind you as you go, and do not look back.*

'The bones of my mother?' Deucalion was outraged. 'She's dead and buried. I don't carry her bones around with me!'

I just pronounce the prophecies, the Oracle muttered. *I don't explain them. Now, shoo!*

Deucalion and Pyrrha weren't very satisfied, but they left the Oracle.

'How are we supposed to throw the bones of our mother behind us?' Deucalion asked.

Pyrrha wasn't sure, but she covered her head with a shawl, then gave her husband an extra scarf so he could do the same, just as the Oracle had ordered. As they walked away, heads bowed, Pyrrha realized that with her shawl over her head she could only see the ground right in front of her, which was littered with rocks.

She froze. 'Husband, I have an idea. *The bones of our mother.*

What if the prophecy doesn't *literally* mean the bones of our mother? It might be a . . . what do you call those things? Limericks?'

'No, a limerick is a naughty poem,' Deucalion said. 'You mean, a metaphor?'

'Yes! What if *the bones of our mother* is a metaphor?'

'Okay. But a metaphor for *what*?'

'The mother of everything . . . *Mother Earth*,' Pyrrha suggested. 'And her bones —'

'Could mean these rocks!' Deucalion cried. 'Wow, you're smart!'

'That's why you married me.'

So Deucalion and Pyrrha started picking up rocks and chucking them over their shoulders as they walked. They didn't look behind them, but they could hear the rocks cracking apart like eggs as they hit the ground. Later, the king and queen found out that each rock had turned into a human. When Deucalion threw one, it turned into a man. When Pyrrha threw one, it turned into a woman.

So Zeus let the human race repopulate itself.

I'm not sure if that means we're still the bronze race, or if we're the stone race, or maybe the rockers? Either way, Zeus was glad to let the humans back into the world, because without them he wouldn't have had any pretty mortal girls to chase after.

You can't swing a cat in Ancient Greece without hitting at least one of Zeus's ex-girlfriends. We've already covered a lot of his romances, so I don't think we need to talk about many of them here. I'll just mention that Zeus had absolutely no shame and was endlessly creative when it came to wooing women. With each girlfriend, he shape-shifted into some weird form to get her attention. He rarely appeared in the same guise twice.

Once he got cuddly with a girl while in the form of a swan. Another time, he visited his girlfriend as a shower of golden light. He cornered other women in the forms of a snake, an eagle, a satyr and an ant. (Seriously, how do you corner somebody when you're an ant, and how would you . . . never mind.) Zeus even tricked some women by appearing as their husbands. That's just low.

One particularly sneaky trick was when he kidnapped this lady named Europa. She was a princess. (Naturally. Aren't they always princesses?) Zeus spied her one day at the beach, hanging out with her friends.

Zeus didn't want to appear to her in his real godly form, because a) Hera might notice and get mad, b) when gods showed up, girls tended to run away for good reason, and c) he really wanted to talk to Europa alone. Don't you hate it when you want to talk to a girl alone, but they always seem to travel in packs, like wolves? It's annoying.

So Zeus transformed into a bull and galloped across the beach. He wasn't a scary bull, though. He had soft grey eyes and a butterscotch-yellow hide with a white spot on his forehead. His horns were pearly white. He stopped on a grassy hillside near the beach and started grazing, like, *Ho-hum. Don't mind me.*

All the girls noticed him. At first, they weren't sure what to think. But the bull didn't do anything threatening. It looked kind of cute and gentle, as far as bulls go.

'Let's check it out,' Europa said. 'He looks pretty!'

So the girls swarmed around the bull and started petting his back and feeding him handfuls of grass. The bull made gentle lowing sounds. He gave Europa the big soft eyes and generally acted cuddly and sweet.

'Awwwwwww,' all the girls said.

Europa noticed that the bull also smelled wonderful – like a combination of leather and Old Spice. She had an over-powering urge to adopt him and take him home.

Bull Zeus nuzzled her dress and then lowered his head, sinking to his front knees.

'OMG!' Europa cried. 'I think he wants to take me for a ride!'

Generally speaking, princesses weren't supposed to ride bulls, but this bull seemed so sweet and tame that Europa climbed right on his back.

'Come on, girls!' Europa called. 'Let's all – WHAA!'

Before she could help her friends climb aboard, the bull bolted straight for the ocean. Europa clung to his neck, terrified that she might get thrown. She was much too afraid to try climbing off while the bull was rampaging.

In no time, the bull was three hundred feet out to sea. Europa's friends called to her desperately, but the beach was getting further and further away, and Europa wasn't a good swimmer. She had no idea where the bull was taking her; her only choice was to hang on and hope for the best.

Zeus swam all the way to the island of Crete. Once there, he turned back into a god and said, 'Finally, we're alone! How you doing? I'm Zeus.'

Well, one thing led to another, and since Europa couldn't get back home she ended up staying on Crete, where she had three sons with Zeus. Because nobody back home knew where Europa had disappeared to, her name eventually came to mean *those lands we don't know much about*. The Greeks started calling the lands to the north of them *europa*, and eventually the name stuck as *Europe*.

Zeus didn't always get his way with women, though.

After that little rebellion when the gods tried to overthrow him, he spent some time flirting with the Nereid Thetis – the lady who had released him from his bonds. Then Zeus heard a prophecy that Thetis was destined to give birth to a son who was greater than his father.

That freaked Zeus out pretty good.

'A kid greater than *me*?' he muttered to himself. 'I don't think so!'

So he broke off flirting with Thetis, and their relationship never went anywhere. Thetis eventually married a great hero named Peleus, and they had a son who was an even greater hero than his dad. In fact, he turned out to be the most powerful and famous hero in all of Greek history. His name was Achilles. So we can be thankful Zeus didn't marry Thetis. None of us needs a super-powerful Zeus Junior running around.

Zeus by himself was powerful enough to handle anything . . . well, *almost* anything.

The only time he got schooled, fooled and totally tooled was when he faced a monster called Typhoeus.

The stories about him are pretty confused. They can't

even agree on his name. Sometimes it's Typhoeus. Sometimes it's Typhon. Sometimes Typhon and Typhoeus are treated like two different monsters. To keep things simple, let's call him Typhoeus.

What did he look like? Hard to say. He was always shrouded in storm clouds. BIG, for sure. Like, so big that his head seemed to scrape the top of the sky. His shape was more or less humanoid from the waist up, but his legs were like the bodies of boa constrictors. On each hand, he had a hundred fingers that were tipped with serpent heads, each of which had fiery eyes and spat venom, so that when he got mad he just showered poison all over the place. This also made it totally impossible for him to get a manicure. He had massive leathery wings, long matted hair that smelled like volcanic smoke, and a face that was constantly shifting and changing so that it seemed like he had a hundred different faces – each one uglier than the last. Oh, and he breathed fire. Did I mention that?

Typhoeus was born and raised in the pit of Tartarus. The spirit of the pit – the primordial god Tartarus – was his dad. His mom was Mother Earth. I guess that explains why Typhoeus was both big and evil. His parents must have been so proud.

Typhoeus had a lovely wife named Echidna down in the pit. Okay, she wasn't really lovely. She was a hideously foul she-monster, but they must have got along, because they had lots of kids together. In fact, just about every horrible monster you can think of was a child of Typhoeus and Echidna.

Despite this, one day Typhoeus got restless and decided to leave his comfy home in the pit of eternal damnation.

'Honey,' he told Echidna, 'I'm going upstairs to destroy the gods and take over the universe. I'll try to be back by dinner.'

'This is your mother's idea, isn't it?' Echidna complained. 'She's always telling you what to do! You should stay at home. The Hydra needs his father. The Sphinx needs her dad!'

Typhoeus shuddered. It was true that Mother Earth was always goading him to destroy the gods. Gaia *hated* the gods ever since they defeated the Titans. But this trip was Typhoeus's idea. He needed a vacation from his monstrous kids and his she-monster wife. Taking over the universe sounded like just the ticket.

'I'll be back,' he promised. 'If I'm late, don't wait up.'

So the storm giant Typhoeus broke into the upper world and began destroying everything in his path. It was pathetically easy. He ripped up a mountain and smashed a city. He summoned a hurricane and drowned an entire island.

'Is this all you've got?' Typhoeus yelled towards Mount Olympus, far in the distance. 'Where are the gods?'

The gods, in fact, were assembling for war . . . until they saw the size of Typhoeus, how he raged across the earth, flattening nations, blowtorching forests, turning the oceans into poison with his serpent-headed fingers.

'Uh . . .' Poseidon gulped. 'That guy is huge.'

'Massive,' said Athena, for once agreeing with the sea god. 'I do not like these odds.'

'Guys!' Zeus protested. 'There are twelve of us, and only one of him! We defeated the Titans. We can do this!'

Actually, Zeus was shaking in his sandals. He wanted to

run, too, but he was the king of the gods, so he had to set a good example.

'Come on,' he said, hoisting his best lightning bolt. 'Charge!'

The gods jumped on their flying chariots and followed him into battle. They yelled, 'Charge,' but they were so nervous it sounded more like 'charge?'

When Typhoeus saw them coming, he experienced something he'd never felt before . . . *joy*. The gods were ridiculously tiny! They would be so easy to destroy that it made him giddy. He could already imagine himself taking over Zeus's throne on Mount Olympus and ruling the universe, though he'd probably have to get a bigger throne.

'DIE, IMMORTALS!' he bellowed, which wasn't a logical challenge, since technically immortals *can't* die, but I guess Typhoeus was planning to blast them into tiny piles of dust and sprinkle them into the abyss, which is pretty close to being dead.

Anyway, the storm giant spewed poison and belched fire and rose to his full height, so his head scraped the sky. Clouds of darkness swirled around him. The ground melted, and the seas boiled around his reptilian feet.

The gods changed their war cry to: 'RUN!' 'HELP!' And: 'MOMMY!'

Everybody except Zeus turned and fled.

It wasn't their finest moment. Some stories say they turned into animals to hide from the giant's wrath. One story even claims they hid in Egypt. While they were there, in the forms of animals, they gave rise to all those Egyptian myths about animal-headed gods.

I'm not sure what the Egyptians would say about that, seeing as their myths are thousands of years older than the Greek ones, but that's the Greek story.

Whatever the case, Zeus was left alone to face Typhoeus.

The god of the sky screamed after the fleeing Olympians: 'Are you *serious*? Get back here, you wimps!'

But his voice was drowned out by the laughter of Typhoeus. 'Poor little Zeus, all alone! You'd better flee, too, tiny god, before I smash you like an ant!'

Zeus had changed into an ant once to woo one of his girlfriends, so he had a fondness for ants. Typhoeus couldn't go around insulting ants like that! Anger gave him courage.

'You're going down, big boy!' Zeus yelled. He charged in for the kill.

He threw a lightning bolt that impacted Typhoeus's chest like a fifty-megaton hydrogen bomb. The storm giant staggered backwards, but he didn't fall.

Zeus blasted the giant again and again. The explosions fried the air, vaporized the water and blistered the surface of the earth, but still Typhoeus kept coming.

The giant swiped at Zeus's chariot and smacked it right out of the sky. As Zeus fell, Typhoeus snatched him up in a snake-fingered hand and began to squeeze.

Zeus changed his size, growing as large as he possibly could, which was still tiny compared to Typhoeus. Zeus struggled to free himself, but even the god's massive strength was of no use against the giant.

'Let me go!' Zeus bellowed.

'Sure,' Typhoeus growled, belching fire so close to Zeus's

face that it burned his beard off. 'But I can't have you making trouble, so I'll need a security deposit.'

'A what?'

Typhoeus's snaky fingers wrapped around Zeus's arms and legs. The snake heads sank their poisonous fangs into his forearms and his calves and . . .

Okay. Prepare yourself. This is gross.

. . . they ripped out Zeus's tendons.

What does that mean? Well, the tendons hold your muscles to your bones, right? At least that's what my basketball coach told me. They're extremely strong bands of connective tissue – like the body's natural duct tape. And without duct tape *nothing* works.

Typhoeus yanked out the immortal sinews, glistening white slimy cords of godly connective tissue (I did warn you it was gross), and Zeus went as limp as a doll. He couldn't move his arms or legs. He was completely helpless, and in so much pain he couldn't even see straight.

'There we go!' Typhoeus yelled. 'Oh, and I'll just take these lightning bolts. They'll make excellent toothpicks.'

The giant grabbed the lightning bolts that were hanging off Zeus's belt. Then he bent down and picked up the extra ones from the wrecked chariot that lay smoking on a nearby island. 'That's good! Now you're free to go. You can enjoy watching me destroy Olympus and taking over the world. Then I'll come back later and step on you.'

Typhoeus tossed Zeus aside like a clod of dirt. The lord of the universe landed in a crumpled heap on the side of a mountain and whimpered, 'Ouch.'

Typhoeus stormed off, heading for Olympus, with Zeus's lightning bolts and gross sinews safely tucked in his pouch (or man purse, or whatever the fashionable evil storm giants were wearing back then).

Well, gang, at this point things weren't looking too good for the gods. Or for humans. Or for anything that lived on the face of the planet. Zeus was lying on a mountainside helpless and in agony, watching as Typhoeus marched off to destroy Olympus.

Zeus thought, Why did I want to be king? This bites.

Meanwhile the other gods were hiding, and Typhoeus raged across creation, almost unopposed. An army of Poseidon's sea monsters and whales did try to stop him, but Typhoeus just kicked them out of the way and poisoned their waters. Some of the sky gods tried to fight him — the spirits of the stars, and Selene, the Titan of the moon. In fact, the Greeks believed that the scars and craters on the moon were left over from when Selene rode the moon chariot into battle.

Nothing helped. The seas kept boiling. Whole islands were destroyed. The sky turned into a red-and-black boiling mass. Every so often Typhoeus would stomp on the earth, open a huge crevice and reach inside to pull out some magma-like yolk from the inside of an egg. He'd throw fiery globs of lava all over the earth, setting fields on fire, melting cities and writing burning graffiti on the sides of mountains like ZEUS SUX and TYPHOEUS WUZ HERE.

He would've made it to Mount Olympus, no problem, but fortunately a couple of gods decided to circle back and see what had happened to Zeus.

They weren't the bravest gods. They were just the sneakiest.

One was Hermes the messenger, who could fly very fast and was good at staying off the radar. The other was a minor satyr god named Aegipan, who had furry legs and hooves like a goat, and generally looked like a regular satyr except that he was immortal.

Aegipan had managed to hide from Typhoeus by turning into a goat with the tail of a fish. (Why such a weird disguise? Maybe he panicked. I don't know.) Anyway, he dived into the sea and escaped.

Now he was feeling bad about being a coward, so he hitched a ride with Hermes, and they flew around until they spotted Zeus lying in a heap.

'Ouch,' Hermes said when they landed. 'What happened to you?'

Zeus wanted to chew them out for running away and leaving him to fight Typhoeus alone, but he was in too much pain, and he needed their help too badly.

He could barely speak, but he managed to tell them about the missing lightning bolts and the sinews that Typhoeus had ripped out of his arms and legs.

Aegipan looked like he wanted to throw up. 'So we're finished. Game over.'

'We can't give up,' Zeus said. 'I need my tendons and my bolts back. If I can get the drop on Typhoeus, hit him at point-blank range, I think I can take him out. But how to get back my weapons and my sinews . . .'

He stared at the panpipes hanging around Aegipan's neck.

Bringing a musical instrument with you into battle might sound silly, but Aegipan always carried his pipes. He had a reputation for playing very well.

Suddenly, Zeus got a crazy idea. He remembered how he'd tricked Kronos into barfing up the other Olympians years ago, how he'd posed as a cupbearer and won the Titans' praise by singing songs and dancing . . .

'When strength doesn't work,' Zeus said, 'trickery might.'

'I like trickery,' Hermes said.

Zeus told them his plan.

Fortunately, Hermes was a fast flyer. He picked up Aegipan and Rag Doll Zeus and zipped at top speed around Typhoeus's path of destruction. The gods landed on the Greek mainland near the foot of Mount Olympus, right where the storm giant would have to walk.

Hermes deposited Zeus in a nearby cave, where the lord of the sky would have to wait like a useless sack of rocks while the plan either failed or succeeded.

Hermes hid out of sight in the nearest grove of trees, while Aegipan the satyr god made himself comfortable in a wide meadow, where he couldn't possibly be missed, and started playing his panpipes.

Pretty soon the sky darkened. The ground shook. The air smelled like acid and poison, and the trees began to smoulder. Aegipan kept playing his sweet melodies.

The dark form of Typhoeus appeared on the horizon, like King Kong, Godzilla and one of those evil Transformer dudes all rolled into one. He bellowed his victory cry as he approached Mount Olympus. The whole earth shuddered.

Aegipan kept playing. His melodies were like sunlight in the morning and a cool stream trickling through the woods and the smell of your girlfriend's freshly shampooed hair . . .

Sorry. I got distracted. What was I saying?

Right . . . the satyr god. His music evoked everything good and beautiful. When Typhoeus got close, he heard the sweet song floating in the air, and he stopped in utter confusion.

'That doesn't sound like screaming,' the giant muttered to himself. 'It's not an explosion, either. What *is* that?'

Safe to say that they didn't have a lot of music in Tartarus, and if they did it was more along the lines of funeral dirges and death metal.

Typhoeus finally spotted the satyr god kicking back in the meadow, playing his pipes. Typhoeus could've stomped him flat, obviously, but Aegipan looked completely unconcerned.

Typhoeus was baffled. He knelt down to take a closer look at the satyr. For a few moments, the world was silent except for the burning wake of destruction behind the giant, and the sweet music of the panpipes.

The storm giant had never heard anything so beautiful. It certainly was better than his she-monster wife's nagging voice and the crying of his monstrous children.

Without even meaning to, Typhoeus heaved a deep contented sigh, which was so powerful it parted Aegipan's hair and disturbed his song.

The satyr god finally looked up, but he didn't seem scared.

(In fact, Aegipan *was* terrified, but he hid it well, possibly because he knew Hermes was standing by, ready for a quick extraction if things went bad.)

'Oh, hello,' said Aegipan. 'I didn't notice you.'

Typhoeus tilted his massive head. 'I am as tall as the sky, shrouded in darkness and I have been destroying the world. How did you not notice me?'

'I guess I was busy with my music.' Aegipan started playing again. Immediately Typhoeus felt his massive heart lift with joy that was almost better than when he contemplated destroying the gods.

'I like your music,' Typhoeus decided. 'I may not kill you.'

'Thank you,' Aegipan said calmly, and went back to playing.

'When I destroy the gods, I will take over Mount Olympus. I will make you my court musician so you can perform for me.'

Aegipan just kept playing his soft happy song.

'I will need good music,' Typhoeus decided. 'You can write a great ballad about me – a song of how I conquered the world!'

Aegipan stopped and suddenly looked sad. 'Hmm . . . if only . . . no. No, it's impossible.'

'What?' Typhoeus boomed.

It was really hard for Aegipan to remember the plan and stay calm with a massive storm giant looming over him, the hundreds of snake-head fingers dripping poison and glaring at him with red eyes.

Hermes is nearby, Aegipan reminded himself. *I can do this.*

'Well, I would love to write a song about you,' Aegipan said. 'But such a majestic tune shouldn't be played on panpipes. I would need a harp.'

'You can have any harp in the world,' Typhoeus promised.

'Very gracious, my lord,' Aegipan said, 'but it would need strings made from some incredibly tough sinew . . . *much* stronger than cow or horse guts. Otherwise, the strings would burst when I tried to play a song about your power and majesty. No mortal instrument could withstand such a song!'

This made perfect sense to Typhoeus. Then he had a thought.

'I know just the thing!' Typhoeus set his pack on the ground and dug out Zeus's tendons. 'You may use these to make your harp.'

'Oh, that's perfect!' Aegipan said, though he really wanted to scream, *That's disgusting!* 'As soon as you conquer the universe, I will make a harp worthy of your song.' Aegipan lifted his panpipes and played a few notes of a soft sleepy lullaby. 'But that must be incredibly hard work, conquering the world, even for an incomparable being such as yourself.'

Aegipan played a little more, invoking a lazy afternoon, the cool shade of a tree by a brook, the gentle swinging of a comfortable hammock. Typhoeus's eyes began to get heavy.

'Yes . . . tiring work,' Typhoeus agreed. 'Nobody appreciates how I labour!' He sat down, shaking the mountains. 'Destroying cities. Poisoning oceans. Fighting with the moon. It's exhausting!'

'Yes, my lord,' Aegipan said. 'If you'd like, I will play you some music while you rest for a moment, before your tiring climb to victory on Mount Olympus.'

'Hmm. Music.' Typhoeus's eyelids drooped. 'Perhaps just a short . . . Zzzzzz.'

His massive head slumped against his chest, and the storm giant began to snore. Aegipan played his sweetest lullaby to keep the giant dreaming happily.

Meanwhile, Hermes sneaked out and took the sinews, then stealthily dug around in Typhoeus's man purse until he found Zeus's lightning bolts. He nodded at Aegipan, like, *Keep playing!*, then flew off to Zeus's cave.

It was messy work, sticking tendons back into the sky god's arms and legs, using careful zaps from a lightning bolt to reattach everything. A couple of times Hermes put the tendons on backwards. When Zeus tried to move his arm, he slapped himself in the back of the head.

'Sorry!' Hermes said. 'I can fix that!'

Finally Zeus was back to normal. Being an immortal god, he healed fast; and, once he held his lightning bolts again, anger surged through him, making him feel stronger than ever.

'Time for payback,' he grumbled.

'What can I do?' Hermes asked.

'Stay out of the way,' Zeus said.

'I can do that.'

Zeus marched from the cave and grew in size until he was almost half as tall as Typhoeus – which was *huge* for a god. As soon as Hermes plucked up Aegipan and flew him to safety, Zeus yelled, 'WAKE UP!'

He slammed Typhoeus in the face with a thunderbolt, which was kind of like having a star go supernova right up your nostrils.

Typhoeus fell flat on the ground, but Zeus blasted him again. The giant staggered, trying to rise. He was still half asleep, dazed and confused and wondering what had happened to the nice satyr with the pretty music. Zeus was hitting him with lightning . . . but that was impossible, wasn't it?

BLAM!

KA-BOOM!

The giant went into full retreat. Lightning crackled around him and blew the snakes right off his fingers, shredding his cloud of darkness and blinding him over and over.

Before Typhoeus could recover, he stumbled into the sea. Zeus ripped a mountain from the earth and held it over his head.

'EAT ETNA!' Zeus bellowed. (Because that was the name of the mountain.)

He smashed Typhoeus under the weight of Mount Etna, and the storm giant has been trapped there ever since, rumbling beneath megatons of rock and occasionally causing volcanic explosions.

So that's how Zeus saved the universe, with a little assistance from Hermes and Aegipan. I'm not sure if Hermes got a reward, but Aegipan was given a constellation to honour his bravery. It's in the shape of a goat with a fish's tail, to commemorate the form he took when he escaped Typhoeus. Later on, that constellation became a zodiac symbol. We call it Capricorn.

And finally, hooray, I can stop talking about Zeus.

The bad news: it's time to talk about a goddess who dislikes my dad and isn't very fond of me, either. But I'll try to be fair, because, after all, she's my girlfriend Annabeth's mom – good old crafty, scary-smart Athena.

ATHENA ADOPTS A HANDKERCHIEF

S O ABOUT A MILLION PAGES AGO, I mentioned Zeus's first wife, the Titan Metis. Remember her? Neither did I. I had to go back and look. All these names: Metis and Thetis and Themis and Feta Cheese – I get a headache trying to keep them straight.

Anyway, here's a recap:

Last week on *The Real Gods of Olympus*: Metis was pregnant with Zeus's child. She had a prophecy that the child would be a girl, but if Metis and Zeus had *another* child after that it would be a boy who would grow up to take Zeus's place. Hearing this, Zeus did the natural thing. He panicked and swallowed his pregnant wife whole.

Dun-dun!

What happened next?

Well, immortals can't die, even when they're ingested by

other immortals, so Metis gave birth to her daughter right there in Zeus's gut.

(Feel free to get sick now. Or you can wait. It gets worse . . .)

Metis eventually faded into pure thought, since she was the Titan of deep thoughts anyway. She became nothing more than a nagging voice in the back of Zeus's mind.

As for her daughter, she grew up in Zeus's body, the same way the earlier Olympians had grown up in Kronos's belly. Once the child was an adult (a small, super-compressed, very uncomfortable adult) she started looking for a way to escape into the world. None of the options seemed good. If she erupted from Zeus's mouth, everyone would laugh at her and say she had been vomited. That was undignified. If she followed Zeus's digestive tract the other way – Nope! That was even grosser. She was a strong young goddess, so she might have been able to break out of Zeus's chest, but then everybody would think she was one of the monsters from the *Alien* movies and, again, that was not the kind of entrance she was looking for.

Finally she had an idea. She dissolved into pure thought – a little trick her mother, Metis, had taught her – and travelled up Zeus's spinal cord straight into his brain, where she re-formed. She started kicking and hammering and screaming inside Zeus's skull, making as much racket as she could. (Maybe she had a lot of room to move around in there because Zeus's brain was so small. Don't tell him I said that.)

As you can imagine, this gave Zeus a splitting headache.

He couldn't sleep all night with the pounding in his skull. The next morning, he stumbled into breakfast and tried to eat, but he kept wincing, screaming and pounding his fork on the table, yelling, 'STOP IT! STOP IT!'

Hera and Demeter exchanged worried looks.

'Uh, my husband?' Hera asked. 'Everything . . . okay?'

'Headache!' Zeus bellowed. 'Bad, bad headache!'

As if to prove his point, the lord of the universe slammed his face into his pancakes, which demolished the pancakes and the plate and put a crack in the table, but did nothing for his headache.

'Aspirin?' Apollo suggested. (He was the god of healing.)

'Nice cup of tea?' Hestia suggested.

'I could split your skull open,' offered Hephaestus, the blacksmith god.

'Hephaestus!' Hera cried. 'Don't talk to your father that way!'

'What?' Hephaestus demanded. 'Clearly he's got a problem in there. I could open up the hood and take a look. Might relieve the pressure. Besides, he's immortal. It won't kill him.'

'No, thanks . . .' Zeus grimaced. 'I . . .' Suddenly red spots danced before Zeus's eyes. Pain racked his body, and a voice in his head screamed, *LET ME OUT! LET ME OUT!*

Zeus fell from his chair, writhing in agony. 'Cut my skull!' he wailed. 'Get it out of me!'

The other gods turned pale with fear. Even Apollo froze, and he had, like, a dozen Boy Scout badges in first aid.

Hephaestus rose from his seat. 'Right. I'll get my awl.' (Which was basically an industrial-strength ice pick for making holes in thick surfaces, like metal, or gods' heads.) 'The rest of you, get Zeus on his throne and hold him down.'

The Olympians prepped for emergency brain surgery. They dragged Zeus to his throne and held him steady while Hephaestus retrieved his tools. The blacksmith god wasted no time. He marched up to Zeus, set the point of the awl in the middle of the sky god's forehead, raised his hammer and *BANG!*

After that, they called him One-Hit Hephaestus.

He used enough force to penetrate the skull without turning Zeus into a god-kebab. From the awl point to the bridge of Zeus's nose, a fissure spread – just wide enough for Athena to squeeze her way out.

She sprang from Zeus's forehead and, right in front of their eyes, grew until she was a fully formed adult goddess, dressed in grey robes and battle armour, wearing a bronze helmet and holding a spear and shield.

I'm not sure where she got the outfit. Maybe Athena magically created it, or maybe Zeus ate clothing and weaponry for snacks. At any rate, the goddess made quite an entrance.

'Hello, everyone,' she said calmly. 'I am Athena, goddess of warfare and wisdom.'

Demeter passed out. Hera looked scandalized, since her husband had just given birth to a child from his own forehead, and Hera was fairly certain Athena wasn't *her* daughter.

Ares the war god said, 'You can't be in charge of war! That's my job!'

'I said warfare and *wisdom*,' Athena explained. 'I'll oversee the sort of combat that requires planning, craftiness and high intelligence. You can still be in charge of the stupid, bloody, "manly man" aspects of war.'

'Oh, all right,' said Ares. Then he frowned. 'Wait . . . *what?*'

Hephaestus sewed up the crack in Zeus's head. Despite the misgivings of the other gods, Zeus insisted that they welcome his daughter Athena into their ranks. That's how she became one of the Olympians.

Like you heard, she was the goddess of wisdom, which included good advice and useful skills. She gave the Greeks the olive tree, but she also taught them about calculating numbers, weaving cloth, using oxen to pull their ploughs, flossing after every meal and a bunch of other helpful tips.

As the goddess of warfare, she was more about playing defence than offence. She didn't *enjoy* combat, but she knew that sometimes it was necessary. She always tried to win through good strategy and sneaky tricks. She tried to minimize casualties, whereas Ares loved violence and liked nothing better than a battlefield littered with mangled corpses. (Yeah, he is a sweetheart, that guy.)

Athena's sacred plant was the olive tree, since that was her big gift to the Athenians. Her sacred animals were the owl and the snake. Supposedly, the owl was a symbol of wisdom from the heavens. The snake symbolized wisdom from the earth. Me, I never understood that. If owls were so wise, why would they go around asking *Who?* all the time, like they couldn't remember their own names? Snakes have never struck me as very smart, either, but apparently the Greeks thought that when snakes hissed they were whispering important secrets. *Yeah, that's right, Mr Greek Dude. Hold that rattlesnake a little closer to your ear. He's got something to tell you.*

Athena is easy to spot in the old Greek statues and paintings. She pretty much always wears the same thing. Her helmet is decorated with rams, horses, griffons and sphinxes, and it has a big fancy Mohawk-type plume on the top. She usually carries her shield and spear, and wears a sleeveless Spartan-style dress with a magic cloak called the Aegis draped over her shoulders. According to the legends, the cloak is lined with snakeskin and is pinned with the bronzed head of Medusa, kind of like a corsage. Sometimes you'll hear the Aegis described as the goddess's shield rather than her cloak. I guess nobody has ever looked closely enough to tell for sure which is right, because with the head of the Medusa there . . . well, the whole point of that thing is to make you run away screaming.

In a lot of stories, Athena gives the Aegis to Zeus as a present, so it's technically *his*, but she borrows it from time to time, like, *Hey, Dad, can I borrow the severed head of Medusa tonight? I'm going out with my friends.*

Okay, honey, just bring it back by midnight, and don't petrify anyone.

One of the biggest mysteries about Athena is why she's called *Pallas Athena*. For the longest time, I thought people were saying Palace Athena, like it was a hotel in Vegas, or maybe Athena's secret lair.

Even the Greeks couldn't agree on why their favourite goddess had the nickname *Pallas*, but here's the way *I* heard it.

When Athena was a young goddess, fresh out of Zeus's forehead, her dad sent her to live with the nymphs of Lake Tritones in Libya on the North African coast.

'You'll like them,' Zeus promised. 'They're warlike women, just like you. They might even teach you a few combat tricks!'

'I doubt that,' Athena said. 'Why are you sending me away?'

Zeus tried for a smile, which wasn't easy, since his forehead still hurt. 'Look, my little war-muffin –'

'Don't call me that!'

'You've been stuck inside my guts your whole life,' Zeus said. 'This'll give you a chance to learn about the wide world.

231

And it'll give the other Olympians time to get used to the idea of you being on the gods' council. Honestly, you're a little intimidating to them. You're smart *and* powerful.'

Athena was flattered, so she agreed to spend some time in Africa.

She loved it there, just as Zeus had predicted. The nymphs of Lake Tritones were excellent fighters and athletes, maybe because they lived in such a harsh environment. Athena learned all sorts of super-secret ninja-nymph combat techniques. The nymphs thought Athena was the best thing since sliced ambrosia.

Her dearest friend was Pallas, the only nymph who could occasionally beat Athena in hand-to-hand combat. They shared the same taste in armour and weapons. They had the same sense of humour. They thought so much alike they could finish each other's sentences. In no time, they became BFFs.

Then one day Athena and Pallas were sparring by the lakeside when Zeus happened to look down from the sky to see how Athena was doing.

Zeus was shocked. Athena and Pallas fought with such speed and intensity that Zeus couldn't believe it was a mock combat. Athena looked like she was about to be killed! (And, yeah, I know she was immortal so she couldn't actually be killed, but Zeus was an overprotective dad. In the heat of the moment, he forgot.)

Pallas thrust her javelin at Athena's chest and Zeus over-reacted. He appeared in the sky right behind Athena and held up the Aegis (which he was keeping at the time) so Pallas couldn't help but see it.

The bronzed face of Medusa startled the nymph. Athena

knocked aside her friend's javelin and counterattacked, stabbing her spear right at Pallas's gut.

Normally, Pallas would've had no trouble dodging. Athena expected Pallas to move.

But this time, Pallas was too slow. Athena's spear went straight through the nymph's stomach and out the other side. Pallas crumpled to the ground.

Nymphs are magical creatures. They can live a long time and withstand a lot, maybe even the sight of Medusa, but they aren't immortal. If you impale a nymph with a spear, she will die.

Pallas died.

Athena fell to her knees, sobbing in shock and horror. She cradled her poor friend's lifeless body and glared at Zeus, still hovering in the air with the Aegis.

'DAD!' Athena screamed. 'WHY?'

Looking in his daughter's stormy grey eyes, Zeus felt almost as scared as he had when he'd faced the giant Typhoeus. 'I thought . . . I didn't mean to . . . Oops.'

He disappeared and fled back to Olympus.

Athena was miserable in her grief. Her friend's body dissolved back into the waters of Lake Tritones, the way water nymphs often do, but Athena decided to honour Pallas with a sacred monument. The goddess built a wooden replica of Pallas and painted it with such skill that it looked almost lifelike. Then Athena cut off a small section of the Aegis cloak (which, being god-size, was pretty huge) and draped it over the shoulders of the replica Pallas.

The statue became an important artefact. Eventually it ended up in the city of Troy, where it stood in a special shrine called the Palladium, meaning *the place of Pallas*. Women could go there and claim sanctuary from Athena. No one would be allowed to harm them. Men, on the other hand, weren't even allowed to look at the statue. The punishment for doing so was death.

The statue of Pallas looked so much like Athena that people began to call it the Pallas/Athena. Then people got confused and started calling the *goddess* Pallas Athena.

Athena was fine with that. In a way, by taking her friend's name, the goddess was keeping Pallas's memory alive.

So feel free to call her Pallas Athena, but don't ask her if you can book a room at the Palace Athena. I can tell you from personal experience, she doesn't think that's funny.

Come to think of it . . . Athena doesn't have a great sense of humour in general.

The way she dealt with Arachne, for instance? *Harsh.*

Arachne started life with no advantages at all. She lived in a kingdom called Lydia, which was in the country we now call Turkey. It was nothing special, sort of the South Dakota of Ancient Greece. (Sorry, South Dakota.) Arachne's parents were lower-class wool dyers, which meant they spent all day stirring bolts of cloth in buckets of stinky, steaming purple soup – kind of the equivalent of flipping burgers at McDonald's.

They died when Arachne was young, leaving her with no friends, family or money. Yet Arachne became the most famous girl in the kingdom because of pure skill. She could weave like nobody's business.

I know, you're thinking, *Wow. Weaving. South Dakota is starting to sound exciting.*

But, dude, *you* try weaving. It's hard! I mean have you ever looked at the fabric of your shirt up close? Next time you're in a boring chemistry lecture, check it out. The cloth is made of threads – millions of them going up and down, back and forth. Somebody had to take the material, like wool or cotton or whatever, brush it out so all the fibres go in the same direction, then spin it and twist it into those tiny little threads. Then they had to line up a zillion sideways threads, all parallel to each other like guitar strings, and weave the up-and-down threads into them.

Sure, now we've got machines to do that. But imagine, back in the day, doing it all by hand. Every square inch of cloth took hours and hours to make. Most people could only afford one shirt and one pair of trousers, because they were so freaking hard to make. Curtains or sheets? Forget about it!

And that's if you just made it one colour, like white. What if you wanted a pattern? Then you had to plan out which threads to dye what colour and you had to get them all in exactly the right place, like a massive puzzle. With my ADHD, I could never do that.

Weaving was the only way to get things made out of cloth, so, unless you wanted to run around naked all the time, you'd better find yourself a good weaver.

Arachne made it look easy. She could make you a Hawaiian shirt with pictures of flowers and frogs and coconuts woven into the fabric, and she could do it in about five minutes. She could make curtains with silver and blue thread so when the fabric rustled it looked like actual clouds moving across a blue sky. Her favourite thing was making tapestries – which were big pieces of fabric art that you could hang on your walls. They were only for decoration, and they were so hard for most weavers to make that nobody but kings and pro basketball players could afford them, but Arachne made them for fun and handed them out like party favours.

That made her popular and *very* famous.

Pretty soon the local folks were gathering at Arachne's hut every day to watch her work. Even the nymphs left their woods and their streams to gawk at her weaving, because her tapestries were more beautiful than nature.

Arachne's hands seemed to fly. She picked up a tuft of wool, spun it into thread, dyed it whatever colour she wanted and looped it on the frame of her loom in less than a second. When she had a whole row of strands going up and down, she attached the sideways thread to a long piece of wood called a shuttle, which was kind of like a giant sewing needle. She slid the shuttle back and forth as fast as a ball in a tennis game, weaving the threads together into a solid piece of cloth and, because she'd planned out her colours so perfectly, a picture appeared in the cloth as if by magic.

Shuttle, shuttle, shuttle, shuttle: WHAM!

Suddenly you were looking at an ocean scene woven from cloth, but so realistic that the waves seemed to break on the beach. The water glittered in blue and green metallic thread. The woven people on the shore were so carefully crafted you could make out the expressions on their faces. If you held a magnifying glass up to the sand dunes, you could pick out each individual grain of sand. Arachne had basically invented high-definition weaving.

One of the nymphs gasped. 'Arachne, you are *amazing!*'

'Thanks.' Arachne allowed herself a smug smile as she prepared to weave her next masterpiece.

'Athena herself must have taught you weaving!' the nymph said.

Now, this was a huge compliment. Arachne should've just nodded, said thank you, and let it go.

But Arachne was too proud of her own work. She had no use for the gods. What had they ever done for her? Arachne had built herself up from *nothing*. Her parents had died and left her penniless. She'd never had a bit of good luck.

'Athena?' Arachne snorted. 'I taught *myself* how to weave.'

The crowd shuffled nervously.

'But, surely,' one man said, 'you should thank Athena for your talent, since the goddess invented weaving. Without her –'

'No tapestry for you!' Arachne hit the man in the face with a ball of yarn. 'Weaving is *my* thing. If Athena is so great, she can come down here and test her skills against mine. We'll see who gets schooled.'

You can guess what happened. Athena heard about this challenge. When you're a goddess, you really can't let somebody get away with calling you out like that.

The next day, Athena descended to the earth, but, rather than come in with spears blazing, she decided to visit Arachne in stealth mode and check things out. Athena was careful that way. She liked to get her facts straight, and she believed in giving people a second chance. After all, she'd accidentally killed her own best friend Pallas. She knew that mistakes happened.

She took the shape of a feeble old woman and hobbled over to Arachne's hut, joining the crowd that had gathered to watch the weaver do her thing.

The mortal was good. No doubt about it. Arachne wove scenes of mountains and waterfalls, cities shimmering in the afternoon heat, animals prowling in the forests, and sea monsters so terrifying they looked ready to leap out of the fabric and attack. Arachne churned out the tapestries with inhuman speed, flinging them into the crowd as prizes, firing them from her T-shirt cannon, making all the spectators happy with valuable parting gifts.

The girl didn't seem greedy. She just wanted to share her work with the world.

Athena respected that. This mortal Arachne hadn't come from a rich family or gone to a fancy school. She had no advantages, and she'd made something of herself from skill alone. Athena decided to give Arachne the benefit of the doubt.

The goddess pushed her way through the crowd and began to speak to Arachne as the young girl worked.

'You know, dearie,' said Old Lady Athena, 'I may be old, but I've gained some wisdom with my age. Would you accept some advice?'

Arachne just grunted. She was busy with her weaving and didn't want any words of wisdom, but she said nothing.

'You're very talented,' Athena continued. 'There's absolutely no harm in gaining the praise of other humans. You've earned it! But I hope you've given the goddess Athena proper credit for your talent. She invented weaving, after all, and she grants talent to mortals like you.'

Arachne stopped weaving and glared at the old lady. 'Nobody *granted* me anything, Grandma. Maybe your eyes have gone bad, but look at this tapestry. *I* made this. I don't need to thank anyone else for my hard work!'

Athena tried to keep her cool. 'You are proud. I see that. And rightly so. But you are dishonouring the goddess. If I were you, I would ask her forgiveness right now. I'm sure she would grant it to you. She is merciful to all who –'

'Get lost, Grandma!' Arachne snapped. 'Save your advice for your daughters and stepdaughters. I don't need it. If you love Athena so much, go tell her to come find me and we'll see who owns the art of weaving!'

That was it.

Athena's disguise burned away in a burst of light. The goddess stood before the crowd, her shield and spear gleaming. 'Athena has come,' she said. 'And she accepts your challenge.'

Pro tip: if you're a mortal and a goddess appears right next to you, and if you want to survive the next few minutes, the proper thing to do is to fall on your face and grovel.

The crowd did exactly that, but Arachne had guts. Of course she was terrified inside. Her face went pale, then flushed red, then turned pale again. But she managed to stand and glare at the goddess. 'Fine. Let's see what you've got, old lady!'

'Ooooo,' said the crowd.

'What *I've* got?' Athena shot back. 'The little girl from Lydia's going to show me how to weave? When I get through, this crowd's going to be using your tapestries for toilet paper!'

'Burn!' said the crowd.

'Oh, yeah?' Arachne sneered. 'Must've been *dark* inside your daddy's head if you think you can weave better than me. Zeus probably swallowed your mama just to keep you from getting born and *embarrassing* yourself.'

'Snap!' the crowd yelled.

'Oh, yeah?' Athena growled. 'Well, *your* mama . . .' The goddess took a deep breath. 'You know what? That's enough trash talk. It's time to weave. One tapestry each. Winner gets bragging rights.'

'Uh-huh.' Arachne put her fists on his hips. 'And who decides the winner. *You?*'

'Yes,' Athena said simply. 'On the River Styx, I promise a fair judgement. Unless you'd like these mortals to decide between us.'

Arachne looked at the terrified mortals and realized she was in a hopeless situation. Obviously the mortals would decide for Athena no matter how good Arachne's weaving was. They wouldn't want to get zapped into ashes or turned into warthogs for angering the goddess. Arachne didn't believe for a minute that Athena would be fair, but maybe gods really *did* have to keep their promises if they swore on the River Styx.

Arachne decided she had no choice, so she might as well go out in style. 'Bring it on, Athena. You want to borrow my loom, or do you need a special one with training wheels?'

Athena clenched her teeth. 'I've got my own loom. Thanks.'

The goddess snapped her fingers. A glowing loom appeared right next to Arachne's. The goddess and the mortal both sat down and furiously began to work. The crowd chanted, 'WEAVE! WEAVE!' and pumped their fists in the air.

The Lydians totally should have sold advertising and got corporate sponsors, because it would've been the highest-rated weaving smackdown in Ancient Greek television history.

As it turned out, Athena and Arachne's trash talk continued – but in the language of tapestries. Athena wove a scene of the gods in all their glory, seated in the council hall of Mount Olympus, as if to say, *We are the best. Don't bother with the rest.* She depicted the temples on the Acropolis of Athens to show how wise mortals *should* honour the gods.

Then, for good measure, Athena wove little warnings into

the cloth. If you looked closely, you could see all the different famous mortals who had dared to compare themselves to the gods and had been turned into animals or flattened into roadkill.

Meanwhile, Arachne wove a different story. She depicted every ridiculous and horrible thing that the gods had ever done. She showed Zeus turning into a bull to kidnap the princess Europa. She showed Poseidon as a stallion chasing Demeter as a white mare, and then poor Medusa, an innocent girl wooed by Poseidon and turned into a hideous monster by Athena. She made the gods look stupid, and evil, childish, and no good for mortals . . . and, I'm sorry to say, she had a lot of material to choose from.

When the tapestries were done, the crowd was absolutely silent, because both were amazing. Athena's was majestic and breathtaking and made you feel the power of the Olympian gods. Arachne's was the most scathing critique of the gods ever created, and it made you want to laugh and cry and get angry all at the same time – but it was still beautiful.

Athena looked back and forth between the tapestries, trying to judge which one was better.

Some stories will tell you that Athena won the contest, but that's not true. In fact, Athena was forced to admit that the two tapestries were exactly equal in quality.

'It's a tie,' she said grudgingly. 'Your skill, your technique, your use of colour . . . As much as I want to, I can't find any fault.'

Arachne tried to stand up tall, but the work had taken something out of her. Her hands hurt. Her back was sore and she stooped from the effort. 'What now, then? A rematch? Unless you're scared . . .'

Athena finally lost her temper. She took the shuttle out of

her loom — a length of wood like a square baseball bat. 'Now, I beat the crud out of you for insulting the gods!'

WHACK! WHACK! WHACK!

The goddess hit Arachne over the head as the mortal weaver scuttled around, trying to hide. At first, the crowd was horrified. Then they did what humans often do when they're frightened and nervous and somebody *else* is getting a beating . . . They began to laugh and make fun of Arachne.

'Get her, Athena!' one cried.

'Yeah, who's the boss now, little girl?' said another.

The same mortals who had gazed in wonder at Arachne's work and had stood around her hut for days hoping for free tapestries now turned against her, calling her names and jeering as Athena hit her.

Cruel? You bet. But, if you ask me, that mob painted a picture of humans that's just as true and just as scathing as Arachne's tapestry about the gods.

Finally Athena's anger subsided. She turned and saw all the mortals laughing and pointing at Arachne, and Athena realized maybe she'd gone too far with the punishment.

'Enough!' the goddess yelled at the crowd. 'Would you turn on one of your own people so quickly? At least Arachne had some talent! What makes *you* people so special?'

While Athena was occupied chewing out the crowd, Arachne struggled to her feet. Every part of her body hurt, but most of the damage was to her pride. Weaving was her only joy, and Athena had taken that away. Arachne would never be able to take pleasure in her work again. The townspeople she'd tried so hard to please had turned against her, too. Her eyes stung with shame and hatred and self-pity.

She rushed to the loom and gathered up a thick row of threads — enough to form a makeshift rope. She tied a noose and put it around her neck, then looped the other end of the rope over the rafter beam above her.

By the time Athena and the crowd noticed, Arachne was hanging from the ceiling, trying to kill herself.

'Foolish girl,' Athena said. She was overcome with pity, but she also hated suicide. It was a cowardly act. 'I will not let you die. You will live on and weave forever.'

She changed Arachne into a spider, and, from then on, Arachne and her children have continued to weave webs. Spiders hate Athena, and Athena hates them right back. But spiders also hate humans, because Arachne never forgot her shame and her anger at being ridiculed.

So what's the moral of the story? The old preachy storytellers will claim: *Don't compare yourself to the gods, because you can't be that good.* But that's not true.

Arachne *was* that good.

Maybe the lesson is: *Know when to brag and when to keep your mouth shut.* Or: *Sometimes life isn't fair, even if you are as gifted as Athena.* Or maybe: *Don't give away free tapestries.*

I'll let you decide.

Athena tore up the tapestries from that contest, as beautiful as they were. Because, honestly, I don't think anybody came away from that encounter looking very good.

You may be getting the idea that Athena . . . well, how to put this delicately? She might've been the wisdom goddess, but she didn't always make the smartest choices.

For one thing, she was self-conscious. For instance, the

way she invented the flute. She was walking in the woods near Athens one day when she heard a nest of snakes hissing, and she thought, Huh, a bunch of long tubular things that make noise. And just like that she got the idea for a new musical instrument. She hollowed out a reed, made some holes in it, blew on one end, and beautiful music came out.

At first she was really proud of her flute. She wasn't even the goddess of music and here she'd invented a cool new sound. She took her flute up to Olympus, eager to show the other gods, but, as soon as she started playing, the other goddesses started giggling and whispering to each other.

Athena stopped mid-song. 'What's so funny?'

'Nothing,' said Aphrodite, the goddess of love.

'The music is lovely, my dear,' Hera said, trying not to laugh.

Now, honestly, the other goddesses were intimidated by Athena, because she was so smart and strong. Naturally, they made fun of her behind her back and tried to shut her out of the clique. Athena disliked the other goddesses. She thought most of them were silly and shallow. But she also wanted to fit in and it made her mad when they teased her.

'Why are you laughing?' Athena demanded.

'Well . . .' Demeter suppressed a smile. 'It's just that when you play the flute, your eyes cross and your cheeks puff out, and you make this funny shape with your mouth.'

'Like this . . .' Aphrodite demonstrated, doing her best imitation of Athena's flute face, which looked sort of like a constipated duck's.

The gods and goddesses burst out laughing. Athena fled in humiliation. You would think, being the goddess of wisdom, she'd be able to laugh it off and not let it get under her skin, but she felt so burned she threw the flute away, letting it fall to the earth.

She even issued a curse. 'Whoever dares play *that* thing again,' she muttered to herself, 'let the *worst* fortune befall him!'

Eventually the flute would get picked up, but that's a story for later . . .

After that, Athena became even more self-conscious about her looks. As a warrior goddess, she'd already decided that she would never get married. She didn't want any man claiming to be her master, and she didn't have time for that silly love nonsense Aphrodite was always gossiping about.

Because of this, Athena was very sensitive about her privacy. One night she decided to go to a swimming hole in central Greece, just to relax. She bathed naked, and while she was washing off in the waterfall, enjoying the peace and quiet, she heard this choking, whimpering sound.

She looked over at the riverbank and saw this old mortal dude just staring at her with his jaw hanging open and his eyes as big as drachmas.

Athena screamed.

The dude screamed.

Athena splashed water in his eyes and yelled, 'Blindness!' Instantly, the man lost his sight forever. His eyes turned pure white. He stumbled backwards, bumped into a tree and fell on his butt.

'M-m-mistress!' he wailed. 'I – I'm so sorry! I didn't –'

'Who are you?' Athena demanded.

The poor guy explained that his name was Teiresias. He had just been out for a walk from the nearest city, Thebes. He had no idea Athena was there, and he was really, really sorry.

Athena's anger cooled, because obviously the man was telling the truth.

'You must remain blind,' she said, 'because no man may see me nude without being punished.'

Teiresias gulped. 'Um . . . okay . . .'

'However,' Athena continued, 'since this was an accident, I will compensate you for your blindness by giving you other gifts.'

'Like . . . another set of eyes?' Teiresias asked.

Athena managed a smile. 'Sort of. From now on, you will be able to understand the language of birds. I will give you a staff, and with the help of the birds you will be able to walk almost as if you had your own sight.'

I'm not sure how that worked, exactly. I would've been worried that the birds would play jokes on me, like, *A little further. Turn left. Now, run!* And I'd pitch over a cliff, or ram headfirst into a brick wall. But apparently the arrangement worked out okay for Teiresias, and the birds took care of him. It also shows how Athena could calm down and moderate her punishments.

The one thing she couldn't stand, however, were guys flirting with her. Which brings us to the story of her and Hephaestus. Okay, deep breath, because things are about to get *weird*.

So, Hephaestus was the crippled blacksmith god. More on him later.

Right now, all you need to know is that ever since he helped Athena get out of Zeus's forehead Hephaestus had had a crush on her. This made sense, because they were both into crafts and tools. They were both deep thinkers and enjoyed solving mechanical problems.

The problem was that Athena hated romance and never even wanted to hold hands with a guy, much less *marry* one. Even if Hephaestus had been handsome, Athena would have turned him down. But Hephaestus was most definitely ugly: Grade-A Industrial-Strength Ugly with Extra Gross.

He tried in his own way to flirt with her, like, *Hey, baby, want to see my hammer collection?* And stuff like that.

Athena power-walked away from him, but Hephaestus limped after her. Athena didn't want to scream and run, because she wasn't a helpless mortal girl, or one of those silly 'pink princess' goddesses who fainted and fluttered their eyelashes or whatever. She was the goddess of war!

She just kept moving away from Hephaestus, snapping at him to leave her alone. Finally the poor guy was sweating and panting like crazy, because it wasn't easy for him to move on his crippled legs. He flung himself at Athena, wrapping his arms around her waist.

'Please,' he begged. 'You're the perfect woman for me!'

He buried his face in her skirt and sobbed and snivelled, and some of his godly sweat and snot rubbed off on her bare leg where the skirt was parted, and Athena was like, 'Gross!'

She kicked Hephaestus away and snatched up the nearest piece of cloth she could find — maybe a handkerchief or a napkin or something. She wiped the godly moisture off her leg and tossed the gross piece of cloth off Olympus, where it fluttered slowly down to the earth.

Then she ran away.

That should've been the end of the story, but something

weird happened to that piece of cloth. It contained the essence of both Athena and Hephaestus, and somehow, when it hit the earth, it grew into a mortal baby boy.

Up on Olympus, Athena heard the baby crying. She tried to ignore it, but, to her surprise, motherly instinct stirred inside her. She flew down to the earth and picked up the child. She understood how he had been born and, though the whole thing was still totally disgusting to her, she couldn't blame the little boy.

'I suppose technically you are my son,' she decided, 'even though I am still a maiden goddess. I will claim you as my own, and name you Erikthonius.'

(She gets one chance to name a kid and *that's* what she picks? Don't ask me.)

'If I'm going to raise you,' she continued, 'I should first make you immortal. I know just the thing . . .'

She got a wooden chest and put the baby inside. Then she created a magical serpent and put it in there, too. (By the way, this is *really* not something you should try at home.) The baby boy Erikthonius fell asleep contentedly with the snake curled around him.

'There,' Athena said. 'A few days in that box, and the serpent will enhance your godly qualities. You will cease to be mortal and you'll become one of the gods!'

She closed the chest and took it to the Acropolis in Athens, which was, of course, her most sacred place. She gave the box to the daughters of Kekrops, the first king of Athens.

'Don't open this box!' she warned the princesses. 'It has to stay closed, or bad things will happen.'

The princesses promised, but after only one night they got curious. They were pretty sure they heard a baby in there, cooing and gurgling, and they were afraid the kid was in trouble.

'What kind of goddess puts a baby in a box?' one of them muttered. 'We'd better check.'

The princesses opened the box and saw the snake curled around the baby. I'm not sure why it freaked them out so badly. Maybe they saw godly light in there or something, but the girls went insane. They dropped the box and ran straight off the side of the Acropolis's cliffs, plummeting to their deaths.

As for the baby, he was fine, but the spell was broken before he could become immortal. The snake slithered away and Athena came to cradle the child. She was raging mad, but since she couldn't scold the princesses, seeing as they were dead and all, she took out her vengeance on their dad, King Kekrops. Once Erikthonius grew up, he kicked out Kekrops and took over as king of Athens. That's why the Athenian kings liked to say they were descended from Hephaestus and Athena, even though Athena was an eternal maiden.

So don't tell me Athena can't have kids, because there's the story that says otherwise. Besides, I'm dating one of Athena's daughters, and I'm pretty sure she didn't spring from a dirty handkerchief.

Hmm. Actually, I've never asked her.

Nah, forget it. I don't want to know.

YOU GOTTA LOVE APHRODITE

N O, SERIOUSLY. That's an order. See, Aphrodite had a magical belt that could make anyone fall in love with her on sight. If you saw her and she wanted you to love her, you would.

Me, I'm lucky. I've seen her, but I guess she wasn't interested in winning my praise or whatever. So I still hate her guts.

Some of you are thinking, *OMG! She's so pretty! Why do you hate her?*

Clearly, you haven't met the lady.

She was trouble from the moment she crawled out of the sea. And I mean she *literally* crawled out of the sea.

Aphrodite didn't have parents. Way back when Kronos dumped the chopped-up bits of Ouranos into the sea, the sky god's immortal blood mixed with the salt water and formed a frothy patch that solidified into a goddess.

In other words, Aphrodite was born in the wake of the first murder, which tells you something about her true nature.

After drifting through the Mediterranean for a while, looking for a good place to come ashore, she finally decided on the island of Cyprus. This was a relief to the dolphins and fish, because the floating naked goddess with the glowing aura was starting to freak them out.

Aphrodite rose from the sea and walked across the beach. Flowers blossomed at her feet. Birds gathered in the nearby branches to sing sweet songs. Little bunny rabbits and squirrels and ferrets and other critters frolicked all around her. It was like a Disney cartoon.

Describing Aphrodite is hard, because she was the most beautiful woman in creation. That could mean different things to different people. Blonde, brunette or redhead? Fair complexion or dark? Blue eyes, green eyes, brown eyes? Take your pick. Just picture the most attractive woman you can possibly imagine, and that's what she looked like. Her appearance would change to appeal to each person who gazed upon her.

That day, the three Horai, the goddesses of the seasons, happened to be meeting on Cyprus – maybe planning which products would get placed in the 'seasonal' aisle at the grocery store. I'm not sure.

They saw Aphrodite walking towards them and completely forgot everything else.

'Oh, wow, you're beautiful!' said Summer.

'I am?' asked Aphrodite, though she already knew it. She just wanted to hear them say it.

'Dazzling!' said Spring. 'We should take you to meet the Olympian gods.'

'There are other gods?' Aphrodite was amazed. 'I'm the goddess of love and beauty. What would you need other gods for?'

Autumn and Spring exchanged a wary look.

'Uh . . . a bunch of stuff,' Autumn said. 'But we should get you dressed before we take you to Olympus. Aren't you cold?'

'No,' Aphrodite said. 'Why would I cover myself?'

Autumn wanted to scream, *Because you're too freaking gorgeous and you're making the rest of us feel bad!*

Instead she said, 'If you appear like that, you'll drive the gods insane with desire. I mean . . . they will *literally* go insane.'

'Oh.' Aphrodite pouted. 'But I didn't bring a thing to wear.'

The Horai took care of that. They summoned up some magical clothing and had a fashion show. Spring offered Aphrodite an Easter Bunny costume. Autumn thought Aphrodite would look good as a Halloween witch. Those plans were vetoed. Finally Summer produced a beautiful white gossamer dress. The Horai placed a delicate golden crown on Aphrodite's head, hung gold earrings in her ears and draped a gold necklace at the base of her throat.

Aphrodite looked even *more* amazing with clothes on, which Autumn found infuriating, but the seasonal goddess forced a smile. 'Perfect! Let's get you to Olympus.'

By now you probably know enough about the Olympian gods to figure out what happened when Aphrodite showed up.

The women were immediately, like, *I hate her.*

The guys fell all over themselves, tripping on their tongues and trying not to drool.

'It would be my honour to marry you,' said Apollo, god of poetry and archery.

'No, *my* honour!' barked Ares, god of war.

'My honour!' yelled Poseidon.

'You're already married,' Zeus snapped. 'It would be *my* honour.'

'*You're* already married!' Hera protested. 'To me!'

'Curses!' said Zeus. 'Er, I mean, of *course*, dear.'

The gods argued and shoved each other and offered Aphrodite various gifts for her hand in marriage. Poseidon conveniently forgot his wife Amphitrite and promised the love goddess all the seafood she could eat, a bunch of horses and a set of his-and-hers matching tridents.

Apollo made up some bad haiku in her honour and vowed to give Aphrodite free archery lessons.

Ares offered to take her on a romantic chariot ride over the crushed lifeless bodies of his foes.

The other goddesses got disgusted. They started yelling at the men to grow up and stop acting like fools.

The entire Olympian council was on the verge of civil war. Meanwhile, Aphrodite just stood there batting her eyelashes, like, *All this fuss for little old me?* But inside she was loving it.

Finally, Hera stepped back, took a deep breath and realized that her godly family was about to unravel. Being the goddess of family life, Hera couldn't allow that, even if half the time she wanted to strangle the other gods herself.

She glanced at the far corner of the throne room, where

one god was *not* participating in the argument. He sat in the shadows, quiet and dejected, knowing he had no chance of competing for Aphrodite.

Hera smiled. She had an idea, and I can tell you from personal experience that when Hera gets an idea you should run away ASAP.

She raised her arms and yelled, 'SILENCE!'

The gods were so startled they stopped fighting.

'I have a solution,' Hera said. 'As the goddess of marriage, I am responsible for picking the best husband for our dear new friend Aphrodite. I'm sure my husband Lord Zeus will support my decision . . . with force, if necessary.'

'I will?' Zeus said. 'I mean . . . yes, dear. Of course I will!'

'Well, then?' Ares asked. 'And may I just say, Mother, that you look beautiful today. Who will marry Aphrodite?'

'My son . . .' Hera began.

Ares beamed with joy.

Then Hera pointed to the opposite side of the room. 'Hephaestus, the blacksmith god.'

Hephaestus was so surprised that he fell off his throne, his crutches clattering across the floor.

As he struggled to get up, Ares exploded: 'What?! How can *that* be married to *this*?'

He gestured to the radiant Aphrodite, who was staring in horror at the blacksmith god, with his twisted legs, his misshapen face, his stained overalls, and the remains of several meals in the whiskers of his beard.

'They're perfect together,' Hera said. 'A beautiful woman needs a hard-working, plain-spoken, no-nonsense husband to keep her grounded!'

I'm pretty sure that's the first time the word *grounded* was ever used to mean a punishment.

'Besides,' Hera continued, 'Aphrodite must get married right away, or the fighting over her will never end. We can't allow the council of the gods to be in chaos over a woman. Can we, Lord Zeus?'

'Hmm?' Zeus was distracted, studying Aphrodite's lovely arms. 'Oh! No, indeed, my dear. You're absolutely right.'

Athena stood, her grey eyes gleaming with cruel amusement. 'I think it's a brilliant idea. And I am, after all, the goddess of wisdom.'

'Yes!' Demeter chimed in. 'Aphrodite *deserves* a good husband like Hephaestus.'

The male gods stopped grumbling. They all wanted to marry Aphrodite, but they had to admit Hera was right. If any *decent* god married her, the other guys would never stop fighting about it and feeling offended. But if Aphrodite married Hephaestus . . . well, he was a joke. They couldn't be jealous of *him*.

Besides, if Aphrodite was stuck in an unhappy marriage, that opened up all sorts of possibilities for becoming her secret boyfriend.

'It's decided, then,' Zeus said. 'Hephaestus, come here!'

The blacksmith god staggered over. His face was the colour of Flamin' Hot Cheetos.

'Hephaestus, do you take this woman, et cetera?' Zeus asked.

Hephaestus cleared his throat. 'My lady Aphrodite, I know I'm not, um, very handsome . . .'

Aphrodite didn't respond. She was too busy trying to look

beautiful and revolted at the same time, which wasn't easy.

'I'm not much of a dancer.' Hephaestus's metal leg braces creaked. 'I'm not witty or charming. And I don't smell very good. But I promise to be a loving husband. I'm handy at fixing things around the house, and if you ever need a lug wrench or a power sander –'

'Urgh,' Aphrodite said, swallowing her nausea.

'Well, that's good enough for me!' Zeus said. 'I now pronounce you husband and wife!'

So Aphrodite married Hephaestus and the celebrity ship *Aphrophaestus* completely dominated Olympian tabloid news for like a thousand years.

Did they live happily ever after?

HAHAHAHAHA. No.

Aphrodite stayed away from her husband as much as possible. They never had any kids. Aphrodite had plenty of children . . . just not with Hephaestus. Immediately after getting married, she started an affair with Ares, the god of war, which became the worst kept secret on Mount Olympus.

When she wasn't busy sneaking around behind her husband's back, Aphrodite spent her time making all the other gods and mortals miserable – uh, I mean, helping them discover the joys of love!

Aphrodite took her place among the Olympians as the goddess of beauty, pleasure, sweet-talk, *telenovelas*, steamy romance novels and (of course) love. When she had to travel, she rode in a golden chariot pulled by a flock of snowy doves, though sometimes when the gods went to war Aphrodite rode with her boyfriend Ares in his war chariot and even held the reins while he was busy killing people.

She had a bunch of attendants called *erotes* – miniature winged love gods. Their leader was Eros, son of Aphrodite, who was the god of physical attraction and Aphrodite's hit man. Whenever she wanted somebody to fall madly in love, she sent Eros to shoot the poor schmuck with a magic arrow. Later on, Eros became known as Cupid. He still shows up on those cheesy Valentine's Day displays. He might sound silly, but, if Aphrodite sends him after you, it's no joke. He can make you fall in love with *anyone*.

If Aphrodite likes you, she might cause you to fall for somebody attractive and nice. If Aphrodite is angry, she might make you fall in love with the most repulsive person you know, or a toy poodle, or a telephone pole.

Aphrodite's favourite trick was to make someone fall in love with a person who didn't love them back. She thought that was the best fun ever. If you've ever had a crush on somebody who didn't notice you, that's Aphrodite's fault. I guess the goddess figured that way, more people would pray to her, like, *Oh, please, let him/her notice me! I'll sacrifice a nice box of chocolates to you, I promise!*

Actually, they didn't have chocolate in Ancient Greece, but Aphrodite was fond of apples. That was her sacred fruit, maybe because it was pretty and sweet, just like her. (Insert gagging sound here.)

She had dozens of other sacred plants and animals and stuff, some of which made sense; some not so much. The rose was one of her flowers, which is why we still use it as a romantic gift. She also liked daffodils, and . . . wait for it . . . lettuce. Yep.

That incredibly romantic roughage was considered Aphrodite's sacred salad ingredient. There's a reason for that, which we'll get to in a second. But, if some day you're tossing a Caesar salad and you start feeling lovey-dovey as you shred romaine lettuce, now you'll know why.

Aphrodite's sacred stone was the pearl, since it comes from the sea, just like Aphrodite.

Her favourite animals were the rabbit (because they have lots and lots and lots of baby bunnies!) and the goose, which you'll sometimes see pictures of Aphrodite riding sidesaddle.

Why a goose? Dunno. It must've been a *big* goose.

All I know is that if I ever saw Aphrodite riding one I'd burst out laughing. Then she'd probably curse me, and I'd end up engaged to a '72 Impala or something.

Aphrodite was a popular goddess because everyone wanted love, but she didn't always get along with mortals or her fellow gods.

For instance, one time she got jealous of Athena because everyone was praising her weaving skills.

Aphrodite didn't like it when the spotlight was on anyone except her.

'Oh, weaving is nothing,' Aphrodite said. '*I* could do that if I wanted to.'

'Really?' Athena smiled. 'Care to challenge me?'

Never heard about the great weaving contest between Athena and Aphrodite? That's because it wasn't so great. It was a disaster.

The goddess of love knew nothing about weaving. She

wasn't Athena or even Arachne. She'd never made anything with her own two hands except trouble.

While Athena wove a beautiful tapestry, Aphrodite managed to get herself wrapped in thread, with her foot tied to the stool and her head stuck in the loom.

'I don't like weaving, anyway!' she huffed as her husband Hephaestus cut her free.

From then on, Aphrodite tried not to criticize the other goddesses. In fact, she even *helped* them sometimes.

I mentioned her magical belt? Sometimes it's called a girdle, because she would wear it under her dress so guys wouldn't realize they were being bewitched. But it wasn't a girdle like one of those ugly fabric-and-steel wraps that squeeze the fat in. Aphrodite's belt was a delicate sash embroidered with scenes of courtship and romance and beautiful people doing beautiful things. (Obviously, Aphrodite didn't embroider it herself or it would've looked like a kindergarten project.)

Anyway, Hera once asked to borrow it, which took guts, considering they didn't get along too well.

'Oh, dear Aphrodite,' Hera said, 'would you do me a huge favour?'

Aphrodite smiled prettily. 'Of course, my wonderful mother-in-law! After everything you've done for me? How could I refuse?'

Hera's eye twitched. 'Great. I'd like to borrow your magical belt.'

Aphrodite leaned in close. 'Got a thing for some handsome mortal?'

'No!' Hera blushed furiously. She was the goddess of

marriage. She never cheated! She managed to calm herself. 'I mean . . . no, of course not. Zeus and I had an argument. He's being *impossible*, refusing to talk to me or even be in the same room. But if I wore your belt –'

'You would be irresistible!' Aphrodite agreed. 'Oh, dear mother-in-law, I'm *so* glad you came to me for help. I've been wanting to offer you some beauty tips for a while now, but I didn't want to overstep my bounds. It must be hard being such a matronly goddess without looking . . . *matronly*.'

Hera gritted her teeth. 'Yes, well . . . the belt?'

Aphrodite lent Hera the magic love girdle, and Hera had no trouble getting Zeus to make up with her. The way the poet Homer put it, she 'beguiled his brain'. Personally, I don't like having my brain beguiled. But, in case you're feeling bad for Zeus, don't.

Occasionally, even *he* asked Aphrodite for help, and it wasn't for anything beautiful or loving.

You remember back in the early days of mortals the Titan Prometheus gave men fire? Well, even after Zeus punished Prometheus by chaining him to the rocks and giving him a liver-eating eagle for company, the lord of the sky was still angry.

He looked around for other people to punish. Then he decided: 'You know what? I'll just punish everyone. *All* mortals will suffer for accepting the gift of fire. And I'll find some sneaky way to do it, so they won't blame me for their problems. I'll fix it so that they blame Prometheus's family . . . That'll make my revenge even sweeter!'

Turns out Prometheus had a younger brother, Epimetheus, who wasn't exactly the sharpest crayon in the box.

Right before Zeus carted Prometheus off to Torture-ville, Prometheus had warned his brother, 'Epimetheus, stay frosty. Zeus will probably try to punish you just because you're related to me. Don't accept any gifts from the gods!'

'Frosties?' Epimetheus said. 'I like Frosties.'

'You're hopeless,' his brother grumbled. 'Just be careful! I gotta go. I got this thing with a rock and an eagle . . .'

Zeus decided to send Epimetheus a booby-trapped present. If he could trick Epimetheus into opening the present, a bunch of evil spirits would escape and cause all kinds of trouble for mortals. The mortals would seek answers from the Oracle, like they always did. The Oracle would say, 'Oh, it's all Epimetheus's fault.' And Zeus would have a good laugh.

The problem was Zeus couldn't get Epimetheus to accept any gifts. Epimetheus remembered his brother's warning and refused to take packages from strangers or gods. Zeus sent Hermes to Epimetheus's house with a Candygram. No luck. Hephaestus dressed up as a cable guy and offered Epimetheus a free HDTV box with all the premium sports channels. Epimetheus turned him away.

Zeus became so exasperated he complained to the other gods. 'This guy, Epimetheus. I just want him to take a stupid present, open it and unleash misery and death on the human race! Is that too much to ask? But he's so stubborn! Any ideas?'

The gods shifted uncomfortably on their thrones.

Finally Aphrodite said, 'Lord Zeus, perhaps you should try a different approach . . . something *no* man can refuse.'

'I already tried free cable!' Zeus said. 'With the premium sports channels!'

'No, my lord.' Aphrodite batted her eyelashes. 'I mean *love*. Perhaps Epimetheus needs a wife. If you could place a wife in his household, *she* could accept the gift you wish to send. If it's all handled correctly –'

'I love this idea!' Actually Zeus hadn't heard a word she'd said. He was too busy staring at her and thinking, *Wow, she's pretty*. But all the other gods were nodding, so Zeus figured her plan must be good.

At Aphrodite's direction, the gods created the perfect woman from scratch. Hephaestus provided the clay and the technical know-how to build her body. Athena gifted her with cleverness and curiosity. Most importantly, Aphrodite instilled her with beauty and charm to make her irresistible.

They named her Pandora, which loosely translates as *all the gifts*, or *the whole package*. Some stories say Pandora was the first woman *ever*, and that before she came along all humans were male. I don't know. That sounds kind of lame and boring to me. At any rate, she was a perfect '10'. Aphrodite made sure of that. Pandora would be the gods' ultimate weapon for making mischief.

The gods led Pandora to Epimetheus's front porch, rang the doorbell and ran away giggling. When Epimetheus opened the door, he saw this beautiful woman smiling at him.

'Hi, I'm Pandora, and I love you,' said Pandora. 'Can I come in?'

'Yes,' said Epimetheus.

He totally forgot about Prometheus's warning. No way could this gorgeous lady be part of some trick!

Epimetheus and Pandora got engaged faster than you can say 'Vegas wedding'.

The gods weren't invited to the ceremony, but Aphrodite dropped off a gift. Because it was addressed to Pandora, Epimetheus couldn't refuse it.

It was a large ceramic *pithos*, a big storage jar, with a cork in the top and a large white silk bow tied around the handle.

'Oh, honey, look!' Pandora said. 'It's perfect for holding our olive oil!'

Epimetheus grunted, still suspicious. 'I wouldn't open it.'

'Your husband is right.' Aphrodite nodded earnestly. 'No, Pandora . . . the jar is just for looking at. *Never* open it. You wouldn't want to know what's inside.'

After Aphrodite left, Pandora burned with curiosity. It wasn't her fault – she was *created* to be curious. All she could think about was opening that jar.

Pandora managed to hold out for several days, but one morning, when her husband was out in the garden, she sat in front of the jar and stared at it, trying to imagine what was inside. Why would the gods send her a present and then tell her never to open it? That was just wrong!

'I have to see what's inside,' she muttered. 'Oh, this is going to be awesome!'

She pulled the cork.

It was *not* awesome.

Zeus had packed that jar with a gazillion evil spirits. They spewed out and spread across the world, bringing misery, sickness, athlete's foot, famine, bad breath and death to the human race. Suddenly being a human was a thousand times worse than it was before, and it had *never* been easy. Humans probably would've all killed themselves from despair – running off cliffs like crazy Athenian princesses – but one *good* spirit remained in the jar, maybe because Zeus had some sense of shame. Elpis, the spirit of hope, stayed with humans so they wouldn't give up completely. They could always believe that things might get better.

If you've ever wondered why humans suffer so much, it's because of that stupid jar. At which point we're supposed to say, 'Way to go, Pandora! Thanks a lot!'

Back in the old days, the writers (who were all guys) would say, 'See? This story shows you that women are troublemakers! It's all their fault!'

Epimetheus and Pandora. Adam and Eve. That blame game has been going on for a long time.

But I'm not sure why we're criticizing Pandora for being nosy, or not following orders, or whatever. She was *made* to open that jar . . . by the gods.

My real question: what was Aphrodite thinking? If she knew this whole Pandora thing would give women a bad rep for eternity, why did she go along with it? Me, I think she just didn't care about the consequences. She wanted to make Pandora beautiful. She wanted to prove that love could succeed where the other gods had failed – even if it caused a global disaster.

Way to go, Aphrodite. Thanks a lot!

To be fair, her creations didn't always turn out so bad.

Once Aphrodite took pity on this sculptor named Pygmalion, who lived on Cyprus, her favourite island. This dude wasn't interested in the local women, because they all seemed crude and rude to him. They'd go out with anybody who had money and a nice chariot. They didn't believe in true love. In fact, a lot of them didn't believe Aphrodite *existed*, and that made Pygmalion angry. He was proud of his 'hometown' goddess, even though he hadn't found his one true pairing (OTP) yet. He definitely believed there was someone perfect out there for everyone.

In his spare time, Pygmalion carved a life-size ivory statue of Aphrodite – because she was his ideal of what a woman should be.

He made the statue so beautiful that it brought tears to his eyes. As far as Pygmalion was concerned, all other women looked ugly by comparison.

Oh, why can't I find a woman like this! he thought to himself. She would be kind and gentle and loving and wonderful, just like Aphrodite!

I guess he didn't know Aphrodite's true personality very well.

When the local Feast of Aphrodite rolled around, Pygmalion went to the goddess's temple and offered a big sacrifice of roses and pearls (and probably some lettuce).

He was too ashamed to admit his *real* wish: he wanted to marry his ivory girl. But he knew that was stupid. You can't marry a statue! Instead, he prayed, 'O Aphrodite, let me find a woman as wonderful as you, as beautiful as the ivory statue in my workshop!'

Up on Mount Olympus, Aphrodite heard his prayer. She heaved a big sigh. 'Oh, that is *so* cute!'

When Pygmalion got home, he stared at his ivory statue for a long time. Gradually, he developed an uncontrollable urge to kiss her.

'That's foolish,' he chided himself. 'It's just a statue.'

But he couldn't help it. He made sure no one was looking, then stepped up to the ivory girl and planted a big kiss right on her mouth.

To his surprise, her lips were warm. He kissed her again and, when he stepped back, his ivory girl was no longer ivory. She was a living, breathing woman so beautiful it made Pygmalion's heart ache.

'I love you!' she said.

After Pygmalion came back to consciousness, he proposed to his perfect woman. They got married, had a few kids and lived happily ever after.

The weird thing, though? The stories don't even tell us what the ivory girl's name was. Probably Aphrodite would say, 'Oh, that doesn't matter! She looked like *me*. That's all you need to know!'

Riiiiight.

So Aphrodite was one of those can't-live-with-them, can't-live-without-them Olympians. She helped the gods and mortals from time to time, but she also caused a ton of trouble.

At one point, Zeus got fed up with her meddling. He blamed her for all the affairs he'd had with mortal women, which was much easier than blaming himself.

He sat on his throne, grumbling to himself, 'Stupid love goddess, getting me into trouble with my wife again! Aphrodite is always making *other* people fall in love when it's not convenient. I should make *her* fall in love with a lowly mortal and see how *she* likes it.'

That idea made Zeus feel much better. He put a spell on

Aphrodite. I don't know how. Maybe he dropped something in her nectar, or he tried shock therapy with his lightning. Whatever the case, he caused Aphrodite to fall head-over-heels for a mortal named Anchises.

Anchises was handsome, but he was only a shepherd, so Aphrodite was way out of his league. Nevertheless, Aphrodite looked down from Olympus one day, saw this guy lounging in the grass, just chilling and watching his sheep, and the goddess was completely love-struck.

'Oh, holy me!' she cried. 'Shepherds are *so* hot! Why haven't I noticed before? I have to get together with that shepherd, like, *right now.*'

She thought about using her son Eros as her messenger. Maybe he could take Anchises a note that read: DO YOU LIKE APHRODITE? _____ YES _____ NO

But she decided against it. Anchises might be too afraid to date a love goddess. Even worse, if she appeared to him in her true form, she might scare him away, or accidentally kill him. His poor heart might give out, or he'd burst into flames. That would ruin their first date.

She decided to disguise herself as a mortal maiden.

She took a nice hot bath, put on a silky dress and sprayed herself with flowery perfume. She flew down to the earth and walked up to Anchises, like, *La-dee-da, just happen to be walking through a sheep pasture in my best outfit.*

Anchises's eyes bugged out when he saw her. 'Wow. You *must* be a goddess. Who are you – Athena? Artemis? Maybe even Aphrodite?'

The goddess blushed. She was pleased to be recognized, but she didn't dare admit who she was. 'No, silly. I'm just an incredibly beautiful mortal maiden. I happened to be walking along and . . . oh, wow! Are you Anchises? I've heard all about you!'

Anchises blinked. 'You have?'

'Totally! I'm a big fan. We should get married!'

Anchises should've figured something was up. He didn't normally have amazing girls walk up to him and propose. But he was lonely, and his folks were always nagging him to get married. Imagine what they would think if he brought this lady home!

'Okay, sure!' he said. 'I'll introduce you to my parents. They live just over there.'

One thing led to another. Anchises married the mysterious mortal lady, and they had a wonderful honeymoon.

Then one morning Aphrodite woke up and Zeus's love spell had broken. She realized what she'd done and felt incredibly embarrassed. She wasn't supposed to get suckered into marrying lowly mortals! That was what she did to *other* gods!

She dressed herself hastily, but Anchises woke while she was lacing her sandals. He noticed that his new bride was glowing.

'Uh . . . honey?' he asked. 'Are you sure you're not a goddess?'

'Oh, Anchises!' Aphrodite cried. 'I'm so sorry! I must've been bewitched. Otherwise I never would have fallen in love with someone like you.'

'Gee . . . thanks.'

'It's not you. It's me! I can't marry a mortal. Surely you understand. But don't worry. When our child is born –'

'Our *child*?'

'Oh, yes,' the goddess said. 'I'm extremely fertile. I'm sure

I'm pregnant. At any rate, the baby will be a boy. I'll raise him until he's five, then I'll bring him to you. He'll become a great prince among your people and make you very proud. Just promise me you'll never tell anyone the true identity of his mother!'

Anchises promised. He was a little bummed about being dumped and divorced, but he kept Aphrodite's secret. Five years later, his son arrived from Olympus. His name was Aeneas, and he did in fact become a great prince of the city of Troy. Later on, after Troy fell, Aeneas sailed to Italy and became the first leader of a new people. They called themselves the Romans.

As for Anchises, one day when he was older and not so careful he was partying with his buddies and let it slip that Aeneas's mom was actually Aphrodite.

Word got around. The goddess of love was mortified. She complained to Zeus, 'This is all your fault to begin with!'

To make things right, Zeus whipped out a lightning bolt and blasted Anchises into ashes for breaking his promise.

Another happy ending!

Think Aphrodite swore off mortal men after that?

If you guessed *no*, you're learning.

Here's one last story about her, which shows how Aphrodite's own curses could come back to bite her.

There was this Greek princess named Smyrna who refused to worship Aphrodite, and the goddess got so mad she cursed Smyrna by . . . you know what? It's too horrible and disgusting. I can't go into it.

Let's just say Smyrna got pregnant, and it was a bad, bad situation. So bad that when her father the king found out he ended up chasing her through the woods with a sword and screaming, 'I'll kill you! I'll kill you!'

Smyrna cried out to the gods, 'Please! It's not my fault! Save me! Turn me invisible!'

The gods didn't do that, but they did turn her into a myrrh tree. I'm sure Smyrna was really grateful.

Nine months later, the tree split open and a little baby boy tumbled out. When Aphrodite heard the kid wailing in the woods, she felt a little guilty. She went down and picked him up. He was so cute that she decided to keep him and raise him in secret.

Why in secret? Aphrodite was the jealous type. The kid was adorable. The goddess didn't want to share his affections with anyone else. But since babies are a lot of work, and Aphrodite had a busy social schedule, she quickly realized she couldn't keep the baby *all* the time.

She decided she had to trust somebody to be a babysitter. She picked Persephone, goddess of the Underworld. That might seem like a weird choice, but Persephone lived down in Erebos, so nobody on Olympus ever had to know about the baby. Persephone was pretty lonely. She was glad to have a cute baby to cheer her up. And Aphrodite figured Persephone was no threat – I mean, please! Have you seen her hair? Her outfit? Aphrodite had nothing to be jealous about.

She named the baby Adonis and kept him in a box, which served as his incubation chamber. (Another story about a baby in a box. I'm not sure what that's about, but, again, do NOT try growing babies in boxes at home. It doesn't work.) The two goddesses shared custody, shuffling the kid back and forth between Aphrodite's secret lair on Cyprus and Persephone's palace in the Underworld; so, as Adonis grew up, he was always forgetting where he left his homework and which house his gym shoes were at.

Eventually he grew into a handsome young man.

No, that's an understatement. Adonis grew into the most handsome dude who ever lived. What did he look like exactly? I don't know. I don't pay attention to other dudes, sorry. Just imagine the coolest, most stylish, most awesome A-list celebrity you can imagine. Adonis was hotter than that.

At some point – like, simultaneously – Persephone and Aphrodite both realized Adonis wasn't a kid any more. He was a potential boyfriend. That's when the fighting began.

'He's mine,' Persephone said. 'I raised him most of the time.'

'No way!' Aphrodite said. '*I* found him in that tree! Besides, he *obviously* likes me better. Don't you, sweetcakes?'

Adonis gulped. 'Uh . . .'

There was no right answer. I mean, who would *you* choose? Aphrodite was the most beautiful goddess in the world, but, well . . . she was Aphrodite. Everybody wanted to be with her, and if you were her boyfriend every other guy in the world would hate you. Also, Aphrodite wasn't known for her faithfulness.

Persephone was beautiful in her own way, especially in the springtime, when she was allowed to roam the upper world, but her years in the Underworld had made her cold and pale and a little scary. She rarely fell in love with mortals. She definitely loved Adonis, but he wasn't sure he wanted to be her boyfriend if it meant staying in the dark palace of Erebos, surrounded by ghosts and zombie butlers. Adonis was also pretty sure Hades wouldn't like that arrangement.

'I – I can't decide,' Adonis said. 'You're both amazing.'

So the two goddesses took Adonis up to Mount Olympus and asked Zeus to solve the problem.

Zeus's eyes twinkled. 'You're a lucky guy, Adonis.'

Adonis wasn't feeling very lucky. He was feeling like the last piece of cake at a birthday party with a dozen hungry kids, but he nodded nervously. 'Yes, sir.'

'The solution is simple,' Zeus said. 'A time-share!'

Aphrodite frowned. 'Can you do that with a boyfriend?'

'Of course!' Zeus said. 'Adonis will spend one third of the year with you, one third of the year with Persephone, and one third of the year on his own, to do as he pleases.' Zeus clapped Adonis on the shoulder. 'A guy has to have some time to relax, away from the ladies. Am I right, bro?'

'I – I guess . . . bro.'

Zeus's expression darkened. 'Don't call the lord of the universe *bro.* Otherwise, I think we're all settled!'

The plan worked for a while, but Persephone's share of each year happened to fall during the winter, so she got the worst end of the bargain, and Adonis didn't like the Underworld. He had to spend most of his time hiding in closets or jumping under Persephone's bed whenever Hades knocked on her door, since Hades didn't know about Persephone's secret boyfriend.

Eventually Aphrodite won Adonis over with her sweet talk and her charm. She convinced him to spend his free portion of the year with her as well, so that she got *two* thirds and could look at Persephone smugly and know who was the better goddess. For a while, Aphrodite and Adonis made a happy couple. They even had a daughter together – a girl named Beroe.

How did the relationship end? Badly, of course.

One day Adonis was hunting out in the woods, which he liked to do when he wasn't with Aphrodite. His dogs caught the scent of an animal and went racing ahead. Adonis followed with his spear. By the time he caught up, he was tired and winded.

Unfortunately, his dogs had cornered a wild boar, which was just about the nastiest, most vicious animal you could meet. Some stories say the boar was put there by the god of war, Ares. That makes sense, since the boar was his sacred animal, and Ares was Aphrodite's godly boyfriend. Other versions say Artemis, the goddess of the hunt, put the boar in Adonis's path. Or maybe it was Persephone, since she was feeling jealous and jilted. It could've been almost any god, because like I said, when you're dating Aphrodite, everybody else is going to hate you.

Whatever the case, the boar rushed at Adonis and stabbed its tusks right in the most painful place you can imagine, which might have been funny, except that Adonis bled out and died.

A little while later, Aphrodite came flying by in her dove-powered chariot. She saw Adonis's lifeless body and rushed to his side.

'No!' she wailed. 'Oh, my poor beautiful man! Even in death, you are amazing.'

She laid his body in a big patch of lettuce, which is why lettuce became her sacred plant. The Greeks called it 'dead man's food'. They thought if you ate too much of it you would become listless and unable to experience love, just like dead Adonis.

Anyway, Aphrodite sprinkled godly nectar over Adonis's body, and he dissolved into blood-red flowers. They were called anemones, after the Greek word *anemoi*, which means *the winds.* Whenever the breeze caught them, the red petals fluttered away with a sweet smell that reminded Aphrodite of Adonis's fragrance.

Aphrodite was sad about his death for almost a whole day. Then she went back to her godly boyfriend Ares – the very one who might have been responsible.

Was Aphrodite mad at him? Nope. That's just the way Ares was.

If you want to meet the dude, he's in the next chapter. But bring your flak jacket and your assault rifle. Ares takes no prisoners.

ARES, THE MANLY
MAN'S MANLY MAN

ARES IS THAT GUY.
The one who stole your lunch money, teased you on the bus and gave you a wedgie in the locker room. The one who breaks other kids' bones in varsity football and makes a D– in every class, but is still popular because it's so funny when he gives the scrawny kids swirlies in the toilet.

If bullies, gangsters and thugs prayed to a god, they'd pray to Ares.

As soon as he was born, his parents knew he was bad news. Hera and Zeus wanted to love him, because he was their first child. But, instead of being cute or saying *goo-goo* or even crying for mama, the baby came out raging and shaking his little fists.

Hera could hardly keep hold of him as she held him up for Zeus to see. 'My lord,' she said, 'your newborn son.'

Zeus reached down to tickle the baby's chin. Ares grabbed

his dad's finger with both hands and twisted it. *SNAP!* The baby pounded his tiny chest and yelled, 'RARR!'

Zeus examined his immortal finger, which was now dangling at a funny angle. 'You know . . . perhaps we should get the boy a nanny.'

'Good idea,' Hera said.

'A large, strong nanny. With lots of patience . . . and good medical insurance.'

They hired a lady named Thero. She must've been like a mountain nymph or something, because she was tough and strong and nothing bothered her. She took Ares into the land of Thrace, a harsh, rocky place just north of Greece, full of snow and jagged mountains and warlike tribes – the perfect spot for a baby combat god.

As Ares grew, he never cried for his bottle or his binky. He roared for blood. Early on, he learned to chuck rocks at birds and knock them out of the sky. He pulled the wings off insects to practise his fine motor skills. He would laugh and laugh as he learned to walk by stepping on flowers and crushing small animals. Meanwhile Thero sat on a rock nearby, reading her Olympian gossip magazines and yelling, 'Keep it down, ya little delinquent!'

Yes, those were happy days.

Eventually Ares grew up and returned to Mount Olympus to take his rightful place on the Olympian council. Of course, he became the god of war (and just a friendly warning: if you ask him whether he's that dude from the video game *God of War*, he will rip your arm off and beat you over the head with it). He also became the god of violence, bloodlust, weapons, bandits, pillaging, levelling cities and good old-fashioned family fun.

He was the god of strength and manly courage, too, which was kind of funny, since the few times he actually got into one-on-one combat with another god he ran away like a coward. I guess that's typical of bullies. Ares was the first one to flee when the storm giant Typhoeus came knocking. Another time, during the Trojan War, he got stabbed in the gut by a Greek mortal's spear. He roared so loud it sounded like ten thousand men. Then he fled back to Mount Olympus, crying and moaning to Zeus, 'It's not fair! It's not fair!'

Zeus told him to shut up.

'If you weren't my son,' the sky god grumbled, 'I'd have stripped away your godliness and kicked you to the kerb years ago. You're nothing but trouble!'

Heartwarming, how the Olympian family got along.

Despite his occasional cowardice, Ares was a bad dude to make angry. When he went into battle, he wore golden armour that burned with harsh light. His eyes were full of flames and, with his war helmet on, he was too scary for most mortals to look at, much less fight. His favourite weapon was his bronze spear. His shield always dripped with blood and gore, because that's just the kind of friendly guy he was.

When he didn't feel like walking, Ares rode a war chariot pulled by four fire-breathing horses. His twin sons, Phobos and Deimos (Fear and Panic), were his usual charioteers, holding the reins and amusing themselves by seeing how many people they could run over: *Fifty points if you can smash that line of archers! A hundred points if you can hit that old dude!*

You can see why Ares's sacred animal was the wild boar, which will charge anything, is almost impossible to kill and has *major* attitude.

One of his sacred birds was the vulture, since it feasted on corpses after a battle. His favourite reptile was the poisonous snake. In a lot of pictures, you'll see Ares holding one, or he'll have one painted on his shield.

Ares didn't have a sacred flower. Go figure.

In addition to his apartment on Olympus, where he liked to hang out with his girlfriend Aphrodite, Ares had his own fortress in the mountains of Thrace. It was the first and ultimate man cave.

The castle was made entirely of iron – black metal walls, metal gates, dark towers, spiked turrets and a central keep with bars on all the windows. The sunlight barely made it inside, as if it was afraid to enter.

The halls and rooms were piled high with loot from various wars – some trophies that Ares had claimed himself, some that had been sacrificed to him by mortal warriors. He had about ten million swords and shields, enough armour to outfit the entire population of India, heaps of broken chariots and siege equipment, old banners, spears and quivers of arrows. If you made a crossover TV show about hoarders who were also doomsday survivalists, the camera crew would totally want to film Ares's fortress.

He had a lot of valuables in there. His gun collection alone must've been worth millions. But the fortress was guarded by dozens of minor warlike gods like Mischief, Anger, Threat, Road Rage and Rude Gestures. Ares also had one of those signs on the front door that read: FORGET THE GUARD DOG! BEWARE OF OWNER!

The Greeks didn't worship Ares much. They felt the same way about him as Zeus did. Ares was part of the Olympian family. They had to tolerate him. Sometimes they feared him. But he was whiny and annoying and always got people killed.

Sure, there were exceptions. The city of Sparta? They *loved* Ares. Of course, they were the manly men of Greece who ate nails and steroids for breakfast, so I guess that made sense.

In the centre of town they had a statue of Ares all chained down, the theory being that if they kept Ares in shackles he couldn't desert them, so the Spartans would always have courage and victory.

Still. Chaining down the god of war? That's *hard-core*.

The Spartans also made human sacrifices in honour of Ares, so you can see why they got along with him so well, though the sacrifices did cut down on Spartan tourism.

Up in Thrace, in the northern lands where Ares was raised, the mortals worshipped him in the form of a sword. Maybe they painted a smiley face on the blade and called it Mr Ares. I'm not sure. But when it was time to sacrifice the sheep, or cows or people, they sharpened the sacred sword and made a big mess.

Another one of Ares's fan clubs? The queendom of the Amazons. In their culture, the women were in charge, and those ladies knew how to fight. The first of them were demigod daughters of Ares. He gave the original Amazon queen a magical belt that bestowed super-awesome combat skills. The Amazon queens passed it down from generation to generation.

Ares always looked out for the Amazons when they went to war. Those female warriors liked Daddy War God so much they built him a temple on a nearby island, which was guarded by some of Ares's sacred birds. Imagine a flock of six million ravens, each one with feathers like razor-sharp darts that could be fired with enough force to pierce the hull of a ship. Yeah . . . the island was well guarded.

If that wasn't enough war-god love, Ares also had two sacred groves: one in central Greece and one in a land called Colchis, far to the east on the shores of the Black Sea. Each grove was a dark forest of oak trees where you could go to pray for victory in battle, but you had to be brave, because each grove was guarded by a dragon.

These two big monsters were both sons of Ares. Who was the mom? How did a god have dragons for sons? I don't know, but the dragons definitely shared their dad's winning personality. They would attack anything that moved, and they loved feasting on human flesh. If you managed to collect the dragons' teeth – which fell out all the time, kind of like sharks' teeth – you could plant the teeth in the ground and grow yourself some *spartoi*, or skeleton warriors.

Good luck getting the teeth, though. The dragons never slept. They spat poison. They had excellent hearing. And they hated it when mortals came around, looking for souvenirs and not even spending any money in the Sacred Grove gift shop.

Eventually, both of the dragons got killed, which was sad for . . . well, pretty much no one except Ares.

The beastie in central Greece got taken out first. This guy named Cadmus was wandering around, leading a bunch of settlers to found a new city. The Oracle at Delphi had told him to follow this certain cow and when the cow fell down from exhaustion that was the best place to build his city.

I dunno. Would you follow a dude who was following a

cow? Apparently Cadmus's peeps didn't mind. They hung with Cadmus until his special cow fell down, and everybody cheered.

'This is the spot!' Cadmus said. 'Let's start building! Oh, and how about we kill the cow and sacrifice it to the gods?'

At that point, the cow probably wished it had kept walking, but too late!

The settlers went to work. After a few hours, Cadmus and his builders got hot and thirsty.

'I need a drink!' one of the guys said. 'Did you bring an ice chest or anything?'

Cadmus frowned. He *knew* he should've brought an ice chest. And they hadn't seen a convenience store in miles. He scanned the horizon until he spotted a thick grove of oak trees in the distance.

'Trees need lots of water,' he said. 'There has to be a river or a spring over there.' He pointed to some of his guys. 'You five go into those woods with some buckets and bring us back some water. And if you see, like, a KFC or something, that would be good, too.'

As you can guess, the woods were the sacred grove of Ares.

There was a spring, all right. It bubbled up inside a cave right in the middle of the grove, feeding a nice pool of fresh water that also happened to be the dragon's drinking source.

The five guys went into the grove with their buckets.

They found the cave.

'What are all these pointy white things on the ground?' one of them asked.

'Arrowheads?' another guessed.

'Nah, they look like dragons' teeth,' said a third.

They all laughed nervously. No such thing as dragons, right?

Then the dragon burst out of the cave and ate them.

Only, one of guys escaped, probably because the dragon was too full to chase after him.

The guy stumbled back to the worksite, screaming in horror, 'DRAGON! BIG! EATS PEOPLE!'

As the settlers gathered round, Cadmus calmed the survivor down enough to get the full story. Then Cadmus grabbed his trusty spear. 'No dragon is going to eat *my* workers.'

At the back of the crowd, a priest cleared his throat. 'Um, sir? This grove sounds very much like a sacred place of Ares. If you kill the war god's dragon –'

'I have to kill it!' Cadmus said. 'The cow told me to build a city here, and I can't have a dragon living next door! Would you deny the wisdom of the dead cow, old man?'

'Oh . . . no. No, sir.' The priest decided to shut up.

Cadmus marched into the grove with his spear and, because he was such a boss, he walked straight up to the dragon (who was really too full to put up a good fight) and drove his spear straight through its head.

Instantly, a bright light shimmered next to Cadmus, and the goddess Athena appeared.

'Well done, Cadmus!' said the goddess. 'You have killed the dragon of Ares!'

Cadmus blinked. 'So . . . I'm not in trouble?'

'Oh, you're in terrible trouble!' Athena said cheerfully. 'Some day, Ares will have his revenge. But for now you're under my protection. I need you to found a great city called Thebes.'

'At the place where the cow fell down? Because the Oracle was pretty specific.'

'Yes, yes, that's fine. But first things first. You'll need some good fighters to defend your new city. Take the teeth of this dragon and sow them into the ground like seeds. Water them with a little blood and watch what happens!'

Athena disappeared.

Cadmus wasn't sure he should be stealing the dragon's dental work, especially if he was already on Ares's naughty list, but he did as Athena commanded. When he was done with his tooth farming, a bunch of super-elite skeleton warriors sprang from the ground, and these became the first soldiers in the new Theban army.

Cadmus built his city. For a while, everything was copacetic. The gods even granted him a minor goddess for his wife – Harmonia, who was a daughter of Aphrodite and Ares. Harmonia became mortal to share her life with Cadmus, which was a pretty big honour.

Ares was not pleased. First, this guy Cadmus kills his dragon. Then, the other gods are like, *Oh, no, you can't kill him! Cadmus is destined to found an important city!*

Like Thebes was important. Please! What kind of name is *Thebes*? It's not as cool as Sparta. Besides, there was already a city called Thebes in Egypt, so having one in Greece too was going to confuse people!

Then, on top of everything else, the other gods decreed that the dragon-killing jerk got to marry Ares's daughter. Not funny.

For his daughter's sake, Ares tried to keep his cool, but he *hated* his son-in-law. Finally one day he saw Cadmus out by the sacred grove, gazing at the spot where he'd killed the dragon years before.

For some reason, this completely torqued off Ares.

The war god appeared in front of him. 'What are you looking at, punk? The place where you killed my dragon? You hate reptiles, huh? Well, guess what? You *are* one!'

WHAM! Ares turned Cadmus into a snake.

Unfortunately, Queen Harmonia had just been walking up to check on her husband. She saw what happened and shrieked, 'Dad! What did you do?'

'He deserved it!' Ares snarled.

'I love him! Change him back!'

'Oh, you choose him over me? Is that how it is? Maybe you'd like to join him!' *BLAM!* He turned his own daughter into a snake, and the king and queen of Thebes slithered away.

That's how Ares got his revenge. But when the snakes Cadmus and Harmonia died Zeus sent their souls to Elysium so they could live together in peace and happiness forever. (Just don't tell Ares. He'd probably go down there and whammy them all over again.)

As for Ares's other sacred grove, the one in Colchis, things were run a little differently over there. The king was a guy named Aeetes. (As near as I can figure, that's pronounced 'I Eat Tees'.) His big claim to fame was that the Golden Fleece – that magical sheepskin rug I'm related to – ended up in his kingdom, which made the place immune to disease, invasion, stock-market crashes, visits from Justin Bieber and pretty much any other natural disaster.

Aeetes wasn't a son of Ares, but he was a big-time worshipper. He would go out of his way to start wars and kill as many people as possible, just so he could get extra points in the Ares Reward Programme. Pretty soon King Aeetes had scored all kinds of swag.

Ares sent his second dragon son to guard the Golden Fleece, which hung in an oak tree in Aeetes's sacred grove. The dragon was only friendly to Aeetes, so it would let the king gather its teeth. Then Aeetes would go to the special Field of Ares and plant the teeth to get himself a fresh crop of skeletal soldiers whenever he needed some. But he didn't have just any old John Deere tractor. Ares gave the king a special plough pulled by metal fire-breathing oxen. And, to keep the king safe from the fire, Ares gave him a set of fireproof, bulletproof, everything-proof armour that Ares had won during the war with the giants. (Which is a whole other story.)

As if the metal oxen, the skeleton warriors and the dragon weren't enough security, Aeetes also built a wall around the entire area so nobody could get close to the field or the grove. Considering that his kingdom of Colchis was pretty much at the end of the known world, the chances of anybody coming to steal his Golden Fleece were pretty slim.

Of course, somebody came to steal his Golden Fleece. The dude's name was Jason. But that's also a big long story for some other time. For now, we'll leave Aeetes in Colchis, all smug and confident and worshipping Ares and thinking, Yeah, I'm cool.

But even the god of war couldn't get away with killing people *all* the time. Sometimes Ares had to explain himself to the other gods. In fact, he was the defendant in the first and only godly murder trial – the pilot episode for *Law & Order: Olympus.*

Happened like this: there was this jerkish demigod son of Poseidon named Halirrhothius. I'm not going to claim the dude as a brother. His name alone should tell you he was no good. Sounds like some kind of throat disease. I think I'll just call him Hal.

Anyway, Hal lived in Athens. He fell in love with this beautiful Athenian princess named Alcippe, who happened to be the daughter of Ares, but Alcippe didn't want anything to do with him. A son of Poseidon? Gross!

Hal wouldn't give up. He followed Alcippe everywhere, stalked her on Facebook, sabotaged her dates and basically acted like a creep.

Then one night Hal cornered Alcippe in an alley. When she tried to get away, he knocked her to the ground. She started screaming and kicking and yelling, 'Help!'

Finally she thought to say, 'Dad! Ares!'

That did the trick.

Ares appeared in a flash and yanked the young man away from Alcippe.

'MESS WITH MY DAUGHTER?' Ares bellowed so loud he made the kid's cheeks flap from the G-force.

'Sorry, sir!' Hal said. 'I give up! Don't hurt me!'

'Oh, I won't hurt you,' Ares promised. 'I'LL KILL YOU!'

The war god pulled a knife and turned Hal into demigod Swiss cheese. Then he slammed the kid on the ground and kicked his lifeless body a few times for good measure.

The scene was so gruesome it was in the news for weeks. All the mortal commentators were asking, 'Godly violence against mortals – has it gone too far?' and basically giving Mount Olympus a bunch of bad press.

Poseidon demanded that Ares stand trial for murder, since Hal was his son.

Ares exploded. 'It was self-defence!'

Poseidon snorted. 'Self-defence? The boy surrendered to you. Then you stabbed him six hundred times and stepped on his face. How is *that* self-defence?'

'I was defending my daughter, Barnacle Beard! Your punk son was trying to rape her!'

Poseidon and Ares rolled up their sleeves to fight – which would've been sweet, because my dad would have totally owned that idiot – but Zeus stopped them.

'Enough!' he snapped. 'We will have a trial, as requested. I will be the judge. The other gods will be the jury.'

They had a trial for Ares on a hill in Athens. Zeus made a big deal about calling witnesses and hearing the evidence. I'm not sure what would have happened if Ares had been convicted. Maybe Zeus would've thrown him into Tartarus, or sentenced him to a thousand years of community service, picking up trash on the side of the highway. But, in the end, the gods decided Ares was innocent. Sure, he'd gone a little overboard, mangling Hal's body like that, but the guy had been assaulting Ares's daughter. That wasn't cool. Only gods could get away with stuff like that!

The hill where they held the trial is still there. If you're ever in Athens, check it out. It's called the Aeropagus, the Hill of Ares, and in ancient times the Athenians built a law court at the top for all their murder trials. I guess they figured if the place was good enough to try Ares it was good enough for their mortal psychos and axe murderers and whatnot.

Me, I agree that Ares had the right to defend his daughter,

but I still think Poseidon should have beaten the snot out of him, just because that would've been awesome to watch.

One more story about the war god, because I want to end with something that makes him look like a complete loser. (Which, honestly, isn't hard to do.)

One time, these two big giant brothers named Otis and Ephialtes decided they were going to destroy the gods. Why? Probably the Earth Mother Gaia put them up to it, or maybe they were just bored. The twin brothers were called the Alodai, which means *the Crushers*. I don't know if they had matching wrestler costumes or what.

Like most giants, they were . . . well, giant. They started ripping up mountains and piling them on top of each other, trying to make an assault tower from which they could destroy Mount Olympus with boulders – the same way Zeus destroyed Mount Othrys back in the old days.

The gods looked down from their palace and saw these two big giants piling up mountains, getting closer and closer, and Zeus said, 'Someone should stop them.'

'Yes,' Hera agreed.

Nobody volunteered. This was shortly after the fiasco with the storm giant Typhoeus, and all the gods were still a little shell-shocked. The idea of fighting *two* massive giants wasn't very appealing.

Finally, Hera said, 'Ares, you're the god of war. You should go fight them.'

'Me?' Ares's voice got squeaky. 'I mean . . . obviously, I could destroy them if I wanted to. But why *me*? Athena's a war goddess. Send her!'

'Ah, but I'm *wise*,' Athena said. 'Wise enough to make *you* do it instead.'

Ares cursed, but he couldn't argue with her logic. He got on his armour and jumped in his chariot and went barrelling down the side of Mount Olympus, shouting and waving his spear.

The giants weren't impressed. They'd been expecting an attack. In fact, they'd made some super-strong chains for just this occasion and set a trap – laying the chains along the ground right in the chariot's path, covering them with branches and gravel and stuff.

As Ares charged, the giants leaped to either side, yanked the ends of the chain and made a trip line that his horses couldn't avoid.

WHAM!

Horses went flying. The chariot exploded into a million pieces. Ares wasn't wearing a seat belt, so he flew about a hundred yards, slammed into the ground and would've broken his neck if he were mortal. While he was still dazed, the giants tied him up in their huge chains and carted him away.

'Oh, bummer,' Athena noted, peering down from Mount Olympus. 'They're kidnapping Ares.'

'Wow, that's a shame.' Poseidon yawned.

'We should help him,' Hera said, but even she sounded half-hearted.

Before any of the gods could decide what to do, the Alodai disappeared into the mountains. They took Ares to a faraway cave and stuffed him in a big bronze jar, where he suffocated and sweltered for thirteen months.

Ares tried to break the chains, but they were way too strong for him. He yelled and screamed and threatened, but as he got weaker and weaker, with no nectar to drink or ambrosia to eat, he just whimpered in the jar and pleaded to be let out.

Zeus couldn't be bothered to launch a rescue mission.

The Alodai kept sending ransom demands. 'Open your gates or we'll destroy your son! No, really! We mean it! Okay, how about a million drachmas' worth of gold? Seriously, we'll hurt him! Come on, guys! We've got your son in a jar! Don't you *want* him back?'

The giants got no reply from Mount Olympus. Ares might have withered away to nothing, which would've been fine with me, but the twin giants had a stepmother named Eriboea, who was kind-hearted and took pity on Ares. Or maybe she just got tired of hearing him whimper in the jar.

One night, she crept out of the cave and found the messenger god Hermes.

'Hey,' she said. 'I can show you where Ares is being kept. You can sneak in and rescue him.'

Hermes wrinkled his nose. 'Do I have to?'

'Well . . . if you don't, my stepsons are going to get tired of trying to ransom him,' Eriboea said. 'Then they'll finish their mountainous siege tower and destroy Olympus.'

Hermes sighed. 'Oh, all right. Fine.'

So Hermes sneaked into the cave and rescued Ares. They flew back to Mount Olympus, where the sight of Ares's sickly pale, withered form made the other gods angry and ashamed. They hated Ares, but nobody should be allowed to treat an Olympian that way.

The gods rallied and eventually managed to destroy the Alodai twins.

As for Ares, he got back to his fighting weight and pretended like the incident never happened, but after that he always had a soft spot for prisoners of war. If you mistreated your captives, Ares would find you and have a heart-to-heart.

Also, Ares developed a serious fear of jars.

I think I'm going to get him a nice one for Christmas.

HEPHAESTUS MAKES ME A GOLDEN LLAMA

(NOT REALLY,

BUT HE TOTALLY SHOULD)

I F YOU WANT TO SEE HEPHAESTUS'S BABY PICTURES, you're out of luck.

He was born so ugly that his loving mother Hera tossed him off Mount Olympus like a bag of trash. If somebody *had* taken a baby picture, it would've shown homely little Hephaestus plummeting through the clouds with a surprised look on his face like, *MOMMY, WHY?*

What happened next? Well, Hera was hoping never to see the kid again.

But eventually Hephaestus came back, just like a boomerang, and smacked her upside the head. I love that guy.

Baby Hephaestus fell into the sea, where he was rescued by the leader of the fifty Nereid sea spirits – Thetis. She's the chick who later freed Zeus when the gods tied him up.

Anyway, Thetis felt bad for this poor little baby. She decided to raise him in a secret underwater cave.

Thetis didn't mind ugly. She lived with jellyfish and eels and anglerfish, so Hephaestus didn't look so bad to her. Sure, his legs were malformed and too scrawny to support his weight without crutches or braces. He had too much man fur, and he had to shave, like, five times a day, even as a baby. His face was red and lumpy like he slept in a hive of African killer bees. But his upper body was strong and healthy. He had clever hands and keen intelligence. As the young god grew, he developed a talent for building and crafting, just like the Elder Cyclopes. Give the kid a bucket of Lego – come back in an hour and he's made a functioning long-range ballistic missile.

Good thing Thetis didn't want to take over the world. All she wanted was jewellery. She put Hephaestus to work making intricate gold necklaces, fancy bracelets of pearl and coral, and neon crowns that lit up and displayed various messages like HAPPY NEW YEAR and YOUR AD HERE, so that she always had the nicest bling whenever she went to parties.

Hephaestus spent nine years under the ocean as Thetis's personal blacksmith. He enjoyed the work and loved his foster mother, but always in the back of his mind he wanted revenge on Hera.

In his spare time, he worked on a special piece of furniture – a dangerous gift for his dangerous mother – and dreamed of the day he could return to Olympus.

Finally he finished his project and told Thetis goodbye.

'Beloved foster mother.' Hephaestus knelt at her feet, which wasn't easy, since his legs were twisted and withered and encased in golden braces. 'I must return home and take my place among the gods.'

Thetis had always suspected this day would come, but she cried anyway. 'They will not appreciate you,' she warned. 'They will only judge you by the way you look.'

'Then they are fools,' Hephaestus said. 'I don't care what anyone thinks. My mother threw me away. She must pay for that insult.'

Thetis couldn't argue. She wished Hephaestus luck, and the god embarked on his journey to Olympus. He rode a donkey up the mountain, because he liked donkeys. They were ugly and stubborn, comical, but strong and sturdy. Hephaestus could relate to that. And if you underestimated or mistreated a donkey you were likely to get your teeth kicked in.

Behind Hephaestus plodded an entire caravan of pack mules, loaded with special gifts for the gods.

Hephaestus rode straight into the Olympian throne room, and the other gods fell silent in amazement.

'Who is *that*?' asked Ares.

Hera made a strangled sound in the back of the throat. 'It can't be.'

'Mother!' Hephaestus grinned. 'It's me, Hephaestus!'

Zeus choked on his nectar. 'Did he just call you *Mother*?'

Hephaestus climbed off his donkey, his leg braces creaking. 'Oh, did she not mention me, Father?'

(Actually, Zeus wasn't *really* his father, since Hera had created the baby all by herself, but Hephaestus decided not to dwell on the technicalities.)

'Probably just an oversight.' Hephaestus smiled grotesquely. 'You see, Hera dropped me from Mount Olympus when I was a baby. But rest easy. As you can tell, dear parents, I survived!'

'Oh,' Hera said. 'How . . . nice.'

Hephaestus told his story about growing up at the bottom of the sea. 'And I brought presents!' He unpacked the big bundles from his mules. 'New thrones for everyone!'

'Thrones!' Ares leaped up and danced with excitement.

The other gods were a little more wary, but they got pretty psyched when they saw Hephaestus's workmanship.

Zeus got a solid gold seat with cup holders on the arms, lumbar support and a built-in rack for lightning bolts. Demeter's throne was shaped from gold and silver cornstalks. Poseidon got a sea captain's chair with a place for his trident and his fishing pole. Ares's iron throne was upholstered in leather with lots of uncomfortable spikes and barbed wire on the armrests.

'I love it,' Ares said. 'Is this Corinthian leather?'

'Mortal skin, actually,' Hephaestus said.

Ares got teary-eyed. 'This is the nicest gift . . . I – I can't even . . .'

All of the gods' new thrones were fully adjustable with wheels, so in no time the Olympians were rolling around the palace and spinning in their seats.

'You *made* these?' Apollo ran his hand along the back of his chair, which was shaped like a giant harp. 'They're awesome!'

'Yep,' Hephaestus said. 'I'm the god of blacksmiths and craftsmen. I can make pretty much anything.' He smiled at Hera. 'Mother, you're not trying your throne?'

Hera stood next to her new chair, which was made of adamantine – a super-strong metal that glittered translucent white, sort of a cross between silver and diamonds. The throne was the most beautiful thing Hera had ever seen, but she was afraid to sit on it. She couldn't believe Hephaestus was being so friendly to her.

Nevertheless, all the other gods were spinning across the room, having a great time, so finally she relented. 'Very well, my . . . er, my son. The throne *is* beautiful.'

She sat down. Immediately invisible cables lashed around her so tightly that she couldn't breathe.

'Agghhh,' she gasped.

She tried to change shape. No luck. The more she resisted, the more the cables tightened. She tried to relax. The invisible cables squeezed until her face turned pale, her eyes bugged out and all the ichor in her body pooled in her hands and feet.

'Mother?' Ares asked. 'Why are you sitting so still? And why are your hands and feet swelling up and glowing gold?'

Hera could only whimper, '*Help.*'

The gods turned to Hephaestus.

'All right,' Zeus grumbled. 'What did you do?'

Hephaestus raised his bushy eyebrows. 'Why, Father, I thought you'd approve. You'll have a much quieter wife now. In fact, she'll never get out of that chair again.'

Hera squeaked in alarm.

'You threw me away,' Hephaestus reminded her. 'I was ugly and crippled, so you tossed me off the mountain. I want you to suffer for that, dear mother. Think about all the things I could've made for you if you'd treated me well. Then maybe you'll understand that you threw away something valuable. You should never judge a god by the way he *looks.*'

With that, Hephaestus limped over to his donkey and saddled up to leave.

None of the other gods tried to stop him. Maybe they were worried that their own thrones would explode, or their seats would sprout Vitamix blender blades.

Hephaestus journeyed down to the mortal world and set up shop in one of the Greek cities. There he made horseshoes, nails and other simple stuff that wouldn't require much thought. He had hoped his revenge would make him feel better, but it hadn't. He felt even emptier and angrier than before.

Meanwhile in Olympus, the other gods got tired of listening to Hera whimper. They tried everything to free her — bolt cutters, lightning, bacon grease, WD-40. Nothing worked.

Finally Zeus said, 'Enough is enough. Ares, go find your brother Hephaestus and convince him to release your mother.'

Ares smiled cruelly. 'Oh, I'll convince him, all right.'

Ares readied his war chariot. He donned his burning golden armour, got his bloody spear and his shield that dripped gore. His sons Phobos and Deimos hitched up the fire-breathing horses, and off they went.

They rode through the city of mortals, causing panic, trampling everyone in their path. They burst into the courtyard of Hephaestus's blacksmith shop, where the crippled god was repairing a teapot.

The horses reared and breathed fire. Phobos and Deimos unleashed waves of pure terror that caused sixty-five heart attacks in the surrounding neighbourhood.

Ares levelled his spear at Hephaestus. 'YOU WILL FREE HERA!'

Hephaestus glanced up. 'Go away, Ares.' He kept hammering on his teapot.

Phobos and Deimos exchanged confused looks.

Ares's spear wavered. He'd been expecting a different reaction.

He tried again. 'FREE HERA OR FACE MY WRATH!'

His horses blew fire all over Hephaestus, but the flames only tickled him.

The blacksmith god sighed. 'Ares, first of all, I don't respond well to threats. Secondly, do you think you're strong because you fight a lot? Try working in a forge all day. Threaten me again and I'll show you strong.' Hephaestus flexed his arms and chest, which rippled with muscles.

'Thirdly,' he continued, 'I'm the god of *fire*. I have to be, since I melt metal for a living. I've forged iron and bronze weapons in the heart of underwater volcanoes, so don't try to scare me with your little ponies.'

Hephaestus waved towards Ares like he was shooing away a fly. A wall of fire roared from the ground and washed over the war god's chariot. When the flames died, the horses' manes were seared off. The chariot's wheels had flattened into ovals. Phobos's and Deimos's helmets were melted onto their heads like fried eggs, and their skin was covered in a fine layer of charcoal.

Ares's armour steamed. The beautiful crest of his war helmet was smouldering.

'Last chance,' Hephaestus said. '*Go away.*'

Ares turned and fled, his chariot *ka-chunk ka-chunking* on its lopsided wheels, leaving a definite smell of charbroiled war god in the air.

The Olympians tried different tactics to convince Hephaestus to free his mother. They sent different ambassadors.

Hephaestus would not be persuaded.

Up on Olympus, Zeus spread his hands and sighed. 'Well, I guess Hera will have to stay on that cursed throne forever.'

'Mrpphh!' said Hera, her face flushing gold with ichor.

Then the most unlikely hero stepped forward – Dionysus, the god of wine. 'Don't worry,' he said. 'I can handle Hephaestus.'

The other gods looked at him.

'You?' Ares demanded. 'What will *you* do? Threaten Hephaestus with a nice Chardonnay?'

Dionysus smiled. 'You'll see.'

Dionysus flew down to the earth. He started hanging around the blacksmith shop. He didn't make any demands on Hephaestus. He didn't threaten or lay on any guilt trips. He just chatted, told funny stories and acted friendly.

Now, *my* experience with Mr D has been pretty different, but apparently he could be pretty charming when he wanted to be. He had once been a mortal guy and had only recently become a god, so he wasn't high and mighty like some of the other Olympians. He didn't mind slumming with humans and ugly blacksmiths. He got along with Hephaestus just fine.

After weeks hanging out together, Dionysus said, 'Man, you are working too hard. You need a break!'

'I like work,' Hephaestus muttered.

The truth was blacksmithing took his mind off his pain. Despite his successful revenge against Hera, Hephaestus couldn't get rid of his anger and bitterness. He was still an outcast god, no happier than he'd been before.

'I'm gonna take you out tonight,' Dionysus said. 'We'll hit the taverns and I'll introduce you to this thing I created. It's called wine.'

Hephaestus scowled. 'It is a machine?'

Dionysus's eyes twinkled. 'Well . . . it has its uses. You'll see.'

Now, kids . . . wine is *alcohol*. That's a drink for grown-ups.

Gee, Mr Percy Jackson, you say, *can't we have some wine?*

No, no, kids. Wine is dangerous. I don't want any of you to drink alcohol until you're at least thirty-five years old. Even then, you should get a doctor's note and your parents' permission, drink responsibly (like one swig a month) and never operate heavy machinery while under the influence!

Okay . . . I think that covers my legal bases. On with the story.

That night, Dionysus took Hephaestus out drinking. In no time, Hephaestus was crying into his cup, pouring out his life story to Dionysus.

'I – I love you, man,' Hephaestus sobbed. 'Nobody else understands me. Well . . . except these guys.' Hephaestus pointed to his bowl of salted peanuts. 'They understand me. But . . . but nobody else.'

'Mmm.' Dionysus nodded sympathetically. 'It must have been hard, living at the bottom of the sea, cast away by your own mother.'

'You've got no idea. It was . . .' Hephaestus sniffled, searching for the right word. 'It was *hard*.'

'Exactly,' Dionysus said. 'You know what would make you feel better?'

'More wine?' Hephaestus guessed.

'Well, possibly. But, also, to forgive.'

'*What*, now?'

'Hera can be a witch,' said Dionysus. 'Believe me, I know. But we're a family, we gods. We have to stick together.'

Hephaestus glared cross-eyed into his cup. 'She threw me out like a bad spark plug.'

'I'm not sure what that is,' Dionysus said. 'But, still, you can't hold a grudge forever. If you bottle it up, well . . . even the finest wine eventually turns to vinegar. Did your revenge make you feel any better?'

'Not really.' Hephaestus scowled. 'I need more wine.'

'No,' Dionysus said firmly, which *really* wasn't like him, refusing somebody a drink. 'You need to go back to Olympus with me right now and let Hera go. Be the good guy. Show everyone you're better than her.'

Hephaestus grumbled and muttered and cursed his bowl of peanuts, but he decided Dionysus was right.

He rode back to Mount Olympus on his donkey – which was really dangerous, because he could've been pulled over for DWI (donkey-riding while intoxicated).

Fortunately he got there safely, Dionysus walking at his side. Hephaestus approached Hera, and the other gods gathered around.

'Mother, I forgive you,' Hephaestus said. 'I will let you go, but you have to promise: no more tossing babies away. *Everybody* has gifts, no matter what they look like. Do you agree?'

'Mrhph,' said Hera.

Hephaestus hit the secret deactivation switch on the back of the throne, and Hera was freed.

According to some stories, Hephaestus demanded a price

301

for letting Hera go. Supposedly Poseidon (who hated Athena) suggested that Hephaestus ask Zeus for the wisdom goddess's hand in marriage, and that's why Hephaestus went chasing after her in the infamous handkerchief incident.

I can't confirm that. Personally, I think Hephaestus just got tired of holding a grudge against his mom. Afterwards, he and Dionysus stayed pretty good friends, and Hephaestus and Hera set aside their resentment.

In fact, the next time Hephaestus got into trouble it was for *helping* his mom.

Fast-forward to when the gods rebelled against Zeus. As you might recall (or maybe not), once Zeus got free, he punished the rebel scum. Apollo and Poseidon lost their immortality for a while. Hera got tied up and hung over the abyss.

During all that, Hephaestus hadn't taken sides. He thought the rebellion was a stupid idea, but nobody bothered to ask his opinion. As a result, Zeus didn't punish him. Still, the blacksmith god didn't approve of his mom getting tied up and dangled over the abyss like live bait.

Hephaestus could hear her screaming day and night. It annoyed him that Zeus could bind Hera and nobody objected, but when *Hephaestus* had tied her up everybody acted like he was a horrible villain. And maybe, just maybe, Hephaestus was starting to love his mom just a little – at least enough not to want to see her hanging over the maw of Chaos.

One night he couldn't stand it any more. He got out of bed, grabbed his tool kit and went to save his mom. With the help of some grappling hooks, a safety harness, a tree trimmer, some rope and of course some duct tape, he managed to cut her down and haul her to safety.

Hera was incredibly grateful. She sobbed and hugged Hephaestus and promised never to call him ugly or disgusting again.

Zeus was less than pleased. When he found out what had happened, he marched into Hephaestus's room with electricity crackling around him and his face as dark as a thundercloud.

'WITHOUT MY PERMISSION?!' Zeus bellowed. 'You will learn to respect my authority!'

Most dads would just yell a lot, or ground you, or take away your Xbox. Zeus grabbed Hephaestus by the ankle, yanked him off his feet and dragged him to the nearest window.

Now, Hephaestus was strong, but his legs were weak. Once he was off-balance, he couldn't defend himself very well.

Also, Zeus was *swole*. He did, like, six hours of upper-body stuff in the gym every week.

He yelled, '*Sayonara*, Tool Guy!' and flung Hephaestus right off the mountain – again.

It took Hephaestus an entire day to fall, which gave him plenty of time to contemplate why he'd ended up with such horrible parents. Finally he hit the earth on the island of Lemnos with a huge *ka-blam!* The impact didn't do much for his deformed body or his crippled legs or his ugly face. He broke every bone in his immortal body and lay there for a long time, unable to do anything but experience blinding, burning, mind-searing pain.

Eventually he was discovered by a tribe called the Sintians, some non-Greek folks who made a living as pirates along the

Aegean coast. They had a bad reputation among the Greeks, but they were kind to Hephaestus. They carried him to their village and cared for him as best they could. Because of that, Hephaestus became their patron god. He set up a new workshop on Lemnos, which became his main headquarters. For centuries afterwards, Greeks visited Lemnos to see the spot where Hephaestus fell to earth the second time. They believed that the soil from the crash site had amazing healing properties, maybe because of all the godly ichor that had soaked into the ground. A little Lemnos mud on your skin and your bruises would fade. Your wounds would heal. The soil was even supposed to cure snake poison.

So next time you're bitten by a cobra, don't worry! Just book a flight to Lemnos and eat a clod of dirt. You'll be fine.

Hephaestus healed. Eventually he made his way back to Olympus. After that, Zeus and he were wary of each other, but they both pretended the *Sayonara, Tool Guy* incident never happened. I guess Zeus was sorry he had overreacted, and Hephaestus didn't want to push his luck. He was getting really tired of being thrown off the mountain.

Hephaestus spent most of his time at his various workshops on Lemnos, or under the ocean, or on other islands dotted across the Mediterranean. Wherever you saw a volcano bubbling and smoking and spewing lava, there was a good chance Hephaestus was in residence, heating up his forges.

Because he used volcanoes to power his workshops, Hephaestus was the god of volcanoes. In fact, the word *volcano* comes from his Roman name, *Vulcanus*, or Vulcan. And, no, he's not one of those pointy-eared dudes from *Star Wars*. Or is it *Star Trek*? I can't keep that stuff straight.

His sacred animal was the donkey, of course, but he also liked dogs. His favourite bird was the crane, probably because it had weird skinny legs that didn't match the rest of its body, kind of like a certain blacksmith.

Mostly, Hephaestus was known for his craftsmanship. Read those old Greek writers and they go on and on for pages about every shield or piece of armour Hephaestus made, describing every colour and decoration, what size grommets he used, how many nails and zzzzzzzzzzzzzz.

Sorry. I fell asleep just thinking about it.

I'll just give you the basics, but Hephaestus *did* do nice work. He made thrones for all the gods, and most of them weren't even booby-trapped! He made a fleet of magical tripods – three-legged tables that had wheels on their feet and raced around Mount Olympus, bringing people drinks and hors d'oeuvres and whatever. If you were staying in Mount Olympus and said, 'Now, where did I put my iPhone?' pretty soon one of the tripods would come puttering up to you, open its drawer, and there would be your phone. Kind of handy, those little guys.

Hephaestus also made the best armour and weapons. Sure, the Elder Cyclopes and the telkhines were good craftsmen, but nobody could touch the blacksmith god. Hercules, Achilles, all the greatest Greek heroes? They *only* used Hephaestus-brand equipment. I don't even think Hephaestus paid them an endorsement fee.

He made chariots for the Olympians with better suspension,

all-wheel drive, rotating blades on the wheels and all kinds of optional upgrade packages. He designed everything from jewellery to palaces. He made this one guy, the king of Chios, an entire underground mansion like a secret bunker.

But Hephaestus's speciality was automatons – mechanical creatures that were basically the first robots. In Hephaestus's workshop, he had a bunch of mechanical women assistants made out of gold. He crafted four of those for Apollo's temple, too, so they could sing Apollo's praises in four-part harmony. For King Alcinous, Hephaestus made a pair of metal guard dogs – one gold and one silver – that were smarter and more vicious than real dogs. For King Laomedon, he made a golden vine that actually grew. For King Minos, he made a giant metal soldier named Talos, who patrolled the borders of the palace day and night. Metal horses, metal bulls, metal people. You name it. If I ever become a king, I'm totally going to ask him for an army of giant golden acid-spitting llamas.

Okay, sorry. I got distracted again.

Next I should probably tell you how Hephaestus reacted when he found out his wife, Aphrodite, was cheating on him. It's kind of a sad story, and no llamas are involved, but Aphrodite and Ares *do* get badly humiliated, which is always a good thing.

Aphrodite had never wanted to marry Hephaestus. The goddess of love was all about looks, and Hephaestus didn't have any.

Hephaestus tried to be a good husband. It didn't matter. As soon as they were married, Aphrodite started having an affair with the war god Ares, and it seemed like Hephaestus was the only one who didn't know about it.

Why was he so clueless? I don't know. Maybe he wanted

to believe Aphrodite could love him. Maybe he figured if he did the right thing, she would. Sure, he noticed that all the other gods were whispering and snickering behind his back, but Hephaestus was used to that.

He started to suspect something was wrong when Aphrodite had her first child. Hephaestus had been expecting the baby to be crippled like him, or at least have some of his features – the misshapen head, the warty face, perhaps a beard.

But the baby boy, Eros, was perfect – handsome and fit. He also bore a striking resemblance to Ares.

Huh, Hephaestus thought. That's weird.

Aphrodite's next child was a girl named Harmonia, and again she looked absolutely nothing like Hephaestus. The blacksmith started to get uncomfortable. Every time he referred to Harmonia as 'my daughter', the other gods looked like they were trying not to laugh. And why did Aphrodite and Ares keep giving each other knowing glances?

Finally the sun Titan Helios took pity on Hephaestus. Helios saw everything from his sun-chariot chick magnet up in the sky – even stuff he didn't *want* to see – so of course he'd witnessed Aphrodite and Ares being *way* more than 'just friends'.

One night he pulled Hephaestus aside and said, 'Dude, there's no easy way to tell you this. Your wife is cheating on you.'

Hephaestus felt like he'd been hit in the face with a three-pound club hammer – one of the really nice ones with the fibreglass grip and the double-faced drop-forged steel head.

'Cheating on me?' he asked. 'Impossible!'

'Possible,' Helios said grimly. 'I saw them myself. Not that I was looking! But, well, they were kind of hard to miss.'

The sun Titan explained that Aphrodite and Ares often sneaked into Hephaestus's apartment while the blacksmith god was working in the forges. Right there in his own bedroom, they got *extremely* naughty.

Hephaestus's heart felt like it was reforging itself. It melted with misery. It got super-heated with anger. Then it cooled and hardened into something stronger and sharper.

'Thanks for the tip,' he told Helios.

'Anything I can do? You want me to give them a nasty sunburn?'

'No, no,' Hephaestus said. 'I got this.'

Hephaestus returned to his forges and made a very special net. He created gold filaments as thin as spiderwebs but as strong as bridge cables. He enchanted them so that they would stick to whatever they caught, harden more quickly than cement and hold their prey motionless.

He hobbled to his bedroom and wove the netting over the four tall bedposts so they hung like an invisible canopy. Then he put a pressure-activated trip wire across the sheets.

He limped into the living room, where Aphrodite was reading the latest steamy romance novel.

'Honey, I'm going to Lemnos!' Hephaestus announced. 'I may be there for a few days.'

'Oh?' Aphrodite looked up from her novel. 'A few days, you say?'

'Yep. Miss you. Bye!'

Aphrodite grinned. 'Okay. Have fun!'

Hephaestus packed his toolbox, saddled the donkey and headed out. Meanwhile, Ares was watching from a nearby balcony. Once the war god was satisfied that Hephaestus really was leaving for Lemnos, he rushed down to the blacksmith's apartment, where Aphrodite was waiting.

'Hey, baby,' Ares said. 'Miss me?'

They retired to the bedroom, but they didn't have time to get very naughty. As soon as they stripped down to their undies and jumped into bed, the trap was sprung.

The golden net fell on them and stuck like flypaper. The two gods struggled and shrieked. Seriously, Ares had a higher-pitched scream than Aphrodite. But they were plastered to the bed, unable to move or change form.

Hephaestus, who had doubled back, burst into the bedroom with an axe in his hands.

'Daddy's home,' he snarled.

He contemplated getting all Kronos on them and turning the bedroom into a horror-movie scene, but he decided against it. To Hephaestus's mind, there was nothing more shocking and embarrassing than leaving the lovers as they were – trapped in the act of cheating, Aphrodite with her make-up smeared and her hair messed up, her limbs flattened awkwardly against the bed like she'd hit a car windshield. Screaming and whimpering next to her, Ares wore nothing but a pair of red socks and his G.I. Joe boxer shorts.

Hephaestus marched into the Olympian throne room, where the gods were assembling for lunch.

'Don't eat yet,' he told everyone. 'I have something to show you, and it'll probably make you hurl.'

Intrigued, the gods followed him back to the bedroom, where they stared at the new piece of performance art Hephaestus had created.

'You see?' Hephaestus demanded. 'This is what I get for

trying to be a good husband. The moment I'm gone, these two start with their hanky-panky. My own wife hates me because I'm crippled and ugly, so she sneaks around behind my back with – with *this* fool. It makes me sick. It makes me want to throw up. Isn't this the most disgusting thing you've ever seen?'

The other gods were silent. Hermes started trembling, trying to keep it together.

Zeus said to himself, *I'm not going to laugh. I'm not going to laugh.*

Then he caught Demeter's eye, and it was all over.

'BWA! BWA-HA!' He doubled over, chortling so hard he thought his ribs would break. All the other gods joined in.

'G.I. Joe boxers!' Apollo screamed. 'OH – oh, I can't even … HAHAHAHAHA!'

'Aphrodite,' Athena giggled. 'You look simply *lovely*.'

The gods couldn't stop laughing. Soon they were rolling on the floor, wiping tears from their eyes, taking photos with their phones to post on Tumblr.

At first, Hephaestus was furious. He wanted to yell at them to take this seriously. He was in pain. He was humiliated!

Then he took a deep breath and realized: no, *Aphrodite and Ares* were humiliated. The other gods would be telling this tale for centuries. Every time the two lovers walked into the throne room, the Olympians would smirk and try not to laugh, remembering Aphrodite's messed-up hair and Ares's stupid boxers and red socks. Every time people told embarrassing stories at family get-togethers, this would be Embarrassing Story Number One.

After a long time, the gods managed to collect themselves.

'Okay,' Poseidon said, wiping his eyes. 'That was hilarious. But you should let them go now, Hephaestus.'

'No,' Hephaestus grumbled. 'Why not leave them here on permanent display?'

Zeus cleared his throat. 'Hephaestus, I thought we'd decided not to tie each other up any more. You've had your revenge. Now release them.'

Hephaestus glared at his father. 'All right. Aphrodite can go . . . as soon as you repay *all* the gifts I made for her dowry. I don't want her in my apartment any more. I don't want her in my life. She's not *worthy* of being my wife.'

Zeus turned pale. Back in those days, if you wanted to marry a woman, you had to give her family a bunch of presents called a dowry. Since Aphrodite didn't technically have a dad, Zeus had given her away, which meant he got all the cool Hephaestus-made swag. If Hephaestus demanded the dowry back, that meant the marriage was over. It also meant Zeus would have to give back the bronze toaster, the set of golf clubs, the plasma-screen TV and a bunch of other fun toys.

'Uh . . . well,' Zeus said, 'I suppose Aphrodite could stay in the net.'

'Zeus!' Hera chided. She didn't like Aphrodite, but she also didn't approve of goddesses being imprisoned.

'All right, all right,' Zeus said. 'Hephaestus can have the dowry back. Aphrodite is officially kicked out of Hephaestus's life.'

'Like she was ever *in* it,' Hephaestus muttered.

Poseidon still looked troubled. Despite his past differences with Ares, the two of them usually got along okay. He felt like he should speak up for the war god, since no one else would.

'You need to let Ares go too,' Poseidon said. 'It's only right.'

'*Right?*' Hephaestus bellowed. 'He made me a fool in my *own* bedroom, and you want to talk about *right?*'

'Look,' Poseidon said, 'I get it. But ask any price to settle the debt. I will personally vouch for Ares. He will pay it.'

Ares made a whimpering sound, but he didn't dare object. The golden net was really starting to chafe his delicate skin.

'All right,' Hephaestus said. 'If Poseidon guarantees payment, I'm good with that. I want a hundred wagonloads of the best armour, weapons and war spoils from Ares's fortress, and *I* get to pick the stuff.'

That was a punishing price, because Ares loved his spoils of war, but he nodded in agreement.

Hephaestus let the two lovers go. As he expected, the story got told and retold around the Olympian dining table for centuries, so Ares and Aphrodite were the butt of everybody's jokes. Aphrodite and Hephaestus never lived together again. Were they technically divorced? I don't know. But it's not like they were ever married in anything but name.

Afterwards, Hephaestus felt free to have relationships with other women. He had kids with a lot of them. Also, from then on he hated the children Aphrodite and Ares had had together, even if they didn't deserve it . . .

Case in point: Harmonia. I mentioned her before. She was the minor goddess who became a mortal and married that king Cadmus, and later they both got turned into snakes.

As if that wasn't enough bad luck for one lifetime, Harmonia also got a cursed wedding present from Hephaestus. He hated her, because she was a constant reminder of Aphrodite's affair with Ares. Not like that was Harmonia's fault, but, hey, even the nicer gods like Hephaestus could be jerks.

When Harmonia married Cadmus, Hephaestus made her a golden necklace as a wedding present. It was the most beautiful piece of jewellery you can imagine, all dripping with precious jewels in delicate golden lace, but it was also hexed with some serious juju. It brought bad luck to Harmonia (which is kind of obvious, since she got turned into a snake), but it also got passed down to her descendants. Everyone who wore that necklace for generations had some horrible tragedy happen to them. We won't go into the details, but it shows you that Hephaestus had a dark side. If you ever find one of his necklaces, be sure to check the engraving. If it says, *Congratulations, Harmonia!*, throw that thing away.

After Aphrodite, Hephaestus's first rebound relationship was with this goddess named Aglaia. She was one of the Charities. And, by Charity, I don't mean Goodwill or the Salvation Army. The Charities were three divine sisters in charge of grace and pleasure. They served as Aphrodite's handmaidens, so it must have really irritated Aphrodite when Hephaestus started dating one of them.

Like, *Yeah, I dumped you, and I'm going out with your handmaiden. Deal with it.*

Anyway, Hephaestus and Algaia had several godly daughters.

Then Hephaestus dated a bunch of mortal princesses and had a slew of demigod kids who became kings of this or that Greek city.

He even had a fling with a nymph named Etna, who was

the goddess of Mount Etna over in Sicily. If you're keeping track, that's the mountain Zeus used to smash Typhoeus the storm giant. I'm not sure why Hephaestus wanted to date a slightly smashed mountain nymph, but they had some children together called the *palikoi*, who were the spirits of hot springs and geysers. If you ever go to Yellowstone Park to see Old Faithful doing its thing, be sure to yell, 'Hephaestus says hello! Call your dad more often, ya bum!'

Hephaestus's most interesting kids were twin boys he had with a sea nymph named Kabeiro. They were called the Kabeiroi, after their mother, but their real names were Alkon and Eurymedon. (And, no, you will not have to remember that for the test. If your teacher says different, your teacher is WRONG.)

The Kaberoi were a lot like Hephaestus, meaning they were good at metalwork and incredibly ugly. Sometimes they're described as dwarfs, though maybe they just looked small next to their dad. They would help out around his forges in Lemnos and even go to war in his name. Once they rode east with Dionysus when he marched to India. Then they got in trouble, and Hephaestus had to rescue them.

You didn't know the wine god had declared war on India? Sure. We'll get to that in a bit. But, right now, I feel like some poetry.

You feel like poetry? No?

Well, TOO BAD. Apollo is getting impatient. He wants me to write his chapter and, since he's the coolest Olympian god (even if he does say so himself), you can only put off the Golden Boy for so long.

APOLLO SINGS
AND DANCES AND
SHOOTS PEOPLE

YOU HAVE TO PITY APOLLO'S MOM.

Being pregnant is hard enough. (Not that I would know, but my mom has told me about a million times.) Apollo's mother, the Titan Leto, was pregnant with *twins*, and she couldn't go to the hospital when she went into labour. Instead she had to run for her life, rushing from island to island, pursued by a vengeful goddess and a giant snake.

Would it surprise you to learn that the whole thing was Zeus's fault?

Old Thunderbritches fell in love with Leto and convinced her it would be totally fine to have kids together.

'Hera will never find out!' he promised.

Zeus had told that lie to so many different women he probably even believed it.

Of course, Hera found out. She glared down from Mount Olympus at the beautiful pregnant Leto, who was glowing with health, sitting in a meadow and patting her swollen tummy, singing to her unborn children.

Hera grumbled to herself, 'How *dare* she be happy? Let's see how happy she is in *eternal pain!*' The Queen of Heaven spread her arms and addressed the entire earth below her. 'Hear me, world! Hear me, Mother Gaia! I forbid any land with roots in the earth to receive Leto when it is time for her to give birth. Any land that dares to oppose me, I will curse for all eternity! Leto will have no bed to lie in, no place to rest! She will be forced to wander without a place to give birth, she will stay pregnant and in labour forever, suffering for the crime of taking my husband! HAHAHA!'

Yeah, Hera was definitely channelling her inner Wicked Witch of the West that day. The ground rumbled. All the nature spirits on every land with roots in the earth promised not to help Leto. Now, you're wondering, why couldn't Leto just buy a boat and give birth at sea? Why couldn't she go underwater, or down into Erebos, or rent a helicopter and give birth one thousand feet in the air?

Near as I can figure, Hera included all that in the curse. She created an impossible situation, where Leto could only give birth on solid ground, but all solid ground was forbidden to accept her. Hera was tricky that way.

When Leto was seven months pregnant, she went into early labour.

'Oh, great,' she groaned. 'These kids aren't going to wait!'

She tried to lie down, but the earth shook. Trees burst into flame. Fissures opened in the ground, and Leto had to run for safety. No matter where she moved, she couldn't find a safe place to rest. She took a boat to another island, but the same thing happened. She tried a dozen different places all over Greece and beyond. In each spot, the nymphs refused to help her.

'Sorry,' they said. 'Hera will curse us for all eternity if we let you come ashore. You can't give birth on any land with roots in the earth.'

'But that means *every* land!' Leto protested.

'Yeah, that's the idea,' the nymphs told her.

Leto drifted from place to place, her body racked with pain, her unborn children getting more and more impatient. Leto felt like she'd swallowed an over-inflated beach ball and a couple of feral cats.

In desperation, she went to Delphi, which had once been her mother Phoebe's sacred place. Leto figured the Oracle would give her sanctuary.

Unfortunately, the Oracle's cave had been taken over by a giant snake called Python. Where did he come from? You'll love this. The word *python* is from the Greek *pytho*, which means *rotting*. The monster Python was born out of the festering, rotten slime left over from the great flood when Zeus drowned the world. Tasty!

Anyway, Python had moved into the area and told himself, *Hey, this is a nice cave. Lots of juicy mortals to eat!* Python proceeded to swallow the priests and the soothsayers and the pilgrims who came looking for aid. Then he coiled up for a nap.

When Leto visited, she was shocked to find a hundred-foot-long snake as thick as a school bus hanging out in her mother's favourite holy place.

'Who are you?' Leto demanded.

'I am Python,' said Python. 'And you must be breakfast.'

The snake lunged at her. Leto fled, but she looked so appetizing, being plump and pregnant and slow, that Python pursued her for miles. A couple of times he almost caught her. Leto barely made it back to her boat.

Where was Zeus this whole time? Hiding. Hera was in a royal snit, and Zeus didn't want to be the target of her wrath, so he let Leto take all the heat. Nice guy.

Leto kept sailing until finally she had a crazy idea. She asked the captain of her ship to sail for the island of Delos.

'But, my lady,' said the captain, 'Delos is a floating island! Nobody knows where it is from day to day.'

'JUST FIND IT!' Leto screamed. Labour pain made her eyes glow red with agony.

The captain gulped. 'One Delos, coming right up!'

Several nerve-racking days later, they found the place. It looked like a normal island – beaches, hills, trees, etc. – but Delos wasn't attached to the earth. It floated on the waves like a giant life preserver, drifting around the Mediterranean, occasionally pinballing off other islands or running over unsuspecting whales.

As the ship got closer, Leto forced herself to stand at the bow. She was in so much pain she could hardly think, but she called out to the main nature spirit of the island: 'O great Delos, you alone can help me! Please let me come ashore and give birth on your island!'

The island rumbled. A voice echoed from the hills: 'Hera will be royally ticked off if I do that.'

'She can't hurt you!' Leto yelled. 'Her curse specified any

land with roots in the earth. You don't have roots! Besides, once my children are born, they will protect you. *Two* Olympian gods on your side. Think about that. Delos will become their holy place. You will have great temples of your own. You can finally settle down in one spot. The tourism alone will make you millions!'

Delos thought about that. The island was tired of drifting around. The forest nymphs were getting seasick from constantly bobbing on the waves.

'All right,' said the voice. 'Come ashore.'

As soon as Leto found a spot to lie down, the whole world trembled with anticipation. It's not every day that two new Olympian gods are born. All the goddesses – except, of course, Hera – rushed to Leto's side to help her give birth.

Leto had two beautiful babies – a boy named Apollo and a girl named Artemis. They were born on the seventh day of the seventh month, when Leto was seven months pregnant, so their holy number was thirteen. (*Just kidding. It was seven.*)

We'll talk about Artemis in a bit, but Apollo wasted no time taking the spotlight. As soon as he'd tasted nectar from his baby bottle, he hopped out of his mother's arms, stood on his own two feet and grinned.

''Sup, folks?' he said. 'My name's Apollo, and I need a bow and arrows, stat! Also, a musical instrument would be good. Has anybody invented the lyre yet?'

The goddesses looked at each other in confusion. Even the Olympians were not used to grinning babies who spoke in complete sentences and demanded weapons.

'Erm, I've never heard of a lyre,' Demeter admitted.

In fact, the lyre would be invented later, but that's another story.

Apollo shrugged. 'Fine. A guitar will do. Or a ukulele. Just not a banjo, please. I don't do banjos.'

The goddesses rushed off to find what the kid wanted. Hephaestus made him a beautiful golden bow and a quiver of magic arrows. The best musical instrument they could come up with was a *keras*, which was like a trumpet.

By the time the goddesses returned to Delos, Apollo had grown so much he looked like a five-year-old, though he wasn't even one day old. He had long golden hair, a super-bronze tan and eyes that shone like the sun. He'd found himself a Greek robe woven from gold, so he was almost too flashy to look at.

He slung the bow and quiver over his shoulders and grabbed the keras. He played a beautiful melody on the trumpet, then began to sing a cappella.

'*Oh, I am Apollo, and I'm so cool! La-la-la, something that rhymes with cool!*'

Actually I have no idea what he sang, but he announced that he would be the god of archery and song and poetry. He also announced that he would become the god of prophecy, and interpret the will of Zeus and the words of the Oracle for all the poor little mortal peons.

When his song was finished, the goddesses clapped politely, though they still thought the whole scene was a little weird. The island of Delos rejoiced that it had a new patron god. Delos put down roots and anchored itself in the sea so that it wouldn't move around any more. The island covered itself with golden flowers in honour of the golden god Apollo. If you visit Delos today, you can still see those fields of wildflowers stretching out among the ruins, though thankfully Apollo doesn't play the trumpet there very often.

Apollo grew with super-speed. In about a week, he'd become a regular adult god, which meant he totally skipped school, got an honorary diploma and stopped ageing when he looked twenty-one years old. Then he stayed that way forever. Not a bad deal, if you ask me.

His first act was to avenge his mother for her pain and suffering while she was trying to find a place to give birth. Sadly, he couldn't destroy Hera, since she was the queen of heaven and all, but when he heard about the giant snake Python, who'd chased his mother out of Delphi, Apollo was enraged.

'Be right back,' he told Leto.

Apollo flew to Delphi (yes, he could fly) and called out Python.

'Yo, snake!'

Python opened his eyes. 'What do you want?'

'To sing you a song about my awesomeness!'

'Oh, please. Just kill me now.'

'Okay!' Apollo drew his bow and shot the snake between the eyes. *Then* he sang a song about his awesomeness. He threw the snake's body into a fissure below the cave, where it rotted eternally and spewed all kinds of cool odours.

Apollo took over the Oracle of Delphi. He welcomed back the priests and the pilgrims. Because the Oracle had once belonged to his grandmother, Phoebe, he was sometimes called Phoebus Apollo. The main priestess who told the future became known as the *Pythia*, after the snake Python. Or maybe she was called that because she spoke a bunch of rot. Anyway, she would get her prophecies straight from the god Apollo, and the lines would always be riddles or bad poetry, or both.

She dwelt in the cave where the snake had died. Usually she sat on a three-legged stool next to one of the big fissures that vented gross volcanic gas, which smelled of dead snakes. If you made an offering, the Pythia would tell your fortune or answer any question. That didn't mean you would understand the answer. If you did understand it, you probably wouldn't like it.

Apollo claimed his place among the Olympian gods, and even Hera didn't dare object. He just looked so . . . *godly.*

He was as tall and muscular and bronze as a *Baywatch* lifeguard. He kept his blond hair long, but tied back in a man bun so it didn't interfere with his archery. He sauntered around Olympus in his gleaming robes with his bow and arrow, winking at the ladies and high-fiving the dudes, or sometimes winking at the dudes and high-fiving the ladies. Apollo didn't care. He figured *everybody* loved him.

He was great with poetry and music . . . or, at least, some people liked it. Me, I'm more of a straight-ahead rock 'n' roll kind of guy, but whatever. Apollo was always popular at parties, because he could entertain you with songs, tell your fortune and even do cool trick shots with his bow, like intercepting a dozen ping-pong balls at once or shooting a wine cup off Dionysus's head.

Apollo also became the god of shepherds and cowherds. Why? You got me. Obviously Apollo liked premium cuts of meat. He raised the finest cattle in the world. *Everybody* wanted to steal them, but Apollo kept them under constant guard.

If anybody got near his sacred herd, they were likely to start World War C (for cow).

When Apollo got mad, he didn't mess around. He could punish any mortal anywhere in the world simply by drawing his bow and firing. The arrow would arc through the sky and find its mark, no matter how far away. If Apollo was hanging out in Greece and some guy in Spain muttered, 'Apollo is stupid!' . . . *BAM!* One dead Spanish guy. The arrow would be invisible, too – so the other mortals would never know what hit him.

In Ancient Greece, anytime somebody dropped dead unexpectedly, they assumed Apollo had struck him down – maybe as a punishment, maybe as a reward for one of the guy's enemies.

Considering that, this is going to sound strange: Apollo was the god of healing. If you wanted plasters or aspirin, Apollo could help you out. But he also had power over plagues and epidemics. He could cure or kill off an entire army or a whole nation. If he got mad, he'd shoot a special arrow that exploded into a foul vapour and spread smallpox or black plague or anthrax. If a zombie apocalypse ever comes around, you'll know who to blame.

Apollo was the god of so many different things that even the Greeks got confused. They'd be like, 'Hmm, I forgot who the god of basket weaving is. Must be Apollo!'

Maybe that's why, later on, the Greeks and Romans started calling Apollo the god of the sun. That was actually Helios's job, but the mortals sort of forgot about Helios and decided to give Apollo the sun chariot instead. Since Apollo was all flashy and golden like the sun, it made sense.

In this book, though, let's not think of him as the sun god. The dude's got enough other stuff on his plate. Plus, the idea of Apollo driving the sun chariot freaks me out, 'cause you know he'd be talking on his cell phone most of the time with the radio cranked to max, the subwoofers rattling the whole chariot. He'd have his dark shades on and be checking out the ladies, like, *How you doing?*

Anyway, his symbols were the bow and arrow – no surprise. Later, when the lyre (like a small harp) was invented, that was his symbol, too.

The main thing to know about Apollo: never underestimate the guy. One day he might be the god of limericks and stupid earworm songs and first-aid classes. The next day he's the god of chemical weapons and world-destroying plagues. And you thought *Poseidon* had a split personality.

Apollo wouldn't kill you for no reason. He just didn't need much of a reason.

Example: one time his mom, Leto, was coming to see him at Delphi. Along the way she got harassed by a giant named Tityos. I know. Terrible name, Tityos. Nothing I can do about that.

Anyway, Tityos was a nasty piece of work. He was one of Zeus's most monstrous kids. His mom was your typical mortal princess, Elara, but when she was pregnant Zeus had the brilliant idea of hiding her from Hera by sticking her in an underground cave. Something about the cave vapours made Elara's unborn child grow ugly and so huge that his mom's body simply couldn't contain him. It's a little disgusting, but . . . well, *KA-BLAM!* Elara died. However, the child kept growing until the entire cave became his incubation chamber. Then Gaia, good old Dirt Face herself, decided to be Tityos's surrogate mom. She completed his training in the Dark Side. When Tityos finally emerged from the earth, he looked less like the son of Zeus and more like the son of Frankenstein's monster.

Anyway, Hera got hold of him and figured she could use this giant to get her long-awaited revenge on Leto.

'Hey, Tityos,' Hera said to him one day.

'Blood!' Tityos screamed. 'Meat and blood!'

'Yes,' Hera said. 'Those are very nice. But how about a pretty wife for you, too?'

'Meat!'

'Okay. Maybe later. A woman will be walking this way soon, heading to Delphi. She just *loves* it when big strong giants try to abduct her and drag her to their underground lair. Interested?'

Tityos scratched his massive head. 'Blood?'

'Why, certainly.' Hera smiled. 'If she resists, shed all the blood you want!'

Tityos agreed, so Hera gave him a cookie for good behaviour and left him lying in wait on the road to Delphi. Soon Leto came along, and Tityos leaped out to grab her.

Thanks to her experience with Python, Leto had had a lot of practice running away from monsters, and this time she wasn't pregnant. She dodged the giant and took off full-speed for Delphi.

'Hey, son?' she yelled. 'A little help back here?'

Apollo heard his mother's call. He grabbed his bow and fired. *THWACK.* Tityos bit the dirt with a golden arrow straight through his heart.

But that revenge was too quick for Apollo. He went down to see Hades in the Underworld and said, 'This guy Tityos . . . I guess he still counts as a mortal demigod. Not sure. Anyway, if his spirit shows up, torture him for me. Something cool . . . like

Zeus did with Prometheus. Except not with an eagle. Maybe vultures or something.'

'Vultures or something?' Hades asked.

'Yeah! Perfect!'

Hades must not have been feeling very creative, because he followed Apollo's suggestion exactly. When the spirit of Tityos turned up, the giant was convicted of assaulting Leto. He was sent to the Fields of Punishment, where he was chained down, given a regenerating liver and cut open so that vultures could feast on it forever. (I think Prometheus filed a copyright infringement suit later on.)

Another time, Apollo avenged an insult by committing mass murder. That seems fair, right? The queen of Thebes, a lady named Niobe, had fourteen kids – seven boys and seven girls. The children were all healthy and attractive and made good grades in school, so Niobe was always bragging about them. You've probably met moms like that. You say, 'Yeah, I scored a goal in the football game last night.' And she says, 'Oh, that's nice. All fourteen of my children are the *captains* of their teams, and they make straight As and can play the violin.' And you just want to smack her.

Well, Niobe was *that* lady. One day the city of Thebes had a festival in honour of Leto. The priests were praising the Titan for being so beautiful and courageous and giving birth to not one but *two* amazing gods, Apollo and Artemis. As the prayers were going on and on, Queen Niobe couldn't stand it any more.

'Oh, that's not so special!' she said to the audience. 'I don't think Leto's any more beautiful or courageous than *I* am. Besides, she only had two children. I had *fourteen* amazing children!'

O-o-o-o-kay. Bad move.

Halfway across the world, Apollo and Artemis heard the insult and came flying with their bows at the ready.

They descended on Thebes and a wave of terror spread across the city. Everyone turned to stone except for the queen and her family.

'Proud of your kids?' Apollo bellowed. 'Maybe we need to put things in perspective for you.'

He shot seven golden arrows and murdered all of Niobe's sons on the spot. Artemis shot down all seven of the daughters. Niobe's husband, the king, wailed in outrage, drew his sword, and charged at Apollo, so the god struck him down, too.

Niobe's heart was shattered. She fled to a mountain in Asia Minor – the country we call Turkey – and wept for years and years, until finally she turned to rock. The Greeks used to visit the spot on Mount Sipylus where a weathered sandstone figure of a woman stood, water seeping from its eyes. Maybe she's still there.

As for her dead family, they weren't buried for nine days. The bodies just lay in the streets of Thebes, attracting flies and getting grosser and more, um, *python*, while the rest of the townspeople were frozen as statues.

Finally, Zeus took pity on Thebes. He unfroze the people and allowed them to bury the royal family. Nobody in Thebes ever insulted Leto again, but I'm pretty sure Apollo and Artemis weren't very popular there, either.

And *still* Apollo could find new and horrifying ways to punish people.

The most horrible thing he did was to the satyr Marsyas.

This goat-legged dude lived in Phrygia, over in Asia Minor, kind of near the spot where Niobe turned to stone. One day Marsyas was trotting along the riverbank, minding his own business, when he spotted a strange instrument lying in the grass. It happened to be the flute Athena had made – the very first one in the world. Maybe you remember that the other goddesses teased her about the way she looked when she played it, so she threw it off Olympus and swore that anyone who played it would suffer a terrible fate.

Well, poor Marsyas didn't know that. It wasn't like Athena had put a warning label on it. The satyr picked up the flute and began to play. Since it had been filled with the breath of a goddess, the flute sounded amazing. In no time, Marysas had mastered the fingering and was playing so beautifully that all the nature nymphs for miles around came to hear him.

Pretty soon he was signing autographs. He scored six number-one hits on *Billboard*. His YouTube channel attracted seven million followers, and his first album went platinum in Asia Minor.

Okay, maybe I'm exaggerating. But he got popular for his music. His fame spread.

Apollo didn't like that. He only had *five* number-one hits on *Billboard*. He didn't want some stupid satyr on the cover of *Rolling Stone* when it should have been him.

Apollo came down to Phrygia and floated invisibly above the crowd that had gathered to hear Marsyas play. The guy was good, no question. That made Apollo even angrier.

He waited and listened, knowing it was only a matter of time . . .

Soon enough, a starry-eyed nymph in the front row screamed, 'Marsyas, you're the new Apollo!'

The praise went right to Marsyas's head. He winked at the nymph. 'Thanks, babe. But, seriously, whose music do you like better – Apollo's or *mine*?'

The crowd cheered wildly – until Apollo appeared on stage in a blaze of golden light. Everyone went absolutely silent.

'What a great question, Marsyas!' Apollo cried. 'Was that a challenge? 'Cause it sounded like a challenge.'

'Uh . . . Lord Apollo . . . I didn't – I wasn't –'

'A *music contest*, you say?' Apollo grinned ear to ear. 'I accept! We'll let the crowd choose who is better and, just to make things interesting, the winner can do *whatever he wants* to the loser – demand any price, inflict any punishment! How does that strike you?'

Marsyas turned pale, but the crowd cheered and hollered in approval. Funny how quickly a flute concert can turn into a public execution.

Marsyas didn't have much choice, so he played the best he could. His flute music brought tears to the nymphs' eyes. The satyrs in the audience cried, held torches in the air and bleated like baby goats.

Apollo followed with a song on his lyre (which had been invented by this time – more on that later). He strummed and sang and did a blazing extended solo. The girls in the front row fainted. The audience roared enthusiastically.

It was impossible to tell who had won the contest. Both musicians were equally talented.

'Well . . .' Apollo scratched his head. 'Tiebreaker, then. Let's see who can do the best *trick* playing.'

Marsyas blinked. '*Trick* playing?'

'Sure, you know. Fancy moves! Showmanship! Can you do *this*?'

Apollo put his lyre behind his head and played a tune without even looking at the strings. The crowd went nuts. Apollo windmilled his arms. He slid across the stage on his knees while shredding sixteenth notes, then hit the reverb button on his lyre and leaped into the mosh pit, ripping out a solo as the crowd pushed him back onto the stage.

The applause died down after about an hour. Apollo grinned at Marsyas. 'Can you do that?'

'With a flute?' Marsyas cried. 'Of course not! That's not fair!'

'Then I win!' Apollo said. 'I have just the punishment for you. See, Marsyas, you think you're special, but you're a fad. *I'll* be famous forever. I'm immortal. You? All glitter, no gold. Scratch the surface, and you're just another mortal satyr – flesh and blood. I'm going to prove that to the crowd.'

Marsyas backed up. His mouth tasted like python slime. 'Lord Apollo, let me apologize for –'

'I'm going to flay you alive!' Apollo said cheerfully. 'I'm going remove your skin, so we can all see what's underneath!'

Grossed out yet?

Yeah. It was pretty horrible.

Marsyas suffered a grisly death just because he dared to make music as good as Apollo's. The satyr's body was buried in a cave near the site of the music contest, and his blood became a river that gushed down the side of the hill.

Apollo made the cover of *Rolling Stone*. From his smiling face, you'd never guess the guy sewed curtains out of satyr skin.

Final thing about Apollo: he was a confirmed bachelor and a real ladies' man. Hey, a mass-murdering psychopath who plays the lyre? It doesn't get much more charming than that!

According to some stories, he dated each of the Nine Muses – the goddesses who oversaw different kinds of art, like tragedy, comedy, docudrama and whatever. Apollo couldn't decide between them. They were all too lovely; so he vowed never to marry, just date around.

Only once was he tempted to break that promise. He fell in love and got his heart broken – and it was his own fault.

One afternoon Apollo happened to be walking through the palace at Mount Olympus when he ran across Eros, Aphrodite's son. The hitman of love was sitting on a window ledge restringing his bow. The kid looked so young, his bow so tiny, that Apollo burst out laughing.

'Oh my gods!' Apollo wiped a tear from his eye. 'You call that a *bow*? Those arrows look like darts. How can you *hit* anything?'

Eros was seething inside, but he managed a smile. 'I do all right.'

'*This* is a bow, kid!' Apollo pulled out his own golden longbow, made by Hephaestus. 'My enemies tremble when they see me coming. I can destroy anyone with a single arrow from any distance! You ... well, I suppose you'd be a fearsome gerbil hunter.'

Apollo strode off, still laughing.

Eros gritted his teeth. He muttered to himself, 'We'll see about that, Mr Big Shot. Maybe you can bring down your enemies, but I can bring down *you*.'

The next morning, Apollo was walking by the riverside in

Thessaly, just playing his lyre and enjoying the sunshine, when Eros shot an arrow straight into Apollo's heart.

By chance, a naiad was bathing nearby – one of the daughters of the local river spirit. Her name was Daphne. By anybody's standards, Daphne was beautiful. Most naiads were. But the moment Apollo saw her he thought she was even hotter than Aphrodite. All the other women he'd dated suddenly seemed like complete losers. Apollo decided he *had* to marry Daphne.

Sadly, like a lot of smart nymphs, Daphne had long ago sworn off dating gods, because bad things happened to their girlfriends. Not all the time, maybe. Just, like, 99.9 percent of the time.

'Hey!' Apollo called out. 'What's your name?'

Daphne leaped out of the water and wrapped herself in her robe. 'I'm – I'm Daphne. Please, go away.'

'Oh, Daphne Please-Go-Away,' Apollo said, 'I love you! Marry me, and I will make you the happiest naiad in the universe.'

'No.'

'I insist! Come; let me kiss you. I will prove my affection and . . . Hey, where are you going?'

Daphne ran.

Apollo was fast, but Daphne was faster. Apollo was burdened with his bow and his lyre and he was dazed with love, so he kept stopping to compose new haiku in her honour.

Eventually, though, Daphne began to tire. She reached a cliff that looked out over a canyon. Apollo climbed the slope behind her. There was no way Daphne could double back.

That left her with two options: leap to her death, or agree to marry Apollo. Hearing him spout love poetry, she thought leaping off the cliff sounded pretty good.

In desperation, she tried one last thing: 'O Gaia, protector of all nature spirits, hear me! Save me from becoming this god's girlfriend!'

Gaia took pity on Daphne. Just as Apollo reached the cliff and threw his arms around the naiad, Daphne changed into a laurel tree. Apollo found himself hugging a tree trunk, caressing arms that had turned into branches, running his hands through hair that had become leaves.

Apollo sobbed in despair. 'Oh, beautiful naiad! I will never forget you. You were my one true love. You should have been my wife! I failed to win your love, but from now until the end of time you will be a symbol of victory. Your leaves shall adorn my head, and I will totally start a new fashion trend!'

That's why you'll often see pictures of Greeks and Romans wearing laurel wreaths on their heads. Apollo made it stylish. Laurels became a sign of honour. If you won a contest or a sporting event, you got to wear laurels. If you conquered an enemy nation, more laurels! If you got tired of doing amazing deeds and you had enough wreaths to stuff a mattress, you could retire and rest on your laurels!

All because Apollo bragged about his big fancy golden bow.

Eros had the last laugh, but, generally speaking, Apollo was right to brag. He *was* the best archer in the world. Only one person was as good as he was, maybe even better.

That would be his sister Artemis. If you want to read about her, fine. But, guys – be on your best behaviour. I'm warning you now: Artemis doesn't have a sense of humour.

ARTEMIS UNLEASHES THE DEATH PIG

I T'S NOT THAT ARTEMIS HATED ALL MEN, just most of them. From the moment she was born, she knew one critical fact: *Guys are kinda gross.*

Of course, she'd spent those seven months in the womb with her twin brother, Apollo, waiting to be born. That much time alone with Apollo would give anyone a bad impression of the male gender.

Artemis was born first, probably because she was anxious to get out. She immediately grew to the size of a six-year-old girl and looked around at the other goddesses who had assembled to help Leto.

'Right,' Artemis said. 'I'll assist with my brother's delivery. He's going to be a pain. Boil some water! Get some extra sheets! I'll scrub up.'

Sure enough, Artemis helped deliver her own twin brother.

From that point on, she became a goddess of childbirth, the protector of newborn babies and young children. (Along with the other childbirth goddess, Eileithyia; they shared the duties.) Once Apollo was born and started dancing and singing about how great he was, Artemis just stepped back and rolled her eyes.

'He's always like this,' she confided to Hestia. 'Seven months in the womb, he wouldn't shut up.'

Hestia smiled kindly. 'And you, dear? Do you sing and dance?'

'Ugh, no. But I do have plans. Could you take me to see my dad?'

Hestia whisked young Artemis off to Mount Olympus, where her father, Zeus, was sitting on his throne, listening to the wind gods give their weekly report on cloud formations. It was *so* freaking boring; Zeus was delighted to have a distraction.

'Hey, look!' Zeus said, interrupting the South Wind's PowerPoint presentation about low-pressure zones. 'It's Hestia and . . . and some kid. Come in!'

Hestia stepped into the throne room, leading Artemis by the hand. 'Lord Zeus, this is your new daughter, Artemis. We can come back later if you're busy.'

'Busy?' Zeus cleared his throat. 'No, no! They're important stuff, weather reports, but, darn it, they'll have to wait!'

He shooed away the wind gods and held out his arms to Artemis. 'Come to Papa, little one! Let's take a look at you!'

Artemis wore a simple knee-length *chiton* – a sort of T-shirt dress tied with a cord at the waist. She had shoulder-length raven-black hair and strikingly beautiful silver-grey eyes. I use the word *strikingly* because you got the feeling those eyes could strike you dead if Artemis got angry.

She was less than a day old, but she already looked like she was in elementary school. Even for a nine- or ten-year-old, she would have been tall. She could've totally dominated the fourth-grade basketball team. As she approached the throne, she gave Zeus a brilliant smile that melted his heart.

'Daddy!' She threw herself into his arms. 'I love you, I love you! You're the best daddy ever!'

Maybe she didn't like guys that much, but she knew *exactly* how to wrap her father around her little finger.

Zeus chuckled. 'Well, shock me silly. You are the cutest little goddess I've ever seen. Tell Daddy Zeus what you want for your birthday present, honeycakes, and it's yours.'

Artemis batted her eyelashes. 'Anything?'

'Anything! I promise on the River Styx!'

Boom. Magic words. You'd think the gods would've been smarter about not making rash promises on the River Styx, but Zeus never seemed to learn. Now he would have to give Artemis whatever she wanted.

Some girls might've asked for a pony or a new phone or a shopping spree with their friends at the mall. Some might've asked for front-row tickets to the hottest boy-band concert, or a date with somebody really awesome – like, I don't know, Percy Jackson, or somebody. (*What? It could happen.*)

Artemis didn't care about any of that. She knew *exactly* what she wanted. Maybe it was because her mom, Leto, had been on the move so much while she tried to give birth, wandering from island to island. Maybe it was because the snake Python had almost devoured Leto before the twins could be born. Whatever the case, Artemis had a restless spirit. She wanted to roam the world and hunt dangerous creatures, and she *definitely* never wanted to get pregnant. She'd seen how much trouble that had brought her mom. Artemis was happy assisting with deliveries, but she never wanted to go through that herself.

'Let me be a maiden forever, Father,' Artemis said, twirling her finger in Zeus's beard. 'I never want to get married. I want a bow and arrows – Wait. You know what? Forget that. If *you* gave me the bow and arrows, they might not be the best quality. I'll go see the Cyclopes and get them to custom-make my weapons. But you can grant me a bunch of followers: ocean nymphs, river nymphs, wood nymphs – what the heck, how about mortal girls, too? Any girls who want to join me can become my followers, as long as they remain maidens like me. They should probably make the decision when they're about nine years old, before they get interested in boys, because after that they'll be all distracted and of no use to me. I think we can start with about eighty followers, okay? We'll see how it goes. They can hunt with me, clean my kills, take care of my hunting dogs. Oh, that reminds me! I want hunting dogs.'

She took a deep breath. 'I also want the right to hunt any dangerous animals anywhere in the world. I want all mountains to be sacred to me, because that's where I'll spend most of my time, out in the wilderness. As far as cities . . . I don't know. Just pick any old city to be my special place. I'll only visit towns when the women need my help with childbirth, or when the little kids need a protector.' She smiled up at Zeus with her big silvery eyes. 'And . . . yeah, I think that's it.'

Zeus blinked, momentarily stunned.

Then he burst out laughing. 'You're my daughter, all right! You think *big!*' He kissed Artemis's forehead and set her on her feet. 'You know, when I have children like you, it's totally worth dealing with Hera's wrath. I'll give you everything you asked for, my sweet. Not only that, I'll give you *lots* of cities. I have a feeling you're going to be very popular!'

Zeus was right. Artemis was worshipped by all kinds of people: pregnant women, little kids, parents, young maidens who wanted protection from gross guys, and of course anyone who hunted, which back then were a *lot* of folks. Guy or girl, if you hunted, Artemis was on your side — as long as you didn't trash the wilderness, and you actually *used* what you killed. But she was also the goddess of wild animals, so if you went crazy and killed too many animals for no good reason Artemis would have a few things to say to you.

After talking with Zeus, Artemis went to see the Cyclopes, who were working at one of Hephaestus's forges on the island of Lipara. She got them to make her a special silver hunting bow and a quiver full of enchanted gold and silver arrows.

Then she went to visit Pan, the satyr god of the wild. She adopted his best wild dogs for her hunting pack. Some were black and white, some were reddish, some had spots like Dalmatians, but they were all fierce. They ran faster than the wind, and each one was strong enough to pull down a full-grown lion. Imagine what they could do as a pack.

Next, Artemis assembled her group of followers. It wasn't hard. A lot of nymphs and mortal girls liked the idea of living free in the wilderness, never having to worry about getting married. Maybe you're thinking, *Oh, but I want to get married some day!* Yeah, but back then most girls didn't get to pick who they married. Your dad just said, *Hey, go marry that guy. He offered me the biggest dowry.* It didn't matter if the dude was fat, old, ugly and smelled like month-old cheese. You had no choice but to marry him.

Artemis's followers never had to deal with that. They also never had to look over their shoulders, wondering if some lovesick god was going to ambush them. Artemis's hunters were off-limits. Anybody who tried to kidnap them, or even flirt with them, would find himself on the wrong side of Artemis's silver bow.

Usually Artemis only took about twenty followers hunting with her at a time. You can't exactly sneak up on your prey with eighty girls. The rest of her followers would either hunt in different groups or stay back at camp and butcher the kills, or cure the leather, or make campfires . . . or whatever nature-type people do when they're camping. I'm from Manhattan. I don't know these things.

Early on, Artemis realized she would be travelling long distances and moving quickly – sometimes more quickly than even a goddess could move on foot. She decided it would be a good idea to get a chariot. She just wasn't sure what type of animals should pull it. Horses were Poseidon's thing. Besides, they were domesticated. Artemis wanted something wild and fast.

Then one day she spotted a herd of deer.

You're thinking, *Wow, deer. That fills me with excitement.*

But this herd of deer included five huge hinds – adult females the size of bulls, with hooves and antlers made of solid gold. How did Artemis know it was real gold and not spray-paint? She's the goddess of wild animals. She could just tell.

She turned to her followers and whispered, 'Those noble deer would be *awesome* pulling my chariot. This will be our first big capture, ladies!'

Now, Artemis preferred not to kill harmless animals like

deer. Mostly she just killed animals that hurt humans, like bears or lions or enraged badgers. But she had lots of clever ways to catch animals without hurting them. Among her followers was a nymph named Britomartis, who was so good at making nets that Artemis would eventually make her a minor goddess – the Lady of Nets. (Did she play basketball? I don't know.)

Britomartis set some snares and concealed nets. Then the followers of Artemis started making noise. Just as they hoped, most of the regular-sized deer ran away, but the giant hinds with the golden horns turned to face the enemy and protect their herd.

Four of them charged straight into the nets and were caught, but the smartest of the five turned at the last second and dashed to safety.

'My lady,' said Britomartis, 'should we go after that one?'

Artemis smiled. 'No. Four deer are enough to pull my chariot. That fifth one has earned her freedom. She's a smart hind! From now on, she will have my blessing. I forbid any hunter to harm her.'

That lucky deer lived a long time. She became famous for hanging out in an area of Greece called Ceryneia, so she was known as the Ceryneian Hind. Later on, Hercules would be ordered to capture her, but that's another story.

Artemis now had everything she needed: her weapons, her followers, her hunting dogs and her chariot pulled by magical hinds with fourteen-carat horns. The goddess spent her time roaming the mountains, hunting monsters, punishing anyone who was needlessly cruel to animals or didn't respect the wilderness. Occasionally she would pop into town to check on the children, help mothers give birth and maybe do a little recruiting among the young girls who might want to join the Hunt.

In some ways, she and her brother Apollo were very much alike. They were both freakishly good archers. While Artemis was the protector of young maidens, Apollo was the protector of young men. Both had healing powers. Both could punish disrespectful mortals with a sudden death-arrow or a horrible plague. Later on, Artemis became known as the goddess of the moon, taking over from the Titan Selene, the same way Apollo took over from Helios, the sun Titan. Sometimes you'll see Artemis with a silvery crescent-shape emblem on her headband, which either means she's the moon goddess or that she has a boomerang duct-taped to her forehead. Let's go with the first option.

In other ways, Artemis was totally different from her brother. Apollo dated *everybody*. Artemis had no time for that nonsense. She was absolutely immune to love magic.

Her brother Apollo liked to make music. Artemis preferred the sounds of the crickets at night, the crackle of the campfire, the hooting of owls and the gurgling of rivers. Apollo liked to draw attention to himself. Artemis preferred to slip away into the wilderness and be left alone with just her followers.

Her symbols? No surprise: the bow, the deer and sometimes the crescent moon.

You might think only women worshipped her, but guys respected her as well. The Spartans used to pray to her for good hunting and success with archery and whatnot. Gross-out alert: to honour her, they used to tie a young guy to Artemis's altar and whip him until he bled all over the place. Why they thought that would make Artemis happy, I'm not sure. Did I mention the Spartans were complete freakazoids?

Other Greeks sacrificed goats to her, or even dogs.

I know. *Dogs?* Artemis loved dogs. Why anyone would sacrifice them to her, I don't know. Hopefully Artemis made her displeasure known by sending a plague down on those idiots.

She was popular all over Greece, but her biggest temple was in the city of Ephesus in Asia Minor. The Amazons founded the place, which makes sense. A nation of women warriors? They totally got what Artemis was about.

Sure, Artemis was mostly into hunting, but she was an excellent warrior when she had to be. For instance, when those twin giants the Alodai attacked Olympus, stacking up mountains to make a siege tower? It was Artemis who took them down.

It happened like this. After Ares, the war god, got sprung from that bronze jar, the twin giants started bragging about how they were going to take over Olympus and make the gods their slaves. Ephialtes wanted Hera for his wife. Otis wanted to force Artemis to marry him.

When word of that got back to Artemis, she said, 'Okay. Those two need to die *now.*'

Maybe she could have taken them down from a distance with her bow, but she wanted to get up-close and personal so that she could see the pain on their faces.

She charged down the mountain and harassed them with arrows, shooting them in the legs, the hands and some very sensitive places. The twin giants tried to impale her with their massive spears, but she was too fast.

Finally she ran between the giants. They both stabbed at her, but she dodged at the last second, and the giants skewered each other. Giants killed. Problem solved. It also made for a great blooper reel on *Olympus's Funniest Battles.*

Most of the time, though, Artemis let wild animals do the killing for her.

One time in the Greek city of Kalydon, this dude King Oineus forgot to make proper offerings to Artemis. It was harvest time. The Kalydonians were supposed to offer the first fruits of their labours to the gods. They poured out olive oil for Athena. They burned some grain for Demeter. They sacrificed fish sticks with tartare sauce for Poseidon.

But they forgot Artemis. All she wanted was a few apples from the orchards. She would've even settled for lemons. But her altar remained empty.

'Okay,' she grumbled to herself. 'I might be dishonoured, but I won't be unavenged!'

She summoned the most ferocious pig in the history of pigs.

This wild boar was the size of a rhinoceros. His eyes were blood-red and blazed with fire. His steel-thick hide was covered with bristles as rigid as spear shafts, so even if he just brushed up against you he would shred you like brisket. His mouth shot lightning and sour clouds of acid, withering and burning anything in his path, and his massive razor-sharp tusks ... well, if you got close enough to see the tusks, you were pretty much already toast.

He was, in short, the Death Pig.

Artemis unleashed him on the fields of Kalydonia, where he uprooted all the orchards, trampled the fields and killed all the animals, farmers and any soldiers stupid enough to try fighting him.

At this point, King Oineus was really wishing he'd given

Artemis some apples. He turned to his son Meleager and said, 'You're the best hunter in the kingdom, my son! What should we do?'

'Hunt the boar!' said Meleager. 'Artemis is the goddess of hunting, right? The only way she'll forgive us is if we launch the biggest and most dangerous hunt in history. If we bring down the boar with bravery and skill, surely she will forgive us.'

King Oineus frowned. 'Or she might get even angrier. Besides, you can't possibly kill that monster yourself!'

'Not by myself,' Meleager agreed. 'I'll summon all the best hunters in Greece!'

The king spread the word and offered rewards. Pretty soon hunters from all over the world flocked to Kalydon. They put on the First Annual and Hopefully Last Annual Kalydonian Boar Hunt.

Artemis didn't make it easy on them. One guy named Mopsos, who was the strongest spear-thrower in Greece, launched his spear at the boar with enough force to crack a bronze shield. Artemis caused the point of the spear to fall off in midflight. The spear shaft just bounced harmlessly off the monster.

Another hunter named Ankaios laughed at him. 'That's no way to fight the Death Pig! Watch and learn!' He hefted his double-bladed axe. 'I'll show you how a *real* man fights! This girlie goddess's boar is no match for me.'

He charged in, raising his axe above his head, and the boar rammed his tusk straight into Ankaios's crotch. Ankaios died, and he was remembered forever after as the Crotchless Wonder.

Finally Prince Meleager himself slew the boar with a lot of help from his friends. That was brave and all, but Artemis still wasn't satisfied. She filled the other hunters with envy.

Meleager skinned the boar and hung its hide in the palace as the grand prize of the hunt, but fighting broke out over who really deserved credit for the kill.

The argument turned into a full-scale civil war. Hundreds of people died, all because the king forgot to give Artemis some fruit. Seriously, it's only twelve gods. Next time make a checklist, Oineus.

So, yeah. If you forgot to make sacrifices, Artemis might kill you. But, if you *really* wanted to guarantee yourself a painful death, invade her personal space.

A hunter named Actaeon made that mistake. The weird thing was he really respected Artemis. He *always* made his sacrifices to her on time. He dedicated his best kills to the goddess and tried to be a good hunter. He'd been raised and trained by Chiron himself, the famous centaur who taught all the best Greek heroes. (*Cough*, me, *cough*.) Actaeon kept a pack of fifty dogs. When he wasn't at Chiron's cave learning hero stuff, Actaeon was out with his dogs, tracking down dangerous creatures and bringing home the wild-boar bacon.

One night he was in the mountains, exhausted from a hard day of hunting. He lay down to sleep on a rock overlooking a lake with a waterfall. His dogs curled up in the meadow behind him. He pulled his blanket over his head and went to sleep, only to wake in the morning to the sound of voices.

Actaeon rubbed the sleep out of his eyes. He looked down at the lake and thought he was dreaming. A bunch of beautiful ladies were bathing in the waterfall, like, *without clothes.* The most beautiful one looked exactly like the statues of Artemis that Actaeon had seen in the temples. She was tall with dark hair and brilliant silver eyes. The sight of her bathing made the blood roar in Actaeon's ears.

Now, if he'd just crept away right then, he might've been okay. Artemis didn't realize he was there. Actaeon could have sneaked off and lived to a ripe old age with his secret and considered himself lucky. I mean . . . he wasn't being a stalker *yet*. He hadn't intended on spying.

But no. Of course not. Actaeon *had* to get greedy.

He kept watching. He fell in love with Artemis. He decided he *had* to marry her.

He knew she was an eternal maiden, sure. But she hadn't met *him* yet!

Actaeon respected her. He'd always sacrificed to her. He loved hunting and animals . . . They had so much in common. Why hadn't he thought about this before?

He sprang up from his sleeping spot and yelled, 'Forgive me, my lady!'

The followers of Artemis screamed and scrambled to the shore to retrieve their clothes and their bows. Artemis narrowed her eyes. She made no attempt to cover herself. She walked towards Actaeon over the top of the water.

'Who are you?' she demanded.

'Actaeon, my lady. I am a great hunter, and I have always worshipped you.'

'Indeed?' Artemis didn't sound impressed. 'Yet you spy on me while I am bathing?'

'That — that was an accident.' Actaeon's neck started to feel itchy, like it was covered in fleas. He wasn't feeling so confident now, but it was too late to back out. 'Your beauty . . . it has inspired me to speak. I must have you! Marry me!'

Artemis tilted her head. A silver aura glowed around her entire body.

'*You must have me,*' she said. 'You think I am your prey?'

'N-no, my lady.'

'You think *you* are the hunter and I am some prize to bring down with your pack of dogs?'

'Well, no. But —'

'Let me enlighten you, Actaeon,' said the goddess. 'I am the hunter. I am always the hunter. *You* are the prey. No man who has seen me naked may live.'

Actaeon's body writhed with pain. Just above his eyes, his forehead split open and sprouted two heavy antlers. His fingers fused together into cloven hooves. His back bent and stretched. His legs narrowed. His boots shrank and hardened into hooves.

Actaeon became a deer — a beautiful sixteen-point buck.

Artemis made a high-pitched whistling noise. Actaeon's pack of fifty dogs stirred from their sleep. They didn't smell their master anywhere, but, wow, that huge deer smelled great! Actaeon tried to command his dogs to stay, but he had no voice. They didn't recognize him. He bolted, as deer usually do, but the dogs were too fast.

They tore their old master into tiny pieces.

When the dogs were done, they looked around for Actaeon. They couldn't find him anywhere. They bayed and whined and got very sad, but finally they made their way back home to Chiron's cave. The centaur saw the pieces of Actaeon's clothing stuck in their teeth and the blood on their fur, and he figured out what must have happened. He had warned that stupid kid not to mess with Artemis. To make the dogs feel better, he made a fake Actaeon dummy out of the hunter's old clothes, like a scarecrow, so the dogs would think that their master was still around.

I guess that was nice of Chiron, for the dogs' sake, but it kind of makes me wonder if he's got a Percy Jackson scarecrow stuffed in a closet somewhere for emergencies. I'm not sure I want to know.

That wasn't the only time a guy spotted Artemis bathing. The next time it was a boy named Sipriotes, who was just wandering along and wound up in the wrong place at the wrong time.

When he saw the naked goddess, he yelped in surprise, but he was just a kid. He didn't ask to marry her. He just fell to his knees and begged for mercy.

'Please, lady,' he whimpered. 'I didn't mean it. Don't turn me into a deer and have me ripped apart by dogs!'

Artemis felt bad. She was the protector of young children, after all.

'Well, Sipriotes,' she said, 'here's the problem. No male can gaze upon me naked and live.'

'But – but –'

'Since you're male, I have to kill you. Unless, of course, you weren't male . . .'

Sipriotes blinked. 'You mean . . . wait. What?'

'Death or gender change. Your choice.'

It wasn't much of a choice. Sipriotes didn't want to die. So *shazam!* Artemis turned him into a *her*, and the girl Sipriotes lived happily ever after with the hunters of Artemis.

Weird enough for you? Oh, it gets weirder!

Another time one of Artemis's followers, a girl named Kallisto, caught the eye of Zeus. Now, Artemis's followers were supposed to be off-limits, but this is Zeus we're talking about. Also, Kallisto was a real knockout.

She was Artemis's favourite follower at the time. They were so much alike – both swift and strong, totally not interested in guys. They became best friends as soon as Kallisto joined the Hunt. Like all followers of Artemis, Kallisto had sworn to stay a maiden forever, but Zeus had other ideas.

One day he looked down from Olympus and saw Kallisto alone in a clearing, relaxing and enjoying the sunshine.

'This is my chance!' he told himself. 'I just have to figure out a way to get close to her so she doesn't run off. That girl is fast. Hmm . . .'

Zeus changed form so he looked exactly like Artemis.

I know – a total creep move, right? But, like I said, the guy had no shame when it came to catching women. He would even pretend to be his own daughter.

Fake Artemis came sauntering into the clearing. 'Hey, Kallisto. Whatcha doing?'

'My lady!' Kallisto leaped to her feet. 'I was just resting.'

'Can I join you?' asked Fake Artemis.

Kallisto noticed something strange about the look in the goddess's eyes, but she said, 'Um, sure.'

Fake Artemis came closer. She took Kallisto's hand. 'You're very beautiful, you know.'

Fake Artemis kissed her, and I'm not talking about a friendly peck on the cheek. Kallisto struggled and tried to pull back, but Zeus held her tight, and he was stronger.

'My lady!' Kallisto shrieked. 'What are you *doing*?'

Zeus changed into his true self, and Kallisto shrieked even louder.

'Now, now,' the sky god said. 'Artemis doesn't need to know, my dear. It'll be our little secret!'

So Zeus once again proved himself a godly slimeball. Yeah, sure, he might hear me and get mad. It won't be the first time I've taken a chance with Mr Thunder. But, hey, I call 'em like I see 'em.

If the real Artemis had been within earshot, she would've come running to help Kallisto. Unfortunately, Kallisto was all by herself. Zeus got his way.

Afterwards, Kallisto was too ashamed to say anything. She was afraid it was somehow her fault. Pro tip: if you're attacked by a creep, it's *never* your fault. Tell somebody.

But Kallisto kept her secret as long as she could. She tried to pretend nothing had happened. Sadly, she was pregnant. She couldn't hide that forever. A few months later, after a hot day chasing down monsters, Artemis and the gang wanted to go swimming. They all jumped in the lake except Kallisto.

'What's wrong?' Artemis called. 'Come on!'

Kallisto blushed. She put her hand on her belly, which was starting to swell. She didn't dare take off her clothes, or Artemis would notice.

Artemis sensed the problem anyway. Suddenly she realized why Kallisto had been so distant and sad recently.

The goddess's heart sank.

'You, Kallisto?' she asked. 'Of all my followers, *you* broke your vow?'

'I – I didn't mean to!' Kallisto said. A tear rolled down her cheek.

'Who was it?' Artemis demanded. 'A handsome warrior?

A smooth-talking hero? My brother, Apollo? Oh, no . . . *please* tell me it wasn't him.'

'It – it was you!' Kallisto wailed.

Artemis stared at her. 'Run that by me again.'

Kallisto told the story of how Zeus had appeared to her in Artemis's form.

The goddess burned with rage. She wanted to throttle her father, Zeus, but there's only so much you can do when your dad is the king of the universe. She looked at Kallisto and shook her head in pity.

'You were my favourite,' Artemis said. 'If you had come to me immediately, I could have helped you. I would have found you a rich, handsome husband and let you settle into a new life in the city of your choice. I would have allowed you to retire from the Hunt with honour. You could have gone in peace. Zeus's assault was not your fault.'

Kallisto sobbed. 'But I didn't want to lose you! I wanted to stay!'

Artemis felt like her heart was breaking, but she couldn't show it. She had rules about her followers. She couldn't allow those rules to be broken, not even by her best friend. 'Kallisto, your crime was keeping the secret from me. You dishonoured me, and your sisters of the Hunt, by not being honest. You defiled our company of maidens when you were not a maiden yourself. That I cannot forgive.'

'But . . . but, Artemis –'

'No more talk!' Artemis pointed at Kallisto, and the young lady began to change. She grew in size. Her limbs became shorter and thicker. Her clothes, which had helped her hide her condition, became a suffocating thick coat of brown fur. Kallisto turned into a brown bear. When she tried to talk, she could only roar.

'Go, now,' Artemis said, trying not to cry. 'Your new shape will remind you that you can never be in my sight. If I see you again, I must kill you. LEAVE!'

Kallisto bounded away through the woods. She gave birth to a human son named Arkas, who returned to the world of mortals and eventually became a king. But, soon after, poor Kallisto was killed by hunters.

Zeus felt some remorse. He turned Kallisto into a constellation, Ursa Major, or the Great Bear – as if that could make up for ruining her life.

Kind of strange: after the incident with Kallisto, Artemis's next two best friends were both guys. I'm not sure why. Maybe she figured they couldn't hurt her any worse than Kallisto had, or if they did, at least she wouldn't be surprised, since guys were naturally jerks. Or maybe she was trying to prove to herself that she would never go back on her own vow of maidenhood, even with the most interesting guy she could find.

Her first male friend was Orion, who had a shady past. For one thing, he was a giant. But he was short for a giant, maybe seven feet tall, and he looked humanoid enough that he could almost pass for a mortal. For a long time he worked for the king of Chios as the royal hunter. Then Orion got in a little trouble with the king's daughter. When the king found out, he had Orion blinded with a searing hot iron. Then he kicked him out of the kingdom.

Orion stumbled around Greece until he happened to run

into the blacksmith god Hephaestus. Orion told him his tragic story. The giant sounded genuinely sorry, so Hephaestus — who knew a lot about tragedy and second chances — designed mechanical eyes that allowed Orion to see again.

Orion retired to Delos, where he met Artemis. She thought he was a nice-enough guy. He didn't try to hide his past crimes. He also had incredible hunting skills. His years of blindness had sharpened his other senses, and his mechanical eyes gave him all sorts of cool night vision/targeting abilities. He became the first male ever to join the Hunters of Artemis.

I'm not sure how the other followers felt about that. The Hunters had never been co-ed before. But Orion didn't try anything funny. He kept his distance from the girls when they were bathing. He helped out with the chores just like everybody else. Pretty soon he became fast friends with Artemis.

The only problem: Orion was a little *too* good at hunting. One day he was out by himself, and he got carried away. He shot sixteen bears, twelve lions and several monsters that he couldn't even name. Then he started shooting harmless stuff: deer, rabbits, squirrels, birds, wombats. Maybe he just snapped. Maybe Apollo drove him crazy, because Apollo didn't like how much time this dude was spending with his sister.

Anyway, Orion soon had a mound of dead wombat carcasses piled up around him. He painted his face with squirrel blood and put leaves in his hair and started screaming, 'I will kill all the animals in the world! All of them! Die, stupid furry critters!'

This didn't really fit with the Hunters' nature-friendly mission statement. It also didn't please Gaia the Earth Mother. Orion was screaming so loudly that he got her attention, even while she was sleeping, and Gaia muttered to herself, 'You want to kill something, punk? Try this.'

Just behind Orion, a massive scorpion emerged from a fissure in the ground. The giant turned and got a poisonous stinger right in the chest.

That was the end of Orion. Artemis went searching for him, and when she found his cold, lifeless body, surrounded (for some bizarre reason) by thousands of dead furry critters, her heart was broken again. This time *Artemis* made a constellation. She put Orion in the sky, with a scorpion nearby, so his story would live forever.

I guess the moral is: don't try to massacre bunnies, squirrels and wombats. They didn't do anything to you, and you might find that they have a very big scorpion friend.

Artemis's last best friend was a prince named Hippolytos. The guy was handsome and charming and had no interest in romance at all. He just wanted to spend all his time hunting. In other words, he was Artemis's perfect man. She accepted him into the Hunt, which must have been a challenge for some of her female followers. The guy was a little too attractive for his own good.

Still, Hippolytos was a model follower. He kept his vows and never gave the ladies a second look.

Not everybody liked this, though. Up on Olympus, Aphrodite the goddess of love was outraged.

'Are you *kidding* me?' she wailed. 'A hot guy like that, hanging out with eighty beautiful women, and he's not interested? This is an insult! This is *not* okay!'

The next time Hippolytos went home to visit his dad, King

Theseus (who is a whole other story, that dude), they got into this huge argument. Dad wanted Hippolytos to get married so he could have kids and carry on the family name when he became king, blah, blah, blah.

Hippolytos said, 'No! I want to stay with Artemis and hunt!'

Theseus roared in frustration. 'If you *love* her so much, why don't you marry her?'

'She's a maiden goddess, Dad! You never listen!'

The argument got more and more heated, because up in Olympus Aphrodite was inflaming their passions. Sure, she was the goddess of love, but there really isn't much difference between love and hate. They both get out of control easily, and one turns into the other. Trust me. I know.

Finally, Theseus drew a sword and killed his own son.

Whoops.

Of course the king was horribly ashamed. He placed the prince's body in the royal crypts and ran off to mourn in private. Meanwhile, Artemis heard the news and came rushing to the tomb.

Weeping with rage, she gathered up the body of Hippolytos. 'No! No, no, no! I will *not* lose another best friend. I *won't*!'

She flew out of the city, carrying Hippolytos's body. She searched all of Greece until she found the best physician in the world – a guy named Asklepios. He was a son of Apollo, the god of healing, but Asklepios was even better at healing than his dad. Probably that was because Asklepios spent all his time *actually* healing, while Apollo flirted and gave concerts in the park.

'Aunt Artemis!' said Asklepios. 'Good to see you!'

Artemis laid the body of Hippolytos at his feet. 'Asklepios,

I need you to heal Hippolytos. Please! This is beyond even my powers.'

'Hmm,' Asklepios said. 'What's wrong with him?'

'He's dead,' Artemis said.

'That's a serious condition. It's almost always fatal. But I'll see what I can do.'

Asklepios mixed some herbs, cooked a potion and force-fed it to the dead prince, who immediately woke up.

'Thank the Fates!' Artemis said. 'Asklepios, you're the best!'

'Hey, no problem.'

Actually, it *was* a problem. Aphrodite complained to Zeus. She was *such* a sore loser. Then Hades complained. Asklepios couldn't go around bringing the dead back to life. That would cause chaos in the mortal world and the Underworld. Zeus agreed. He zapped Asklepios with lightning and killed him, which is why you can't go to the doctor today and ask him to resurrect your dead relatives. Zeus declared that level of medicine off-limits.

As for Hippolytos, Artemis made sure he stayed safe. She whisked him off to Italy, where he became a priest at one of her sacred shrines and lived to a ripe old age.

After that, Artemis decided not to get too close to any of her followers. It was just too dangerous for them. She also became wary about inviting any more men into the Hunt.

That's okay with me. I like Artemis, but I don't do well with nature. Also, I don't like hunting. I *do* like girls, but my girlfriend would *not* be okay with me hanging out with eighty beautiful women in the wilderness.

She's kind of possessive that way.

HERMES GOES TO JUVIE

I T WOULD BE FASTER to list the things Hermes *wasn't* the god of, because that guy had a lot going on.

He was the god of travel, so he was the patron of anyone who used the roads. That meant merchants, messengers, ambassadors, travelling performers and herders bringing their livestock to market. It also meant bandits, thieves, drifters and those annoying caravans of retired people in motorhomes heading south for the winter.

Hermes was in charge of guiding dead souls to the Underworld. He was Zeus's personal FedEx service, carrying his boss's messages all around the globe with guaranteed overnight delivery. He was also the god of (take a deep breath) commerce, languages, thievery, cheeseburgers, trickery, eloquent speaking, feasts, cheeseburgers, hospitality, guard dogs, birds of omen, gymnastics, athletic competitions, cheeseburgers, cheeseburgers and telling fortunes with dice.

Okay, I just tossed in the cheeseburgers to see if you were paying attention. Also, I'm hungry.

Basically, Hermes was in charge of anything and everyone you might encounter while travelling – the good stuff and the bad. So, if you take a trip, you'd better hope that Hermes is in a good mood. Otherwise you'll wind up sleeping in the airport, or stuck on the side of the road with a flat tyre. Since everybody in Ancient Greece needed to travel at one time or another, Hermes was an important, well-respected dude.

Hard to believe he was born in a cave and got arrested when he was twelve hours old.

His mom, Maia, tried to keep him out of trouble. She was a Titan, the daughter of Atlas; and when she became pregnant with Zeus's baby (which makes her, what, like girlfriend #458? Is anybody keeping track?) she tried to protect herself so she wouldn't end up like *most* of Zeus's girlfriends – cursed and harassed by Hera.

Maia hid in a cave on Mount Cyllene in central Greece, where she gave birth to cute little Hermes. She realized her kid was a baby god, so she decided she had better be careful. You can never tell when a baby god will start dancing and singing and shooting people. (She'd heard stories from Leto.) Maia nursed Baby Hermes and swaddled him tight in his blankets so he couldn't move or get into trouble. She placed him in a woven basket for a cradle and began singing a lullaby about the different gods and their favourite animals, because even back then baby songs were all about farm animals and stuff. She sang about Artemis and her dogs, Poseidon and his horses, Apollo and his herd of sacred cows – the finest and tastiest cattle in the world. Soon Hermes was sleeping peacefully. Maia stumbled to her bed and passed out, because giving birth was hard work.

As soon as Hermes heard his mom snoring, he opened his eyes.

The young god struggled in his swaddling blankets. 'Seriously?' he murmured. 'Born for thirty minutes, and I'm already in a straitjacket? Mom must really not trust me. Smart lady.'

He wriggled free and jumped out of the crib. Hermes still looked like a newborn, but only because he wasn't ready to start growing yet. He figured a baby could get away with stuff that an older kid couldn't. He stretched his arms, did a few jumping jacks and hiked up his diapers.

'All that singing about cows made me hungry,' he said. 'I could go for a steak!'

He strolled out of the cave, figuring it couldn't be too hard to find Apollo's cattle. He'd only gone a few steps when he tripped on something hard.

'Ow!' Hermes knelt down and realized that he'd stumbled over a tortoise.

'Hey, little buddy,' Hermes said. 'You're the first animal I've run across! I guess you'll be one of my sacred creatures. How would you like that?'

The tortoise just stared at him.

'That's a nice shell you've got.' Hermes rapped his knuckles on the tortoise's back. 'All dappled and pretty. How about I take you inside the cave where I can get a better look? I won't hurt you.'

Hermes was strong for a baby. Actually, he was strong for *anybody*. He picked up the tortoise and brought it inside.

Looking over its shell, he had a sudden idea. He remembered the way his mother's voice had echoed through the cave when she sang her lullaby, becoming louder and richer. Hermes had enjoyed that. This tortoise shell might amplify sound the same way, like a miniature cave – if there was no tortoise inside it.

'You know what, little buddy?' Hermes said. 'I changed my mind. I'm afraid I *will* hurt you.'

Gross-out alert: Hermes chopped off the tortoise's head and legs. He scooped out the rest of it with his mom's soup ladle. (Hey, I'm sorry. Back then, people butchered animals all the time for meat or hide or shell or whatever. This is why my friend Piper became a vegetarian.)

Anyway, once Hermes hollowed out the shell, he blew into it. The sound echoed deeply, but it wasn't quite what he wanted. Outside the cave, he could hear owls, crickets, frogs and a bunch of other critters making sounds at different pitches, all at the same time. Hermes wanted something like that – a bunch of sounds simultaneously. Over by the fire, he spotted some long, stringy sheep tendons that Maia had set out to dry for sewing or whatever.

Hermes thought, Hmm.

He stretched one tendon between his foot and hand. He plucked it with his free hand, and the gut string vibrated. The tighter he made the string, the higher the note.

'Oh, yeah,' he said. 'This'll work.'

He glanced at his mom to make sure she was still asleep. Then Hermes set to work. From his mom's loom, he took a couple of wooden dowels and ran them through the tortoise shell so that they stuck out of the neck hole like horns. Then he fastened a third dowel across the top, between the two braces, so they looked kind of like American football goalposts. He ran seven strings from the top of the neck to the base of the tortoise shell. Then he tuned the strings to different pitches. When he strummed, the sound was amazing. Hermes had invented the first stringed instrument, which he decided to call a lyre. (Why? Maybe because he *was* a liar, I don't know.)

If he'd spent a few more hours working, he probably could've invented the acoustic guitar, the stand-up bass and the Fender Stratocaster, too, but by now he was *really* hungry. He hid his new lyre in the blankets of his cradle and set out to find those yummy magic cows.

He climbed to the top of Mount Cyllene – hey, no big deal for such a buff baby – and peered across Greece, watching and listening. Apollo kept his cows well hidden at night, in a secret meadow in Pieria, which was about three hundred miles north of Cyllene, but Hermes had excellent senses. In no time, he heard a distant 'Mooo'.

Another cow said, 'Shhh. We're hiding!'

The first cow said, 'Sorry.'

Up on the mountaintop, Hermes grinned. 'Ha! I've got you now, cows.'

Three hundred miles? No problem! Hermes ran there in about an hour – which must have looked really strange, this newborn god tearing across Greece, his hands still covered in tortoise blood. Fortunately it was night-time and nobody saw him.

When he got to the secret meadow, Hermes drooled at the sight of so many delicious big fat healthy heifers, hundreds of them grazing in the tall grass between the base of a mountain and the sandy shores of the Mediterranean.

'I don't want to be greedy,' he said to himself. 'Maybe I'll just take fifty or so. But how to cover my tracks?'

He couldn't just stuff fifty cows in a sack and sneak away. And, if he herded them, Apollo would easily be able to follow the hoofprints of so many animals.

Hermes stared at the beach. Then he examined some nearby crepe myrtle trees. Not sure what he was doing exactly, he broke off some twigs and young branches from the myrtles. He remembered that back in Maia's cave his cradle had been a woven basket, and he started to weave the branches and twigs into big paddles. He wrapped these around his feet and created the first snowshoes – which was pretty amazing, since it never snowed in Greece.

Hermes took a few steps in the grass, then on the sand. The paddle shoes left wide, vague impressions that completely masked the size of his feet.

Perfect, he thought. That covers *me*. And now for the cows . . .

He waded across the meadow in his new shoes. He managed to separate the herd, shooing fifty of the fattest, juiciest cows away from the rest. Those fifty he drove sideways towards the beach.

Once they reached the sand, Hermes snapped his fingers and whistled to get the cows' attention. When all fifty of them were looking at him, their tails facing the ocean, he said, 'Okay, guys. Now back it up. Back it up!'

Ever tried to get fifty cows walking backwards? It's not easy. Hermes kept their attention on him, whistling and making back-up noises like, '*BEEP, BEEP, BEEP!*' while he waved his arms and advanced towards the water. The cattle shuffled backwards, right into the surf. Then Hermes turned them south and herded them a few hundred yards through the waves before leading them onto dry land again.

When he looked back, he had to appreciate his own trickery. It looked as if fifty cows had marched *out* of the sea and joined the main herd. No one would be able to tell where the missing cows had gone. Hermes had left no footprints that could be traced to him.

He led the cows south through the fields of Greece.

By this time it was after midnight, so Hermes figured he wouldn't be seen. Unfortunately, one old mortal farmer named Battus was out tending his grapevines. Maybe Battus couldn't sleep, or maybe he always pruned his grapes at night, but when he saw this little baby leading fifty cows down the road the old dude's eyes bugged out of his head.

'What?' he warbled. 'How?'

Hermes forced a smile. ''Sup?' He considered killing the old man. He didn't want any witnesses. But Hermes was a thief, not a murderer. Besides, he already had the blood of an innocent tortoise on his hands. 'I'm just taking my cows for a walk. What's your name, old-timer?'

'Battus.' Battus couldn't believe he was having a conversation with a baby. Maybe he was still asleep in bed, dreaming.

'Well, Battus,' said Hermes, 'it would be best if you forgot you saw me. Anybody asks, I was never here. Do that, and I'll make sure you get some awesome blessings when I take my place on Mount Olympus, okay?'

'Erm . . . okay.'

'Cool. And, hey, is that a knife in your belt? Could I borrow that?'

Battus gave the baby god his pruning knife, and Hermes led his cattle onward.

Finally Hermes found a nice cave where he could hide the stolen cows. He penned forty-eight of them inside so he could eat them later, or maybe sell them on the black market. He hadn't decided yet. Then he used the old man's knife to butcher the last two.

Again, a pretty creepy image – a baby god with a knife, slaughtering cows – but Hermes wasn't squeamish. He built a fire and sacrificed the best cuts of meat to the Olympian gods (including himself, naturally). Then he put more meat on a spit, roasted it and stuffed himself with tasty beef.

'Aw, that was good!' Hermes belched with appreciation. 'Man, it's getting late. Or early, I guess. I'd better get home.'

He cleaned up in a nearby stream, because he didn't think his mom wanted to see her newborn child covered in blood. Then, just for fun, he took a couple of cow bones, hollowed them into flutes and tied them together at one end in a V so that he could play them both simultaneously (because just one flute is boring). He waddled home with a full belly, playing soft music on his new double flute to keep himself awake. He got back to Maia's cave just before dawn, crawled into his cradle and tucked his V-flute under his blankets with his lyre. Then he passed out. Even for a baby god, it had been a long first night.

The next morning, Apollo flew to Pieria to count his cows. He always liked to start the day by admiring his cattle.

When he realized that fifty of them were missing, he freaked. He ran around yelling, 'Here, cows! Here, cows!' He found hoofprints leading out of the sea, as if his cattle had gone for a swim and then returned, but that made no sense. He saw some huge, shallow indentions in the sand, like a very thin guy with size twenty-five shoes had been walking around – but again, that made no sense.

Apollo searched most of the morning, until finally he came across the old farmer Battus, who was still pruning his vines. After the 'talking baby' incident, Battus hadn't been able to get any sleep.

'Old man!' Apollo called. 'Have you seen fifty cows walking this way? Possibly led by a very lightweight giant with size twenty-five shoes?'

Battus winced. He was no good at lying. Apollo could tell immediately that the farmer was trying to hide something.

'I might add,' said Apollo, 'that I am a god. It would be a very good idea to tell me the truth.'

Battus heaved a sigh. 'It was a baby.'

Apollo frowned. 'What, now?'

Battus told him the story, which was so weird that Apollo decided it must be the truth. Apollo knew of only one newborn god. He'd heard rumours that the Titan Maia had given birth last night on Mount Cyllene. (Apollo always tried to keep up with the latest gossip.) It seemed unlikely that a newborn child could be responsible for a cattle theft three hundred miles away, but Apollo himself had started singing and dancing as soon as he came out of the womb, so it wasn't impossible.

He flew down to Maia's cave and woke up the mama Titan. 'Your kid stole my cows!' he told her.

Maia rubbed her eyes. She looked at baby Hermes, still lying in his cradle, swaddled in blankets . . . though his belly did look a lot bigger, and was that a dribble of A1 Steak Sauce on his chin?

'Uh, you must have the wrong baby,' Maia said. 'He's been here all night.'

Apollo snorted. 'It *had* to be him. Look at the steak sauce on his chin! My cows are probably stashed around here somewhere.'

Maia shrugged. 'You're welcome to look.'

Apollo tore through the cave, searching inside pots, behind the loom, under the bedrolls. Amazingly, fifty cows were not hidden in any of those places.

Finally Apollo marched to the baby's cradle. 'All right, kid. 'Fess up. Where are my cattle?'

Hermes opened his eyes and tried to look as cute as possible. 'Goo goo?'

'Nice try,' Apollo grumbled. 'I can smell the beef on your breath.'

Hermes stifled a curse. He knew he should've eaten some breath mints.

'Dear cousin Apollo,' he said brightly, 'good morning to you! You think I've stolen some cattle? Can't you see that I'm just a baby?'

Apollo balled his fists. 'Where are they, you little punk?'

'I have no idea,' Hermes said. 'How could a little guy like me hide fifty cows?'

'Ha!' Apollo cried. 'I never said there were fifty!'

'Ah, tortoise poop,' Hermes muttered.

'You are under arrest for thievery!' Apollo said. 'I'm taking you to Mount Olympus for the judgement of Zeus!'

Apollo picked up the entire cradle and flew off to Mount Olympus. When he set the cradle in front of Zeus and explained that this newborn baby was a cattle thief, the other gods started giggling, but Zeus silenced them.

'This baby is my son,' Zeus said. 'I'm sure he's capable of anything. Well, Hermes, did you steal Apollo's cows?'

Hermes stood up in his cradle. 'No, Father.'

Zeus raised an eyebrow. He casually picked up one of his lightning bolts and tested the point. 'I'll give you a moment to reconsider your answer. Did you steal Apollo's cows?'

'Yes, Father. But, to be fair, I only killed two. The rest are safe and sound. And when I slaughtered the cows I sacrificed the first meat to the gods.'

'And then you stuffed yourself!' Apollo growled.

'Well, I'm one of the gods, too!' Hermes said. 'But all of you got a portion, of course! I would never forget to honour my relatives.'

The gods muttered among themselves and nodded. The baby might be a thief, but at least he was a respectful thief.

'This is ridiculous!' Apollo cried. 'Father Zeus, he stole from me. Put him in juvie! Put him on the chain gang!'

Zeus suppressed a smile. He knew he had to be just, but he also couldn't help admiring Hermes's audacity. 'Hermes, you will immediately show Apollo where you've hidden his cows. Then you will *pay* Apollo whatever price he demands for the two cows you killed.'

'I'll throw him into Tartarus!' Apollo yelled. 'That'll be my price!'

Zeus shrugged. 'You'll have to work that out between yourselves. Now, off with you.'

Hermes sighed. 'As you wish, Father. Apollo, you drive. I'll navigate.'

Apollo picked up the cradle and flew off with Hermes. The baby god directed him to the secret cave where he'd hidden the cattle, but he took a roundabout route. He was furiously thinking about how he could avoid punishment.

When Apollo saw his missing cows, he calmed down a little bit, but he was still angry with Hermes.

'It's Tartarus time,' Apollo snarled. 'I'll throw you so far into the abyss –'

Hermes pulled his lyre from the blankets of his cradle and began to strum.

Apollo listened, spellbound. He didn't dare interrupt until Hermes was through.

'What – where – how –'

'Oh, this?' Hermes said casually. 'I call it a lyre. I invented it last night.'

His fingers flew across the strings, creating a waterfall of beautiful notes.

'I must have it,' Apollo said. 'I'm the god of music. Please! I – I must have it!'

'Oh, but you're going to throw me into Tartarus,' Hermes said sadly. 'I'll need my lyre to cheer me up down there in the dark.'

'Forget Tartarus,' Apollo said. 'Give me the lyre, and we'll call it even.'

'Hmm,' Hermes said. 'And I get to keep the rest of these cows?'

'*What?!*' Apollo demanded.

Hermes played another melody, as bright as sunlight through the trees.

'Yes, yes!' Apollo said. 'Fine, keep the cows. Just give me the lyre.'

'Wonderful!' Hermes tossed the lyre to Apollo.

Then the baby god pulled out his double flute, which he'd decided to call a *syrinx*. He started playing *that*, and Apollo's mouth hung open.

'Don't tell me you invented that, too!'

'Hmm?' Hermes paused. 'Oh, yes. Just a little something I thought up after dinner. It's for sale . . . for the right price.'

Hermes played a little Mozart and some One Direction, and Apollo cried, 'I must have it! The girls will go wild for that! I'll offer you . . . well, I've got some nice magic items back at my apartment: a herald's staff I'm not using, some flying shoes and a sword. You can have all three!'

Hermes considered that. 'Throw in the power of prophecy and it's a deal.'

Apollo scowled. 'I can't do that. Prophecy is *my* gig. Tell you what: I'll give you the power to tell fortunes with dice. Nothing fancy, but it's a good party trick, and you can make some decent money that way.'

'Deal.'

'Deal!'

So Apollo and Hermes ended up becoming good friends. Apollo forgot about the cattle thievery. He didn't even mind that he'd totally been ripped off on the price of the lyre and the syrinx flute. Hermes got his own herd of cattle, which was how he became the god of cattle herders. He got a pair of winged sandals that made him faster than any other god. He got a sword made from adamantine and gold, with a blade so sharp it could cut through almost anything. He got a herald's staff, like human messengers carried when they travelled from city to city to show they had diplomatic immunity, except that Hermes's staff was magical. Normally, a herald's staff had two white ribbons twined around it. Hermes's staff had two living snakes instead. It also had the power to put anyone to sleep, or to wake them up, which was helpful to a god of thieves. The staff became known as a *caduceus* – just because I knew you needed another complicated word to remember.

Oh, and the old dude Battus who told on Hermes? Hermes flew back to the farm and turned Battus into a pillar of stone. Battus is still standing there overlooking the road, wishing he'd never seen that stupid cattle-thieving baby.

Hermes grew into an adult (in a couple of days, being a god and all). Usually he appeared as a handsome teenaged guy with curly black hair and just the beginnings of a wispy moustache. Of course, being a god, he could appear any way he wanted to.

He became the messenger of Zeus, and sometimes he even did secret dirty deeds for the boss man. That was Hermes's favourite part of the job!

Case in point: one time Zeus fell in love with a river nymph named Io. (Yes, that was her name. Just I and O. I guess she came from a poor family that couldn't afford consonants.) She was *amazingly* beautiful, but Zeus had the hardest time convincing her to go out with him. She always hung with a bunch of her nymph friends, so he couldn't ambush her. She totally ignored his texts. He sent her flowers and candy. He put on a beautiful thunderstorm to impress her. He worked at it for weeks and weeks and got totally obsessed.

Finally she agreed to meet him alone in the woods, and Zeus was like, 'YES!'

Unfortunately, Hera got wind of what was going on. Maybe one of the other nymphs told her.

Anyway, Zeus showed up in the clearing and Io was waiting for him in a shimmering white dress. She smiled and said, 'Hey, handsome.'

Zeus nearly whimpered with excitement, but just as he took Io's hand he heard a familiar voice in the woods.

'Zeus!' Hera screamed. 'Where are you, you no-good cheater?'

He yelped and turned Io into the first thing he could think of: a cow.

Not very nice, turning your girlfriend into a heifer. It's like word association: *chocolate – delicious. Sunlight – warmth. Io – cow!* Or maybe Hera's voice made him think of cows, since that was her sacred creature.

Anyway, when Hera stormed into the clearing, she found Zeus leaning casually against a large white cow.

Hera narrowed her eyes. 'What are you doing?'

'Hmm? Oh, hello, dear! Nothing. Nothing at all.'

'What's with the cow?'

'Cow?' Zeus seemed to notice Io for the first time. 'Oh, *this* cow? Um, nothing. Why?'

Hera clenched her fists until her knuckles turned white. 'That cow wouldn't happen to be one of your girlfriends, cleverly transformed?'

'Ha-ha! Oh, come on, dear. You know I wouldn't . . . Um . . . No, of course not.'

'Then why is the cow here?'

A bead of sweat trickled down the side of Zeus's face. He panicked and blurted out, 'It's a gift! For you!'

'A gift.'

'Well, yes.' Zeus tried to smile. 'Since . . . cows are sacred to you, right? I wanted it to be a surprise. But, um, if you don't like it, I can return it to the cow store.'

Hera figured Zeus was more full of manure than the heifer. But she decided to play along.

'Why, thank you, dear,' she said. 'It's wonderful. I'll take it with me right now.'

'You — you will?'

'Yes.' Hera smiled coldly. She summoned a magical rope and put it around poor Io's neck. 'I think I'll put her in my sacred grove in Mycenae, where she'll be safe and well guarded. What's her name?'

'Um . . . Io.'

'Come, then, Io.' Hera led the cow away, softly singing, 'Io, Io, it's off to the grove we go.'

As soon as she was gone, Zeus cursed his horrible luck. He kicked some rocks and summoned lightning to blow up trees.

'I was *this close!*' he yelled. 'I *have* to get that cow back. Who do I know who can steal cows . . . ?'

Of course, he called Hermes.

When Zeus explained the problem, Hermes grinned. 'No worries, boss. I'll sneak into that grove and —'

'It won't be that simple,' Zeus warned. 'Hera said the cow would be well guarded. I'm afraid I know what she meant. She's got this new giant working for her, a dude named Argus.'

Hermes frowned. 'So? I'll either sneak past him or kill him. I've got a sword.'

Zeus shook his head. 'This guy is huge and strong and

quick. You can't beat him in a fair fight, even with your sword. And as for sneaking . . . no way. The guy has eyes in the back of his head, and –'

Hermes laughed. 'I've heard that before.'

'No. I mean he *literally* has eyes in the back of his head. And on his arms and legs and all over his body. A *hundred* eyes.'

'That's disgusting!'

'I know, right? But he never rests, and he's always looking in every direction. If he's guarding Io . . .'

Hermes scratched his head. 'Don't worry, boss. I'll figure something out.'

So off he flew. When he got to Hera's sacred grove, Hermes saw Io the white cow tied to an olive tree. Standing right next to her was the giant Argus.

Just like Zeus had said, Argus was covered with eyes, all blinking and looking around in a dizzy, psychedelic way that made Hermes a little queasy. Argus was about ten feet tall, and the dude obviously worked out. He was holding a big wooden club with iron spikes on the end. Hermes wondered if Argus had eyes in his palms and, if so, whether he got black eyes from holding his club all day.

Hermes changed his form so that he looked like a simple mortal shepherd. His caduceus morphed into a regular wooden staff. He strolled into the grove, whistling casually, and acted surprised when he saw Argus.

'Oh, hello!' Hermes smiled. 'My, aren't you tall!'

Argus blinked several hundred times. He was used to people teasing him about his eyes, but this shepherd didn't seem horrified or disgusted. The giant wasn't sure what to make of that.

Hermes wiped his forehead. 'Hot day, isn't it? Mind if I sit and rest?'

Without waiting for permission, Hermes made himself comfortable in the meadow. He set his staff next to him and secretly willed it to begin working its magic on Argus. The caduceus sent out waves of sleepiness – making Argus feel kind of like how you would in sixth period after lunch on a hot day.

SLEEP, the caduceus seemed to say.

But Argus was a big guy with lots of eyes. He'd been bred specifically *not* to fall asleep. Hermes figured it would take a while. He had to buy time.

'Man, what a day I've had!' he told the giant. He pulled out a jug of water. 'Join me, my friend, and I'll tell you all about it! Happy to share this ice-cold water with you!'

Argus was really thirsty. He'd been standing in the blazing sun all day, watching this stupid cow, as Hera had commanded. But the cow was boring.

Still, he was on duty. He shook his head, which was all he could do. He didn't like to talk, because it would reveal the eyes inside his mouth and all over his tongue.

Hermes started chatting. He was the god of travel, so he knew a *bunch* of good stories. He'd heard jokes from all over the world. And messengers had to be good at speaking, so Hermes knew how to entertain. He regaled Argus with the latest gossip about the gods.

'I heard this one god Hermes stole Apollo's cattle!' Hermes said with a grin. Then he proceeded to tell the story as if it had happened to somebody else.

Meanwhile, the caduceus kept pulsing with magic, filling the air with a heavy layer of drowsiness, like a comfortable blanket.

After half an hour, Argus dropped his club. He sat next to Hermes and accepted some water.

Hermes kept joking with him, telling him stories, until Argus felt like they were old friends.

SLEEP, said the caduceus.

After another hour, Argus's eyes began to get heavy. He knew he was supposed to be on duty, but he couldn't remember why. His imagination was drifting through the wonderful stories that Hermes told.

Finally Hermes started singing a lullaby. 'This is one my mother sang for me when I was just a baby.' He sang the same song he'd heard in his cradle the night he was born, about Artemis's dogs and Poseidon's horses and Apollo's cows.

Argus's head drooped once, twice – *bam*. All his eyes closed, and the giant began to snore.

Hermes kept singing. Very slowly he got to his feet and drew his sword. He crept behind Argus and chopped off the giant's head.

'Nighty-night!' Hermes said cheerfully. (I take back what I said earlier. Hermes *was* a murderer.)

Hermes untied Io the cow and brought her back to Zeus.

Hera was enraged, but she couldn't prove what had happened. Zeus was delighted. Hermes got a nice little bonus in his next paycheck. Poor Io . . . once Zeus was tired of dating her, Hera turned her into a cow permanently and sent a gadfly to sting her for the rest of her life, so Io had to be constantly on the move, roaming from country to country.

But, *c'est la cow!* At least Hermes got the satisfaction of a job well done.

DIONYSUS CONQUERS THE WORLD WITH A REFRESHING BEVERAGE

I SAVED THIS GUY FOR LAST, because he's likely to turn me into a porpoise if I say anything bad about him. And, honestly, I'm not sure I can say anything *good*.

Here goes nothing . . .

A while back I told you about this princess Semele who got vaporized while she was pregnant with Zeus's kid? Anyway, Zeus had to rescue the premature baby by sewing him into his right thigh to keep him alive.

(Yeah, I know. Just another boring day in the life of a god.)

Several months later, the baby was getting big and uncomfortable in Zeus's leg, so Zeus figured the kid was ready to be born. Zeus undid the stitches. Amazingly, the kid came out alive and healthy.

Zeus wrapped him in a blanket, but he didn't know anything about raising babies, so he called in Hermes.

'Hey,' Zeus said, 'take this baby down to the mortal world. I think Semele had a sister or something. Find her and ask her to raise this kid until he's older.'

'Sure, boss.' Hermes took the baby and looked him over. 'Is he a god or a demigod or what?'

'Not sure yet,' Zeus said. 'We'll have to wait and see. But I don't want to be changing diapers in the meantime.'

'I hear you. What's his name?'

The kid started screaming and yelling.

'For now,' Zeus decided, 'let's call him Bacchus.'

Hermes grinned. '*The noisy one?* Nice.'

'One more thing: Hera will be looking for him. She hasn't been able to mess with the kid while he's been stuck in my thigh, but she'll notice that the big lump is gone now.'

'Yeah, that lump was kind of obvious.'

'Might be best if Bacchus's aunt raises him like he's a girl, just for a while. Maybe that will throw Hera off the scent.'

Hermes frowned. He didn't see how raising the baby as a girl would help. Hera wasn't so easily fooled, but Hermes knew better than to argue with the boss.

'Got it,' he said. 'Off I go!'

Hermes had no trouble finding the baby's Aunt Ino and Uncle Athamas. They agreed to raise Bacchus with their own children, and the boy grew up at a normal human rate – not super-accelerated like a god. Everybody decided he must be a demigod, but that just made Zeus more fearful that Hera would try to rip the kid apart.

As requested, Ino and Athamas dressed Bacchus in girl's clothing to keep his identity secret. The first few years of his life, Bacchus was very confused. He wasn't sure why his foster parents called him 'he' in private and 'she' in public. At first he thought *all* kids were treated that way.

Then, when he was three years old, Hera struck. Somehow she discovered where the baby was living, and she flew down from Olympus, intent on revenge. By the time Zeus found out what was happening, he only had a few seconds to act. He managed to zap Bacchus into the form of a goat so that Hera wouldn't notice him, but Bacchus's foster parents weren't so lucky. Hera spotted them and inflicted them with a violent form of madness.

Uncle Athamas thought his eldest son, Learkhos, was a deer and killed him with a bow and arrow. Aunt Ino thought their younger son, Melikertes, needed a hot bath – a *really* hot bath, so she drowned him in a basin of boiling water. Then Ino and Athamas realized what they'd done. In despair, they both leaped off the side of a cliff and plummeted to their deaths.

That Hera . . . she's all about wholesome family values.

Zeus managed to retrieve Bacchus and turn him back into a child, but the experience haunted Bacchus. He'd learned that madness could be used as a weapon. He'd learned that goats were good. (In fact, the goat became one of his sacred animals.) And he'd learned that you couldn't hide who you were just by putting on different clothes. Later on, he became the god of anybody who felt confused about his or her own gender, because Dionysus could relate.

Anyway, Zeus looked around for a new set of foster parents. Big shock: not many people volunteered after hearing what Hera had done to Ino and Athamas. Finally Zeus flew to Mount Nysa on the Greek mainland and convinced the nymphs there to raise Bacchus. Zeus promised to make them immortal if they just did him this favour, and that was a hard deal to refuse. Young Bacchus became known as 'the godly son of Zeus who lives on Nysa', which got shortened to *Dios* (god) of Nysa, which eventually became his new name: Dionysus, though he was still called Bacchus, the noisy one, especially after he ate beans or cabbage. Which is way more than you wanted to know.

Dionysus grew up on Mount Nysa with the nymphs as his foster mothers and the satyrs as his foster fathers. Satyrs are pretty wild and chaotic (no offence to my satyr friends), so it's no surprise Dionysus turned out a little out-of-the-ordinary.

Occasionally he played with mortal kids from the nearby farms, and Dionysus became popular for his magic tricks with plants. He discovered early on that he could produce drinkable nectar by crushing any kind of plant matter – twigs, leaves, bark, roots, whatever. Cypress-tree syrup? No problem. Fennel juice? Yum!

The other kids would challenge him, like, 'Bet you can't make a drink out of that thorn bush!' Dionysus would pick up a rock, smash some branches and golden sap would flow from the wounded plant. Dionysus would collect it in cups, mix some water, add miniature umbrellas and, *voilà*, iced thorn-bush spritzers for everyone.

An entertaining trick – but none of Dionysus's early recipes caught on. Fennel juice just wasn't that popular, after all.

Then one day Dionysus was out in the woods with his best friend, a young satyr boy named Ampelos. They spotted a thick vine curled around the branch of an elm tree about twenty feet above their heads. Dionysus froze in his tracks.

'What is it?' Ampelos asked.

'That vine up there,' Dionysus said. 'What kind of plant is that?'

Ampelos frowned. The vine didn't look like anything special to him. It was thick and bristly, with wide green leaves and no fruit or flowers that he could see. 'Well, it's not ivy. Or honeysuckle. Dunno. Never seen it before. Come on!'

But Dionysus stood transfixed. There was something important about that plant – something that could change the world.

'I have to get a closer look.' Dionysus tried to scale the trunk of the elm, but he was a lousy climber. He fell on his butt in the leaves.

Ampelos laughed. 'If it's so important to you, I'll get it. Leave the climbing to satyrs.'

Dionysus felt a sudden chill of dread. He didn't want Ampelos going up there. But he also wanted the vine.

'Be careful,' he said.

Ampelos rolled his eyes. 'I've climbed higher trees than this!'

The young satyr clambered up the trunk and was soon straddling the elm branch. 'Easy peasy!' He started prising the vine from the branch, feeding the end down to Dionysus like a rope. 'Got it?'

Dionysus reached up and grabbed the vine.

What happened next isn't clear. Maybe Dionysus pulled the vine too hard. Maybe Ampelos reached down too low. Whatever the case, Ampelos lost his balance and fell, tangled in the vine.

Twenty feet isn't so far, but it was enough. Ampelos hit his head on a rock with a sickening *crack*.

Dionysus wailed in horror. He embraced his friend, but

the young satyr's eyes were already dull and empty. He wasn't breathing. Sticky blood matted his hair and stained the leaves of the vine.

Ampelos was dead.

Dionysus sobbed. If he hadn't wanted this stupid vine, his friend would still be alive. His sadness mixed with anger. He glared at the satyr's blood on the green leaves. He snarled, 'You will pay for this, vine. You will bear the sweetest fruit to make up for this bitter loss. BEAR FRUIT!'

The vine trembled. The body of Ampelos dissolved into mist. The satyr's blood soaked into the plant, and clusters of small fruit popped up, ripening instantly to dark red.

Dionysus had created the first grapevine.

He wiped away his tears. He had to make his friend's death mean something. He would learn to use this new plant.

The grapes looked full of juice, so Dionysus picked several bunches. He carried them to a nearby creek bed and found two large flat stones. He crushed the grapes between the rocks, inventing the first winepress.

Dionysus collected the juice in his drinking cup, which he always kept at his belt. He held the liquid in the sunlight and worked his magic, swishing the grape juice around until it fermented into . . . something else. Something new.

He took a sip and his taste buds nearly exploded. 'This,' he pronounced, 'is good stuff.'

Dionysus called it *wine*. He made enough to fill his flask, then looked back wistfully one more time at the place where Ampelos had died. The grapevines were going crazy now, spreading all over the woods, blooming with a vengeance and bearing more grapes.

Dionysus nodded, satisfied. If he had his way, the whole world would be filled with grapevines in Ampelos's honour.

He went back to the cave where he lived on Mount Nysa. He showed his discovery to one of his foster moms, a nymph named Ambrosia. (Yes, she was named after the godly food. I don't know why. At least it's better than Cookie or Snickerdoodle.)

Ambrosia took a sip of wine. Her eyes widened. 'This is *delicious!* Where's Ampelos?'

'Oh . . .' Dionysus hung his head. 'He died, falling from a tree.'

'That's terrible!' Ambrosia took another sip. 'But this is good stuff!'

Soon she was sharing wine with all her nymph friends. The satyrs came by to see what the giggling was about. Pretty soon, the whole mountain was one giant party, with dancing and singing and tiki torches and *lots* of wine. Dionysus kept making the stuff and passing it around. He couldn't keep up with demand. Finally he taught the satyrs and nymphs how to make it themselves, and by the end of the night everybody on the mountain was an expert winemaker.

The satyrs quickly discovered that if they drank *too* much wine they got drunk. They couldn't think straight, see straight or walk straight. For some reason, they found this hilarious. They kept on drinking.

An older satyr, Silenos, threw his arm around Dionysus's shoulders. 'You, sir, are a god! No, I mean that. The god of . . . what's this stuff called again?'

'Wine,' said Dionysus.

'God of wine!' Silenos hiccupped. 'Got any more?'

Now, kids, this is another good time to remind you that wine is for grown-ups! It tastes horrible and could seriously mess up your life. Don't even be tempted until you're at least forty years old!

Aw, but, Percy, you whine (get it, whine?), *it sounds like the satyrs had so much fun drinking wine!*

It might sound that way, kids. But satyrs can be pretty stupid. (Again, no offence to my buddy Grover.) You also didn't see the satyrs the morning after, when they had splitting headaches and were stumbling into the woods to puke their guts out.

Still, the nymphs and satyrs were so impressed with Dionysus that they decided he really must be a god. His invention was just *that* amazing.

Maybe you're thinking . . . *Okay, it's wine. Big deal. How does that rate making Dionysus a god? If I invented tuna salad, would I be a god, too?*

But wine was a major breakthrough in beverage technology.

Sure, people drank water, but water could kill you. Especially in the cities, it was full of bacteria and other people's garbage and . . . well, I'm not really going to go into it. Let's just say that water was gross. Nobody had invented canned soda or even tea or coffee, so you were pretty much stuck with water or milk. Even with milk you had to drink quickly before it spoiled, since there were no refrigerators.

Then Dionysus came along and invented wine. It didn't go bad as long as you kept it bottled up. Sometimes it even tasted *better* if you let it sit for a few years. You could water it down so it wasn't as strong, but the alcohol would still kill germs and stuff, so it was safer to drink than regular water. You could even adjust the taste to make it sweeter with honey, or vary the flavour by using different kinds of grapes.

Basically, it was the super-beverage of Ancient Greece.

Not only that but if you drank a little it would mellow you out. If you drank a lot it would make you giddy and crazy. Some people even thought they had visions of the gods if they chugged enough wine. (Again: do not try this at home. You will not see the Greek gods. You may get a close-up view of your toilet as you are throwing up, but you will not see gods.)

Word spread quickly about the new drink. Nymphs and satyrs from Mount Nysa travelled the countryside, telling anyone who would listen about the awesomeness of wine and the god who made it, Dionysus. They set up tasting booths on the side of the road. They offered starter kits including a potted grapevine, an instruction manual for making a winepress and access to a toll-free customer-service hotline.

Dionysus became famous. Even regular mortals began to gather on Mount Nysa every night for the ultimate party. Sure, they drank too much and got wild, but it wasn't just for fun. The followers of Dionysus considered themselves religious people. They called themselves the *bacchae* – the groupies of Bacchus – and partying was their way of going to church. They believed it brought them closer to all the gods, because Dionysus was destined to be the twelfth Olympian.

How did Dionysus feel about that?

A little nervous. He was still young and insecure. He wasn't sure if he was truly a god or not. On the other hand, he was happy to see people enjoying his new beverage. By spreading the knowledge of wine, he figured he was doing something good for the world, which made him feel better about all the pain he'd been through — his mom dying before he was born, Hera driving his foster parents crazy and, of course, his best friend Ampelos dying in the woods.

Then one day his followers gathered around him and pitched an idea.

'We need to go mainstream!' explained one of the satyrs. 'We should go to the nearest major city and get the king on our side. You can offer to become their patron god. They'll build you a temple, and your fame will spread even faster!'

The nearest king was a dude named Lycurgus, who ran a seaside town at the base of Mount Nysa. The satyrs suggested they start there, to support local business and all.

Dionysus wasn't sure he was ready for prime time, but his followers were enthusiastic. They wouldn't take no for an answer.

'It's a great idea!' they promised him.

As Dionysus soon found out, it was a terrible idea.

Lycurgus was all kinds of evil.

He enjoyed whipping helpless animals like dogs, horses, hamsters and anything else that got in his way. In fact, he had a special whip made just for that purpose — ten feet of black leather braided with iron spikes and jagged pieces of glass.

If no hamsters happened to be around, he would whip his servants. Sometimes, just for fun, he would whip his subjects when they came into the throne room to petition him for stuff.

'My lord, OWWWW! My neighbour killed my horse, and — OWWWW! I'd like him to pay for damages. OWWWW! OWWWW!'

It made his audiences go much more quickly.

Dionysus and his followers didn't know this. They spent all their time partying on Mount Nysa. They marched into town in a happy parade, handing out free grapes, grapevines and glasses of wine, clanging cymbals, singing songs and stumbling into pedestrians. Dionysus noted the nervous faces of the townspeople. Many of them bore scars from whippings. Dionysus didn't like that, but his followers were announcing him as a god, singing his praises and dancing around him. They'd dressed him in expensive purple robes and put a crown of ivy leaves on his head. He was supposed to be the newest Olympian, master of wine and lord of parties. If he ran away, it would probably ruin the effect.

They made their way into the royal palace.

Lycurgus didn't normally get hundreds of satyrs and nymphs bursting into his house in a party mood. For a few moments, he was too stunned to act.

Dionysus approached the throne, mentally rehearsing his lines.

'King Lycurgus,' he said. 'I am Dionysus, the god of wine, and these are my followers.'

The king stared at him. The boy looked no more than fourteen or fifteen, with long dark hair and a pretty face – almost girlish, Lycurgus thought.

'You're a god,' the king said flatly. 'I see. And what exactly is *wine*?'

Dionysus's followers raised their cups in salute. Some laid potted grapevines and bottles of wine at the steps of the throne.

'Wine is a new drink,' Dionysus explained. 'But it's more than just a drink. It's a religious experience!'

Dionysus began to explain wine's other virtues, but Lycurgus held up his hand for silence.

'Why are you here?' he demanded. 'What do you want from me?'

'We simply want to share knowledge about wine,' Dionysus said. 'If you allow your people to learn the arts of grape harvesting and wine making, your kingdom will flourish. Also, I will be your city's patron god. All I ask is that you build me a temple.'

Lycurgus's mouth twitched. It had been a long time since he'd been tempted to laugh. 'A temple. Is that all?'

Dionysus shuffled from foot to foot. 'Erm. Yes.'

'Well, young god, I invented something, too. Would you like to see it? I call it the new and improved whip. I use it to get rid of PEOPLE WHO WASTE MY TIME!'

King Lycurgus started whipping everyone. If he saw it, he whipped it. He whipped it good.

Dionysus's followers scattered. They hadn't expected a fight, and they couldn't defend themselves with grapes and glasses. Many wore only scanty tunics, so the whip really hurt. Dionysus's foster mother Ambrosia got struck in the face and fell down dead at Dionysus's feet.

'NOOOOO!' Dionysus wailed.

Palace guards closed in on all sides, rounding up the satyrs and nymphs and arresting them.

Dionysus fled, pursued by guards. He was almost captured but jumped from a balcony into the ocean, where the Nereid Thetis conveniently came to his rescue. She allowed Dionysus to breathe underwater and bound his wounds while he waited for the king's soldiers to give up the search.

Dionysus cried bitterly as the sea nymph held him. 'Thetis, I can't do anything right! Everyone who gets close to me dies or gets punished for believing in me!'

Thetis stroked his hair soothingly. 'Don't give up, Dionysus. You *will* be a god, but you can't let jealous mortals stand in your way. Go back to Lycurgus and teach him that he cannot disrespect you like this.'

'He's got a whip!'

'You have weapons, too.'

Dionysus thought about that. A fire began to burn in his stomach, as it had when he took his first gulp of wine. 'You're right. Thanks, Thetis.'

'Go get 'em, champ.'

Dionysus marched out of the sea and straight back to Lycurgus's palace.

Was that the moment when Dionysus changed from a demigod into a full god? Nobody really knows. His evolution was gradual, but definitely he got more powerful as his followers increased, and when he decided to confront Lycurgus I think that was the first time he believed in himself as much as the *bacchae* believed in him.

King Lycurgus was sitting on his throne, talking to his eldest son, Prince Dryas, who had just arrived and was wondering why there were a bunch of dead nymphs and satyrs on the floor.

Dionysus stormed in, soaking wet and with a steely gleam in his eyes.

Lycurgus was even more surprised than he had been the first time. 'You again?' asked the king. 'All your followers are dead or in prison. Do you wish to join them?'

'You will release my remaining followers immediately,' said Dionysus.

Lycurgus laughed. 'Or what?'

'Or your kingdom will turn barren. No vines will grow. No fruit will ripen. No plants of any kind will bloom.'

'Ha! Is that all?'

'No,' Dionysus said coldly. 'Also, you will be afflicted with madness. Do you refuse?'

'I refuse!' Lycurgus grinned. 'So where is this madness – ACK!'

Lycurgus doubled over in pain. Then he stood bolt upright and screamed in falsetto.

His son Dryas grabbed his arm in concern. 'Dad! Are you okay?'

Lycurgus looked at the prince, but all he saw was a writhing pillar of grapevines. The king stumbled back in horror. 'The grapes! They're everywhere! The grapes are taking over!'

Lycurgus snatched a double-bladed axe from the nearest guard and chopped at the pillar of vines.

'Dad!' the vines wailed.

'Die, grapes!' Lycurgus chopped and hacked until the wailing stopped. The grapevines lay in pieces all around his feet.

The king's vision cleared, and he saw what he had done. Lycurgus sobbed in misery and fell to his knees, the blood of his dead son glistening on his axe.

If Dionysus felt any regret, he didn't show it. After all, Hera had taught him how to use madness to punish his foes. Dionysus had learned from the best.

'Lycurgus, this is the price of your insolence,' said the wine god. 'Until you free my followers and recognize me as a god, your entire kingdom will suffer.'

'Kill him!' the king screamed.

The guards surged forward, but Dionysus simply looked at them and they backed away. They could see the power and divine anger in his eyes.

'Your king will never bow to me,' Dionysus told them. 'Your land will suffer until he is . . . removed. Think on this.'

Dionysus strode out of the palace.

In the following days, the countryside withered. In the city and the fields, every plant shrivelled up. Fruit rotted. Bread turned to mould. The water in the wells turned warm and scummy. The farmers couldn't grow anything. The towns-people couldn't feed their families.

Finally, after two weeks, the royal guards stormed the palace and captured King Lycurgus. Nobody protested. Nobody had liked the king much anyway. The guards dragged him kicking and screaming into the town square. They tied his limbs to four horses, then thwacked the horses' rumps and set them running in four different directions.

Yeah. The king's death was messy.

The people of the town released Dionysus's followers. Immediately the plants began to grow again. Flowers bloomed. Grapevines overtook the palace walls and bore juicy bunches of grapes.

The townspeople learned to make wine. They started building Dionysus's first temple. And that's how Dionysus won his first victory.

After that, he decided to take his show on the road. He gathered his followers and began the Dionysus Grand World Tour of Madness and Wine-Tasting. (Mr D won't admit it, but he's still got some unsold event T-shirts in a box in his closet — all size adult small.)

Some towns accepted Dionysus and his army of drunken *bacchae* without a fight. When that happened, everything was sunshine and smiley faces. The town got free wine and the knowledge of how to make it. The *bacchae* threw a big party. Everybody honoured Dionysus, and the next morning the army moved on, leaving a bunch of broken glasses, crushed party hats and people with hangovers.

Not everybody liked this new god and his followers, though. King Pentheus of Thebes distrusted Dionysus. The god's army of drunks seemed dangerous and barely under control. But Pentheus had heard what happened to Lycurgus, so he played it cool when Dionysus came to visit.

'Give me some time to think about your offer,' the king said.

Dionysus bowed. 'No problem. We'll be in the woods to the east, holding our nightly revels. I would invite you to join us, but . . .' The god smiled mysteriously. 'They are not open to *unbelievers.* Trust me, though. You're missing quite a party! We'll come back tomorrow to get your answer.'

The army left in peace and made camp in the woods.

King Pentheus was burning with curiosity. What was this new god about? Did he have secret weapons? Why were his revels closed to outsiders?

The king's spies reported that many of his own towns-people had already accepted Dionysus as a god without waiting for the king's permission. Hundreds were planning to sneak out of the city and join the revels in the woods tonight.

'I have to know more about this new threat,' Pentheus grumbled. 'And I can't trust secondhand reports. Too many of my own people already believe in this new god! I need to spy on Dionysus's camp myself.'

His guards warned him it was a bad idea, but the king didn't listen. He put on his black ninja outfit, painted his face with grease and ash, and sneaked out of town. When he reached the edge of Dionysus's camp, Pentheus climbed a tree and watched the revels with fascination and horror.

The *bacchae* parties had got pretty wild as the army moved around Greece. Some of the mortals, nymphs and satyrs were content to drink wine and listen to music. Others put on rowdy comic plays, because Dionysus had become the patron god of theatre.

But a lot of his followers got *much* crazier. They built huge bonfires and leaped through them for fun. Others got drunk and staged wrestling matches to the death. Others . . . well, I'll have to let you use your imagination. Personally, I've never been to Mr D's revels. If I went, my mom would ground me for eternity. But there was some crazy stuff going on.

Dionysus's most hard-core followers were a group of nymphs called the maenads. During the revels they got so frenzied they felt no pain and had absolutely no self-control. They just did whatever came to mind. You had to be careful when the maenads were in the zone, because they could go from super-happy to super-angry in a split second. They were so strong and vicious . . . Imagine thirty drunk She-Hulks with razor-sharp fingernails, and you've got the general idea. They acted as Dionysus's bodyguards and shock troops, so nobody would ever dare to whip the god again.

That night, they were dancing around Dionysus as he sat in his makeshift wooden throne, drinking wine and toasting his followers. He usually wore the same outfit – purple robes and a wreath of oak leaves. As a symbol of his power he held a special sceptre called a *thyrsus*, which was topped with a pinecone and encircled with grapevines. If that doesn't sound like much of a weapon, then you've probably never been smacked upside the head by a pinecone on a stick.

Anyway, Pentheus watched the revels from up in the tree. He started to realize that this new god Dionysus was much more powerful than he'd thought. Hundreds of Pentheus's own townspeople were dancing in the crowd. Then he saw an older woman chatting with some satyrs by a bonfire, and his heart turned to lead.

'Mother?' he whimpered.

He didn't say it very loudly, but somehow the god sensed his presence. At the other end of the clearing, Dionysus casually stood up. He drained his wine cup and strolled over to the tree. Pentheus didn't dare move. He knew if he tried to run he'd never make it.

Dionysus leaped up and grabbed a huge branch. It was heavier than any human would've been able to bend, but he pulled it down easily. King Pentheus was completely exposed.

The music died. Hundreds of *bacchae* stared at the spy in the tree.

'Looky here,' Dionsyus said. 'The king is trespassing,

making a mockery of our sacred rituals.' He turned to the maenads and the rest of the revellers. 'What do we do with trespassers, my friends? Show him!'

The crowd swarmed the tree. They pulled down Pentheus and literally tore him to pieces. Even Pentheus's own mother, overcome with the party spirit, joined the fun.

So, yeah . . . wine, music, dancing, the occasional gruesome murder. Dionysus definitely knew how to put on a show.

After that incident, not many cities stood in his way. Dionysus had a little trouble in Athens, but once he explained the situation (by driving a lot of Athenian women insane), the city welcomed him and started a yearly festival in his honour. Dionysus even travelled into Egypt and Syria, spreading the good word about wine. Sure, he had a few problems here and there, but if I told you about every time Dionysus drove a king mad or flayed him alive we'd be here all day. Dionysus was just a never-ending fiesta of fun.

Hera made one last attempt to destroy him and almost succeeded. She separated Dionysus from his army and drove him insane, but Dionysus got better. He rode a talking donkey to an oracle in Dodona, where Zeus cured him. (Long story, and don't even ask where he got the talking donkey.)

Then one day Dionysus got married. It only happened because he got captured by pirates.

The night before it happened, the *bacchae* had thrown an especially huge party on the coast of Italy. The next morning, Dionysus woke with a massive headache. While the rest of the camp was sleeping, Dionysus stumbled to the beach to go to the bathroom.

(Yes, of course gods go to the bathroom. Um . . . at least I think . . . You know what? Let's just move along.)

Anyway, he *really* had to go. He stood there for a long time doing his business, watching the ocean. Eventually a ship appeared on the horizon. It got closer and closer, its black sails billowing and a black pennant flapping from the top of the mast. As Dionysus watched, the ship weighed anchor. A rowing boat came ashore. Half a dozen ugly-looking dudes got out and marched towards him.

'Arrr!' one said, pulling a sword.

Dionysus grinned. 'Oh, no way! Are you guys *pirates*?'

Dionysus had heard about pirates, but he'd never met any. He was terribly excited.

The pirates glanced at each other, momentarily confused.

'That's right, ye scalawag,' said the one with the sword. 'I'm the captain of these salty seadogs. And you're obviously a rich young prince, so we're taking you hostage!'

(Note to self: get somebody to check my pirate-speak before we publish this. It's been a while since I saw *Pirates of the Caribbean*.)

Dionysus clapped his hands enthusiastically. 'Oh, that's fabulous!' He glanced back towards the sand dunes. 'My army is still sleeping. I can probably spare a few hours before they wake up.'

The captain narrowed his eyes at the mention of an army, but he couldn't see anyone over the tops of the dunes, so he decided the young prince must be bluffing. Dionysus certainly looked rich. Poor people didn't wear purple robes or oak leaf crowns. They didn't have nicely manicured hands, long flowing black hair and good teeth. In fact, the captain had never seen a guy who looked so *pretty*.

'Get moving, then!' the captain ordered. 'In the boat!'

'Yay!' Dionysus hurried to the rowing boat. 'Do I get a tour of your ship? Do I get to walk the plank?'

The pirates took Dionysus aboard and sailed away. They tried to bind him, but the ropes kept falling off no matter what they tried.

The captain asked Dionysus who his father was, so they could demand a rich ransom.

'Hmm?' said Dionysus, examining the rigging. 'Oh, my father is Zeus.'

That made the pirates very uneasy.

Finally the navigator couldn't stand it. 'Can't you see he's a god? I mean *nobody* mortal would look so . . . pretty.'

'Thank you!' Dionysus beamed. 'My secret is wine every day and lots of partying.'

The navigator frowned. 'We should take him back and let him go. This ain't going to end well.'

'Spit on that!' yelled the captain. 'He's our prisoner and we'll keep him!'

'I love you guys!' Dionysus said. 'But all this excitement has made me *really* tired. Can I just take a quick nap? Then maybe we can swab the deck or something.'

Dionysus curled up in a pile of ropes and started snoring.

Since the pirates hadn't been able to tie him up, they let him sleep. When he finally woke up, the sun was high in the sky.

'Oh, um, guys?' Dionysus stood and rubbed the sleep from his eyes. 'It's getting late. My army will be worried. Can we go back?'

'Go back?' The captain laughed. 'You're our prisoner. Since ye wouldn't tell us your real father, we're taking you to Crete to sell you into slavery!'

Dionysus was tired of playing pirates. Also, he woke up cranky from naps. 'I told you my father was Zeus. Now, turn the ship around.'

'Or what?' the captain asked. 'You'll pretty me to death?'

The ship began to rattle. Grapevines sprouted from the deck and crawled up the mast. Pirates yelled in alarm as the vines completely covered the sails and began snaking down the rigging. The crew ran around in a panic, slipping on bunches of grapes.

'Calm yourselves!' yelled the captain. 'They're just plants!' Then he snarled at Dionysus, 'You're more trouble than you're worth, young prince. Time to die!'

The captain advanced with his sword.

Dionysus had never tried changing his form before, but now he was thrilled to discover he could. Suddenly the captain found himself facing a five-hundred-pound bear.

Dionysus the Bear roared at the captain, who dropped his sword and ran, only to slip on some grapes. The rest of the crew fled, heading for the prow, but a huge phantom tiger appeared on the foredeck, growling and ready to pounce. It was just an illusion, but the pirates were terrified. Everywhere they turned, Dionysus created a different phantom predator – a lion, a leopard, a jackalope; you name it.

Finally the pirates dived over the side. Dionysus decided the ocean was a good place for them to stay, so he turned them into dolphins, and off they swam. If you ever see a dolphin with an eye patch, chattering 'Arrr, matey!', now you'll know why.

The only pirate left was the navigator, who had stayed at the wheel, too terrified to move.

Dionysus smiled at him. 'You're the only one who recognized me as a god. I like you!'

The navigator made a squeaking sound.

'Can you take me back, please?' Dionysus asked.

'M-m-my lord,' the navigator managed. 'I would, but with no crew I can't sail far. Plus the grapevines in the rigging . . .'

'Oh, right.' Dionysus scratched his head. 'Sorry about that.'

The god gazed across the water. About a mile to the east, he spotted a small island. 'How about there?'

'Erm, that would be Naxos, my lord. I think . . .'

'Perfect. Can you just drop me off? I'll find my own way back to the army.'

So Dionysus ended up on the island of Naxos, which was uninhabited except for a beautiful young lady, who Dionysus found weeping by the edge of a stream in the woods.

She sounded so heartbroken that Dionysus sat next to her and took her hand. 'My dear, what's wrong?'

She didn't even seem startled, as if she didn't care about anything any more.

'My – my boyfriend dumped me,' she said.

Dionysus's heart twisted into a pretzel. Despite her red puffy eyes and dishevelled hair, the girl was absolutely gorgeous.

'Who on earth would be so stupid as to dump you?' Dionysus asked.

'His . . . his name was Theseus,' the girl said. 'I'm Princess Ariadne, by the way.'

She told Dionysus her sad story – how she'd helped this

handsome guy Theseus escape from her father's maze, which was called the Labyrinth. Theseus had killed the Minotaur, blah, blah, blah. That's a whole other story. In the end, Theseus had promised to take Ariadne home with him to Athens. On the way, he stopped at Naxos for fresh water, dumped her on the beach and sailed away.

And you thought breaking up by *texting* was low.

Dionysus was furious. If Theseus had been around, the god would've turned him into a bunch of grapes and stomped him.

The god comforted Ariadne. He summoned wine and food, and they began to talk. Dionysus was good company. After a while, Ariadne began to smile. She even laughed when Dionysus told her about the pirates. (I guess she had a strange sense of humour.)

As quick as that, the two of them fell in love.

'I will take you with me, my dear,' Dionysus promised. '*I* will never leave you. When I ascend to my throne on Mount Olympus, you will be my queen for eternity.'

Dionysus kept his promise. He married Ariadne, and when he was finally recognized as a god and became the twelfth Olympian he made Ariadne his immortal wife. Oh, sure, he still had occasional flings with mortals. He *was* a god, after all. But, as far as Greek stories go, they lived happily ever after.

Dionysus's last big adventure on earth, before he became a full-time god: he decided to invade India.

Why?

Why *not*?

He had travelled all over the Mediterranean and into Egypt and Syria, but whenever he tried to spread the good news about wine further east he always got stopped by angry locals. Maybe that's because Mesopotamia was where they invented beer. Maybe they didn't want any beverage competition.

Anyway, he decided to make one final push to expand his market share. As far as the Greeks were concerned, India was pretty much the end of the world, so Dionysus decided to go there, take over, teach them about wine and come back home, preferably in time for supper.

His drunken followers gathered by the thousands. Some stories say that Hercules joined Dionysus for the expedition, and they had some major drinking contests along the way. Other stories say that the twin sons of Hephaestus, the Kabeiroi, rode into battle on a mechanical chariot and fought bravely. A couple of times, they got a little *too* brave and were surrounded by enemies, at which point Hephaestus himself had to come down, spray the enemy with his divine flamethrower and bring his kids back to safety.

Dionysus rode at the head of his army in a golden chariot pulled by two centaurs. A lot of towns surrendered to him in Syria. The drunken army made it all the way to the Euphrates River and constructed a bridge to get them across – the first time Greeks had got that far.

The bridge isn't there any more. What did you expect? It was made by a bunch of drunks. It probably fell apart in about a week.

Everything was going great – until the army reached India. Those Indians knew how to fight. They had their own magic, their own gods, their own bunch of nasty secret weapons. Their holy men, the Brahmans, would sit on the field of battle, looking all peaceful, and Dionysus's army would roll up, thinking the enemy was surrendering. As soon as the Greeks got close, the Indians would fire rockets into their midst – jets of flame and blinding light, massive explosions that caused panic in the troops.

After a bunch of tough battles, Dionysus finally made it to the Ganges River, which was the holy river of India. He assaulted one last fortress – a big castle on a hill as tall as the Acropolis back in Athens. His centaurs and satyrs tried a frontal assault, climbing up the rocks, but the Indians set off some magic explosions that were so powerful the Greek front lines were vaporized. Supposedly you can still see the after-images of satyrs and centaurs burned into the cliffs where the battle happened.

At that point, Dionysus decided enough was enough. They'd made it to India. They'd introduced wine. Dionysus had collected a sweet assortment of exotic predator cats, like tigers and leopards. He'd even taken the leopard as his new sacred animal and started a fashion craze by wearing a leopard skin as a cape. The army had taken a lot of treasure. They'd met new and interesting people, killed most of them and generally had a good time.

Dionysus built a pair of pillars on the banks of the Ganges to prove that he'd been there. He bade the Indians a tearful farewell and marched back to Greece. He dropped off a load of treasure at the Oracle of Delphi in honour of the gods, and for a long time there used to be a big silver bowl in the Delphic treasure room inscribed: TAKEN FROM THE INDIANS BY DIONYSUS, SON OF ZEUS AND SEMELE. (One of the old Greek writers saw it. I'm not making this up.)

Anyway, Dionysus finally ascended to Mount Olympus and

became the last of the major gods. Cue the theme music! Cue the closing credits! Our camera pans away from the Olympian throne room, where twelve gods are rolling around on their wheelie thrones. And CUT!

Phew. We did it, gang.

Twelve Olympians — we collected the whole set, plus a few extra bonus gods like Persephone and Hades!

Now, if you'll excuse me, I'm going to sleep. I feel like I just got back from the Dionysian revels, and I've got a splitting headache.

AFTERWORD

So those are the basics.

I know some of you are going to be complaining, like, *Ah, you forgot to talk about Cheez Whiz, the god of mice! You forgot to mention Bumbritches, the god of bad fashion statements!* Or whatever.

Please. There are about a hundred thousand Greek gods out there. I'm a little too ADHD to include every single one of them in a single book.

Sure, I could tell you how Gaia raised an army of giants to destroy Olympus. I could tell you how Cupid got his girlfriend, or how Hecate got her farting weasel. But that would take a whole other book. (And please don't give the publisher any ideas. This writing gig is HARD!)

We've covered most of the major players. You probably

know enough now to avoid getting zapped into a pile of ash if you ever come across any of the twelve Olympians.

Probably.

Me, I'm late to meet my girlfriend. Annabeth is going to kill me.

Hope you enjoyed the stories. Stay safe out there, demigods.

Peace from Manhattan,

Percy Jackson

SO THAT'S THE GREEK GODS COVERED.

Read on for Percy Jackson's
take on the heroes of Ancient Greece
in this sneak peek from

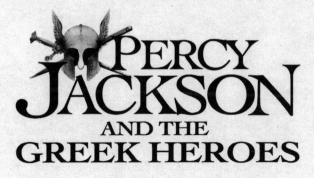

PERCY JACKSON
AND THE
GREEK HEROES

PERSEUS WANTS
A HUG

I HAD TO START WITH THIS GUY.

After all, he's my namesake. We've got different godly fathers, but my mom liked Perseus's story for one simple reason: he *lives*. Perseus doesn't get hacked to pieces. He doesn't get damned to eternal punishment. As far as heroes go, this dude gets a happy ending.

Which is not to say that his life didn't suck. And he *did* murder a lot of people, but what are you gonna do?

Perseus's bad luck started before he was even born.

First, you gotta understand that back in the day Greece wasn't one country. It was divided into a gazillion different little kingdoms. Nobody went around saying, 'Hi, I'm Greek!' People would ask you which city-state you were from: Athens, Thebes, Sparta, Zeusville or whatever. The Greek mainland was a huge piece of real estate. Every city had its own king.

Sprinkled around the Mediterranean Sea were hundreds of islands, and each one of them was a separate kingdom, too.

Imagine if life were like that today. Maybe you live in Manhattan. Your local king would have his own army, his own taxes, his own rules. If you broke the law in Manhattan, you could run away to Hackensack, New Jersey. The king of Hackensack could grant you asylum, and Manhattan couldn't do anything about it (unless, of course, the two kings became allies, in which case you were toast).

Cities would be attacking each other all the time. The king of Brooklyn might decide to go to war with Staten Island. Or the Bronx and Greenwich, Connecticut, might form a military alliance and invade Harlem. You can see how that would make life interesting.

Anyway, one city on the Greek mainland was called Argos. It wasn't the biggest or most powerful city, but it was a respectable size. Folks who lived there called themselves the Argives, probably because 'Argosites' would've made them sound like some kind of bacteria. The king was named Acrisius. He was a nasty piece of work. If he were your king, you would totally want to run away to Hackensack.

Acrisius had a beautiful daughter named Danaë, but that wasn't good enough for him. Back then it was all about sons. You had to have a boy child to carry on the family name, inherit the kingdom when you died, blah, blah, blah. Why couldn't a girl take over the kingdom? I dunno. It's stupid, but that's how it was.

Acrisius kept yelling at his wife, 'Have sons! I want sons!' but that didn't help. When his wife died (probably from stress), the king started getting really nervous. If he died without male offspring, his younger brother, Proteus, would take over the kingdom, and the two of them hated each other.

In desperation, Acrisius took a trip to the Oracle of Delphi to get his fortune read.

Now, going to the Oracle is usually what we call a *bad idea*. You had to take a long trip to the city of Delphi and visit this dark cave at the edge of town, where a veiled lady sat on a three-legged stool, inhaling volcanic vapour all day and seeing visions. You would leave an expensive offering with the priests at the door. Then you could ask the Oracle one question. Most likely, she'd answer you with some rambling riddle. Then you'd leave confused, terrified and poorer.

But, like I said, Acrisius was desperate. He asked, 'O Oracle, what's the deal with me not having any sons? Who's supposed to take the throne and carry on the family name?'

This time, the Oracle did not speak in riddles.

'That's easy,' she said in a raspy voice. 'You will never have sons. One day your daughter Danaë *will* have a son. That boy will kill you and become the next king of Argos. Thank you for your offering. Have a nice day.'

Stunned and angry, Acrisius returned home.

When he got to the palace, his daughter came to see him. 'Father, what's wrong? What did the Oracle say?'

He stared at Danaë – his beautiful girl with her long dark hair and lovely brown eyes. Many men had asked to marry her. Now all Acrisius could think about was the prophecy. He could never allow Danaë to marry. She could never have a son. She wasn't his daughter any more. She was his death sentence.

'The Oracle said that *you* are the problem,' he snarled. 'You will betray me! You will see me murdered!'

'*What?*' Danaë recoiled in shock. 'Never, Father!'

'Guards!' Acrisius yelled. 'Take this vile creature away!'

Danaë couldn't understand what she'd done. She always tried to be kind and considerate. She loved her dad, even though he was scary and angry and liked to hunt peasants in the woods with a spear and a pack of rabid dogs.

Danaë always made the appropriate sacrifices to the gods. She said her prayers, ate her vegetables and did all her homework. Why was her dad suddenly convinced she was a traitor?

She got no answers. The guards took her away and locked her in the king's maximum-security underground cell – a broom-closet-sized room with a toilet, a stone slab for a bed, and twelve-inch-thick bronze walls. One heavily grated air shaft in the ceiling allowed Danaë to breathe and get a little light, but on hot days the bronze cell heated up like a boiling teakettle. The triple-locked door had no window, just a small slot at the bottom for a food tray. King Acrisius kept the only key, because he didn't trust the guards. Each day, Danaë got two dry biscuits and a glass of water. No yard time. No visitors. No Internet privileges. Nothing.

Maybe you're wondering, *If Acrisius was so worried about her having children, why didn't he just kill her?*

Well, my evil-thinking friend, the gods took family murders very seriously. (Which is weird, since the gods basically *invented* family murders.) If you killed your own child, Hades would make sure you got a special punishment in the Underworld. The Furies would come after you. The Fates would snip your lifeline. Some major bad karma would mess up your day. However, if your child just 'accidentally' expired in an underground bronze cell . . . that wasn't strictly *murder*. That was more like *Oops, how did that happen?*

For months, Danaë languished in her underground cell. There wasn't much to do except make little dough dolls out of biscuits and water, or talk to Mr Toilet, so she spent most of her time praying to the gods for help.

Maybe she got their attention because she was so nice, or because she had always made offerings at the temples. Or maybe it was because Danaë was knockout gorgeous.

One day, Zeus, the lord of the sky, heard Danaë calling his name. (Gods are like that. When you say their names, they perk right up. I bet they spend a lot of time Googling themselves, too.)

Zeus peered down from the heavens with his super-keen X-ray vision. He saw the beautiful princess trapped in her bronze cell, lamenting her cruel fate.

'Dude, that is *wrong*,' Zeus said to himself. 'What kind of father imprisons his own daughter so she can't fall in love or have kids?'

(Actually, that was exactly the sort of thing Zeus might do, but whatever.)

'She's kind of hot, too,' Zeus muttered. 'I think I'll pay that lady a visit.'

Zeus was always doing stuff like this. He'd fall in love with some mortal girl at first sight, drop into her life like a romantic hydrogen bomb, mess up her entire existence and then head back to Mount Olympus, leaving his girlfriend to raise a kid all by herself. But really . . . I'm sure his intentions were honourable (*cough* – yeah, right – *cough*).

With Danaë, Zeus's only challenge was figuring out how to get into that bronze maximum-security cell.

He was a god, of course. He had skills. He could simply blast the doors open, but that might scare the poor girl. Plus, then he'd have to kill a bunch of guards, and that would be messy. Causing explosions and leaving a trail of mangled corpses didn't set the right mood for a first date.

He decided it would be easier to turn into something small and sneak in through the air vent. That would give him plenty of privacy with the girl of his dreams.

But what should he turn into? An ant would work. Zeus had done that once before with a different girl. But he wanted to make a good first impression, and ants don't have much of a 'wow' factor.

He decided to turn himself into something totally different – a shower of gold! He dissolved into a swirling cloud of twenty-four-carat glitter and sped down from Mount Olympus. He poured through the air shaft, filling Danaë's cell with warm, dazzling light that took her breath away.

FEAR NOT, said a voice from the glitter. *I AM ZEUS, LORD OF THE SKY. YOU LOOK FINE, GIRL. DO YOU WANT TO HANG OUT?*

Danaë had never had a boyfriend. Especially not a god boyfriend who could turn into glitter. Pretty soon – like in five or six minutes – she was madly in love.

Weeks passed. Danaë stayed so quiet in her cell that the guards outside grew incredibly bored. Then one day, about nine months after the glitter incident, a guard was pushing a food tray through the slot in the door as usual when he heard a strange sound: a baby crying inside the cell.

He ran to get King Acrisius – because this was the kind of thing the boss would want to know about. When the king got there, he unlocked the door, stormed into the cell and found Danaë cradling a newborn baby in a blanket.

'What . . .' Acrisius scanned the cell. No one else was there. No one could've possibly got in, because Acrisius had the only key, and no one could have fitted through Mr Toilet. 'How . . . Who . . .'

'My lord,' Danaë said with a resentful gleam in her eyes, 'I have been visited by the god Zeus. This is our son. I have named him Perseus.'

Acrisius tried not to choke on his own tongue. The word *Perseus* meant *avenger* or *destroyer*, depending on how you interpreted it. The king did *not* want the kid growing up to hang out with Iron Man and the Hulk, and the way Danaë was glaring at him the king had a pretty good idea who she wanted destroyed.

The king's worst fear about the prophecy was coming true – which was kind of stupid, because if he hadn't been such a butt-brain and locked up his daughter it never would've happened. But that's the way prophecies work. You try to avoid the trap, and in doing so you end up building the trap yourself and stepping right into it.

Acrisius wanted to murder Danaë and the little boy. That was the safest bet. But there was that whole *taboo* thing about killing your family. Annoying detail! Also, if Danaë was telling the truth and Perseus was the son of Zeus . . . well, angering the lord of the universe wasn't going to help Acrisius's life expectancy.

Acrisius decided to try something else. He ordered his guards to find a large wooden box with a hinged lid. He had some airholes drilled in the top, just to show he was a nice guy, then he stuffed Danaë and her infant son inside, nailed the lid shut and had the box tossed into the sea.

He figured he wasn't killing them directly. Maybe they would perish from thirst and hunger. Maybe a nice storm would smash them to pieces and drown them. Whatever happened, it wouldn't be his fault!

The king went back to the palace and slept well for the first time in years. Nothing like condemning your daughter and grandson to a slow, horrible death to really ease your mind. If you're an airhole like Acrisius, that is.

Meanwhile, inside the wooden box, Danaë prayed to Zeus. 'Hi, um, it's me, Danaë. I don't mean to bother you, but my dad kicked me out. I'm in a box. In the middle of the sea. And Perseus is with me. So . . . yeah. If you could call me back or text me or something, that would be great.'

Zeus did better than that. He sent cool gentle rain that trickled through the airholes and provided Danaë and the baby with fresh water to drink. He persuaded his brother, the sea god Poseidon, to calm the waves and change the currents so the box would have a smooth journey. Poseidon even caused little sardines to leap onto the box and wriggle through the airholes so Danaë could enjoy fresh sushi. (My dad, Poseidon, is awesome that way.)

So, instead of drowning or dying of thirst, Danaë and Perseus survived just fine. After a few days, the S.S. *Wooden Box* approached the shore of an island called Seriphos, about a hundred miles east of Argos.

Danaë and the baby still might have died, because that

box lid was nailed shut tight. Fortunately, a fisherman named Dictys happened to be sitting on the beach, mending his nets after a hard day of pulling in the fish.

Dictys saw this huge wooden box bobbing on the tide and thought, Whoa, that's weird.

He waded into the water with his nets and hooks, and dragged the box to the beach.

'I wonder what's inside?' he said to himself. 'Could be wine, or olives . . . or gold!'

'Help!' said a woman's voice inside the box.

'Waaaaah!' cried another, tiny voice from inside the box.

'Or people,' Dictys said. 'It could be full of people!'

He got out his handy fishing knife and carefully prised off the top of the box. Inside sat Danaë and baby Perseus – both of them grubby and tired and smelling like day-old sushi, but very much alive.

Dictys helped them out and gave them some bread and water. (Oh boy, Danaë thought, more bread and water!) The fisherman asked Danaë what had happened to her.

She decided to go light on the details. After all, she didn't know where she was, or if the local king was a friend of her dad's. For all she knew, she'd landed in Hackensack. She just told Dictys that her father had kicked her out because she'd fallen in love and had a child without his permission.

'Who's the boy's father?' Dictys wondered.

'Oh . . . um, Zeus.'

The fisherman's eyes widened. He believed her immediately. Despite Danaë's grubby appearance, he could tell she was beautiful enough to attract a god. And, from the way she talked and her general composure, he guessed she was a princess.

Dictys wanted to help her and the little baby, but he had a lot of conflicting emotions.

'I could take you to see my brother,' he said reluctantly. 'His name is Polydectes. He's the king of this island.'

'Would he welcome us?' Danaë asked. 'Would he give us asylum?'

'I'm sure he would.' Dictys tried not to sound nervous, but his brother was a notorious ladies' man. He would probably welcome Danaë a little too warmly.

Danaë frowned. 'If your brother is the king, why are you only a fisherman? I mean, no offence. Fishermen are cool.'

'I prefer not to spend too much time at the palace,' Dictys said. 'Family issues.'

Danaë knew all about family issues. She was uneasy about seeking help from King Polydectes, but she didn't see another option, unless she wanted to stay on the beach and make a hut out of her box.

'Should I get cleaned up first?' she asked Dictys.

'No,' said the fisherman. 'With my brother, you should look as unattractive as possible. In fact, maybe rub some more sand on your face. Put some seaweed in your hair.'

Dictys led Danaë and the baby to the main town on Seriphos. Looming above all the other buildings was the king's palace — a mass of white marble columns and sandstone walls, with banners flying from the turrets and a bunch of thuggish-looking guards at the gate. Danaë started to wonder if living in a box on the beach wasn't such a bad idea, but she followed her fisherman friend into the throne room.

King Polydectes sat on a solid bronze throne that must have offered little in the way of lower-back support. Behind him, the walls were festooned with war trophies: weapons, shields, banners and a few stuffed heads of his enemies. You know, the usual decor to brighten up an audience chamber.

'Well, well!' said Polydectes. 'What have you brought me, brother? It looks like you finally caught something worthwhile in your fishing nets!'

'Um . . .' Dictys tried to think of a way to say, *Please be nice to her and don't kill me.*

'You are dismissed,' the king said.

The guards hustled the poor fisherman away.

Polydectes leaned toward Danaë. His grin didn't make him look any friendlier, since he had some nasty crooked teeth.

He wasn't fooled by Danaë's ragged clothes, the sand on her face, the seaweed and tiny sardines in her hair, or the bundle of rags she was holding. (Why *was* she holding that bundle? Was it her carry-on bag?) Polydectes could see how beautiful the girl was. Those eyes were gorgeous. That face — perfection! Give her a bath and some proper clothes, and she could pass for a princess.

'Do not be afraid, my dear,' he said. 'How I can help you?'

Danaë decided to play to victim, thinking the king would respond to that. She fell to her knees and wept. 'My lord, I am Danaë, princess of Argos. My father, King Acrisius, cast me out. I beg you for protection!'

Polydectes's heart wasn't exactly moved. But his mental gears definitely started turning. Argos — nice city. He'd heard about Acrisius, the old king with no sons. Oh, this was too good! If Polydectes married Danaë, he would become the ruler of *both* cities. He would finally have two throne rooms with enough wall space to display all those stuffed heads he kept in storage!

'Princess Danaë, of course I grant you sanctuary!' he said, loud enough for all his attendants to hear. 'I swear upon the gods, you will be safe with me!'

He rose from his throne and descended the steps of his dais. He meant to take Danaë in his arms to show what a kind, loving dude he was. As soon as he got within five feet of her, the princess's bundle of rags started screaming.

Polydectes jumped back. The screaming stopped.

'What sorcery is this?' Polydectes demanded. 'You have a bundle of screaming rags?'

'It's a baby, my lord.' Danaë tried not to smirk at the king's horrified expression. 'This is my son, Perseus, whose father is Zeus. I hope your promise of protection extends to my poor tiny child as well.'

Polydectes developed a tic in his right eye. He hated babies – wrinkly, pudgy creatures that cried and pooped. He was sorry he hadn't noticed the kid earlier, but he'd been distracted by Danaë's beauty.

He couldn't take back his promise now. All of his attendants had heard him say it. Besides, if the baby was a child of Zeus, that complicated matters. You couldn't chuck demigod babies in the bin without angering the gods – most of the time, anyway.

'Of course,' the king managed. 'What a cute little . . . thing. He will have my protection, too. I'll tell you what . . .'

The king edged closer, but Perseus started screaming again. The kid had evil-king radar.

'Ha, ha,' Polydectes said weakly. 'The boy has a strong set of lungs. He can be raised in the Temple of Athena, far away at the other end of the city . . . I mean, conveniently located in the *best part* of the city. The priests there will take excellent care of him. In the meantime, you and I, dear princess, can become better acquainted.'

Polydectes was used to getting his way. He figured it would take fifteen, maybe sixteen minutes tops to get Danaë to marry him.

Instead, the next seventeen years were the most frustrating time in Polydectes's life. Try as he might to become *better acquainted* with Danaë, the princess and her son thwarted Polydectes at every turn. The king gave Danaë her own suite of rooms at the palace. He gave her fancy clothes, beautiful jewellery, maidservants and an all-you-can-eat coupon book for the royal buffet. But Danaë wasn't fooled. She knew she was just as much a prisoner here as she had been in that bronze cell. She wasn't allowed to leave the palace. Aside from her servants, the only visitors she could have were her son and his nursemaids from the Temple of Athena.

Danaë loved those visits from Perseus. While he was a baby, he would scream every time the king got close to Danaë. Since the king couldn't stand the sound, he would leave quickly and go take some aspirin. When Perseus wasn't around, Danaë found other ways to rebuff the king's flirting. Whenever he came to her door, she would make retching noises and apologize for being sick. She would hide in the palace laundry room. She would weep uncontrollably while her maidservants looked on until the king felt embarrassed and ran away.

For years the king tried to win her affection. For years she resisted.

Their mutual stubbornness was kind of impressive, actually.

Once Perseus got older, things got easier for Danaë and harder for Polydectes.

After all, Perseus was a demigod. The dude had mad talent. By the time he was seven, he could wrestle a grown man to the floor. By the time he was ten, he could shoot an arrow across the length of the island and wield a sword better than any soldier in the king's army. Growing up in the Temple of Athena, he learned about warfare and wisdom: how to pick your fights, how to honour the gods – all good stuff to know if you want to live through puberty.

He was a good son, which meant he continued to visit his mom as often as possible. He didn't scream any more when Polydectes came around, but, if the king tried to flirt with Danaë, Perseus would stand nearby, glaring, his arms crossed and several deadly weapons hanging from his belt, until the king retreated.

You'd think Polydectes would have given up, right? There were plenty of other women to bother. But you know how it is. Once you're told you can't have something, you want it even more. By the time Perseus turned seventeen, Polydectes was out of his mind with irritation. He wanted to marry Danaë before she was too old to have more kids! He wanted to see his own children become the kings of Argos and Seriphos. Which added up to one thing: Perseus had to go.

But how to get rid of a demigod without directly murdering him?

Especially since Perseus, at seventeen, was the strongest and best fighter on the island.

What Polydectes needed was a good trap . . . a way to make

Perseus walk right into his own destruction without any of the blame splashing back onto Polydectes.

Over the years, the king had seen a lot of heroes gallivanting around: slaying monsters, rescuing villages and cute puppies, winning the hearts of princes and princesses, and getting major endorsement deals. Polydectes had no use for such nonsense, but he'd noticed that most heroes had a fatal flaw – some weakness that (with any luck) would get them killed.

What was Perseus's fatal flaw?

The boy was a prince of Argos, a son of Zeus, yet he'd grown up as a castaway in a foreign kingdom, with no money and only his mother for family. This made him a little touchy about his reputation. He was anxious to prove himself. He would take on any challenge. If Polydectes could use that against him . . .

The king began to smile. Oh, yes. He had just the challenge in mind.

Coming Autumn 2015

MAGNUS CHASE

AND THE

GODS OF ASGARD

THE SWORD OF SUMMER